ADVANCED EDUCATIONAL STATISTICS

Dr. Ansari Abdul Aziz
[B.Sc.; M.A. M.Ed., Ph.D.]
Former Vice-Principal
Gokhale Education Society's
College of Education and Research
Parel, Mumbai

Dr. Usha Rao
[M.A. (Phil.) M.A.(Psy.) M.Ed., Ph.D.]
Former-Principal
Gokhale Education Society 's
College of Education and Research
Parel, Mumbai

First Edition: 2011

Himalaya Publishing House

MUMBAI • NEW DELHI • NAGPUR • BENGALURU • HYDERABAD • CHENNAI
• PUNE • LUCKNOW • AHMEDABAD • ERNAKULAM • BHUVNESHWAR • INDOR

First Edition : 2011

Published by : Mrs. Meena Pandey for **Himalaya Publishing House Pvt. Ltd.**,
"Ramdoot", Dr. Bhalerao Marg, Girgaon, **Mumbai - 400 004.**
Phone: 2386 01 70/2386 38 63, Fax: 022-2387 71 78
Email: himpub@vsnl.com Website: www.himpub.com

Branch Offices

New Delhi	:	"Pooja Apartments", 4-B, Murari Lal Street, Ansari Road, Darya Ganj, New Delhi - 110 002. Phone:23270392, 23278631 Fax: 011-23256286
Nagpur	:	Kundanlal Chandak Industrial Estate, Ghat Road, Nagpur - 440 018. Phone: 2738731, 3296733 Telefax: 0712-2721215
Bengaluru	:	No. 16/1 (Old 12/1), 1st Floor, Next to Hotel Highlands, Madhava Nagar, Race Course Road, Bengaluru - 560 001. Phone: 22281541, 22385461, Telefax: 080-22286611
Hyderabad	:	No. 3-4-184, Lingampally, Besides Raghavendra Swamy Matham, Kachiguda, Hyderabad - 500 027. Phone: 040-27560041, 27550139, Mobile: 09848130433
Chennai	:	No. 85/50, Bazullah Road, T. Nagar, Chennai - 600 017. Phone: 044-28144004/28144005
Pune	:	First Floor, "Laksha" Apartment, No. 527, Mehunpura, Shaniwarpeth (Near Prabhat Theatre), Pune - 411 030. Phone: 020-24496323/24496333
Lucknow	:	Jai Baba Bhavan, Church Road, Near Manas Complex and Dr. Awasthi Clinic, Aliganj, Lucknow - 226 024. Phone: 0522-2339329, 4068914, Mobile: 9305302158, 9415349385, 9389593752
Ahmedabad	:	114, "SHAIL", 1st Floor, Opp. Madhu Sudan House, C.G.Road, Navrang Pura, Ahmedabad - 380 009. Phone: 079-26560126, Mobile: 09327324149,09314679413
Ernakulam	:	39/104 A, Lakshmi Apartment, Karikkamuri Cross Rd., Ernakulam, Cochin – 622011, Kerala. Phone: 0484-2378012, 2378016, Mobile: 09344199799
Bhubaneswar	:	5 Station Square, Bhubaneswar (Orissa) - 751 001. Mobile: 9861046007
Indore	:	Kesardeep Avenue Extension, 73, Narayan Bagh, Flat No. 302, IIIrd Floor, Near Humpty Dumpty School, Narayan Bagh, Indore 452 007(M.P.) Mobile: 09301386468
Kolkata	:	108/4, Beliaghata Main Road, Near ID Hospital, Opp. SBI Bank, Kolkata - 700 010, Mobile: 09910440956

Typeset by : Athurva Graphics, Mumbai.

Printed by : New Offset Printer, Delhi.

PREFACE

(Preface is written in the end, put in the beginning and least read)

It is impossible to overemphasize the importance of statistics in modern times. In fact modern age is the of statistics and all the branches of human knowledge make extensive use of statistical methods. In the field of Education statistics and its application occupies an important place.

As teachers of Educational Statistics for a long time the authors have felt that students need one such book on the subject from which they can understand and solve practical questions and find out the accuracy or otherwise of their answers.

The students and scholars busy in research work have different educational background like education, engineering, science, arts, pharmacy and medicine etc. Medium of instruction at school level and their mathematical abilities also differ. No doubt there are many books by foreign as well as Indian authors which give few solved and some problems for practice but there are very few or none which are written for those who have little knowledge of mathematical calculations. This book is an attempt to meet this need. Care is taken to explain the procedure of solving the examples and the steps involved in the solution are increased for better understanding.

After studying the entire book you won't know all the statistics. We hope that you will know enough statistics and enough about statistics to feel that the part you don't know is understandable, not mysterious. Perhaps you will appreciate the great power of statistical methods and appreciate their limitations. We hope that you will have formed the habit of questioning and seeking understanding rather than being satisfied with blind acceptance of dogmatic assertions. We expect that you will share in the excitement of statistics and that you Will feel the rich pleasure that comes with discovery, valid conclusion and interpretation. If most of these hopes are fulfilled than you have had an optimum introduction to Educational Statistics through this book. We have been helped by the writers of other books, some of which, we have referenced in the section of Bibliography. We take the opportunity to express our sincere gratitude and thanks to all these great writers.

Our sincere thanks are due to the very prestigious publishers for the meticulous care they took in publishing this book. This volume it is hoped will be found useful for researchers, teachers, students and others interested in promoting the cause of research in the field of Education. In spite of great care, some errors and omisions might have crept in. We shall be grateful to the readers who will point them out. The suggestions for the improvement of the book will be highly appreciated.

Dr. Ansari Abdul Aziz

26/1/2010 **Dr. Usha Rao**

CONTENTS

CHAPTER I
INTRODUCTION

HISTORICAL BACKGROUND

It is indeed a fact, that the very word 'Statistics' means something that is un-understandable to many minds. But it is not so. A person is really afraid of water, but once he/she learns the tactics of swimming, he or she is no more afraid of water _ how so-ever deep the river or well-water may be. Same is the case with Statistics. Therefore, it is really interesting to see the reputation of statistics. Many people have a feeling that statistics is the only means through which the dishonesty of either the thesis or dissertation can be proved. But making use of statistics for such purposes is not correct; rather it is improper. The best way is to get rid of the ignorance regarding statistics and try to make oneself as familiar with the subject-matter as one can; and this can be achieved only through proper study of the subject-matter. For this, it is very essential to go to the correct concept of the word 'statistics'.

Statistics is as old as science. For the last few centuries, it has remained a part of mathematics as the original work has done by mathematicians like Pascal (1623-1662), James Bernouli (1654-1705), DeMoivre (1667-1754), Lapolace (1749-1827), Gauss (1777-1855), Boyes, Markoff, etc. These mathematicians were mainly interested in the development of the theory of probability as applied to the theory of games and other chance phenomena. However, the development of the science of statistics was very gradual and its field of application widened day-by-day. Slowly, the definition of statistics too changed from time to time depending upon the use and application.

SEVERAL CONCEPTS

The word 'statistics' describes several concepts of importance; hence, it is very essential for the beginner to have a correct understanding of different concepts. Word 'Statistics' appears to have been derived from the Latin word 'status' meaning a political state. In fact, originally the word 'Statistics' was applied only to such facts and figures that were required by the State for official purposes. This indicates that in olden days, it was considered as a science of kings. But, by the advancement of time, the subject became not only more and more popular but also its application became wider and wider.

Then its scope stretched over to all those branches of human knowledge in which numerical treatment became essential. In its origin, therefore, statistics was simply the collection of numerical data, by the kings, on different aspects useful to the state. With still more passage of time, however, the scope of statistics began to include collection of numerical data pertaining to almost every endeavour, calculation of percentages, etc., and the presentation of data in tables and charts. This is how, people started hearing about statistics of births, death, imports, exports, wastage and stagnation in schools, marriages, divorces, mental abilities of people and of population and the like. By the end of nineteenth century, statistics began to concern itself not only with the collection and presentation of data, but also with interpretation and drawing of inferences from data.

DEFINITION

There was a gradual development of the science of statistics and its field of application too went on widening day-by-day. Therefore, it became difficult to give the exact definition of statistics. The definitions also went on changing from time-to-time because of its use and application. Hence, it is better to take a note of the various definitions given by different people. Almost all the definitions reflect the statistical angle as well as the field of activity. Let us now have a look at certain definitions which are as given below –

Word Statistics is known to have been used for the first time in 'ELEMENTS OF UNIVERSAL EDUCATION' by Baron J.F. Von Bielfeld translated by W. Hooper M.D. (3 Vol. London, 1970). Here statistics is defined as :

> "The science that teaches us what is the political arrangement of all modern states of the known world".

As seen earlier, meaning of the word 'statistics' became accumulated with numerical statements. Hence, Bowley defines statistics as 'numerical statement of facts in any department of enquiry placed in relation to each other'.

However, a still better definition is provided by an eminent mathematician Horace Secrist who states –

> "Statistics is an aggregate of facts, affected to marked extent by a multiplicity of causes, numerically expressed, enumerated or estimated according to reasonable standards of accuracy, collected in systematic manner for a pre-determined purpose and placed in relation to each other".

Here, certain characteristics of numerical data are given. If they possess them, then they are statistics otherwise not, as it is a well-known fact that 'all statistics are numerical facts but all numerical facts are not statistics'. One thing is certain and that is, Secrist's definition gives all the characteristics of statistics :

- **(i) Aggregate of facts :** A single isolated figure does not mean statistics. Marks of one student in one subject will not be termed as statistics. But if we take into consideration the marks of all the students in the class in a particular subject, then they will be termed statistics.
- **(ii) Affected by multiplicity of causes :** There are various reasons for the changes in the data-e.g., marks of the pupils is dependent on the intellectual level of the pupils, their capacity, their desire to do the task, etc.
- **(iii) Numerically expressed :** Unless the characteristics have some numerical measurement, they will not be called statistics. The statement 'A pupil writes good English' is not

statistics. However, if marks of the whole class in the subject of English are given, then, they will be termed as statistics.

(iv) Enumerated or estimated according to reasonable standards of accuracy : How so ever much a person may try, it is just impossible to attain perfect accuracy, whether we actually measure or estimate the characteristics. But a certain standard of accuracy, has to be set up according to the problem under consideration. For example, the estimate of the cost of a big project may be correct even upto Rs. 1000/- but for the household expenses, it has to be correct even upto a rupee.

(v) Collected in a systematic manner : There must be a method in the manner of collection. Then only, the figures will be reliable and useful.

(vi) Collected for a pre-determined purpose : The purpose must be correctly made clear. Sometimes, the data collected may not be sufficient or some unnecessary information will be collected which may turn out to be just sheer waste of time, money as well as energy.

(vii) Placed in relation to each other : Only when we want to compare the characteristics that have some relation with each other, we collect statistics. For example, the wages of fathers and ages of sons should not be collected together. But we can have ages and heights of a group of persons, so that the relation between the two can be found out.

A somewhat similar type of definition has also been given by G.A. Ferguson who defined Statistics by saying "Statistics is a branch of scientific methodology. It deals with collection, classification, description and interpretation of data obtained by conduct of surveys and experiments. Its essential purpose is to describe and draw inferences about the numerical properties of population".

According to Webster, "The classified facts representing the condition of the people in a state, especially those facts which can be stated in numbers or in tables of numbers or in any tabular or classified advertisement, is termed as statistics".

A.L. Bowley has given the following definitions:

(i) Statistics is the science of counting.

(ii) Statistics is the science of averages.

(iii) Statistics is the science of measurement of social phenomena, regarded as a whole in all its manifestations.

Concludingly, Bowley has said that the subject of statistics is such which is not confined to any one science.

In a nutshell, it may be said, then, that, statistics is a scientific study of dealing with the numerical data, that has been gathered by the administration of some kind of enquiry form or test, in a classified or tabulated manner involving the method of collection of data, their classification and interpretation in the field of enquiry. The primary objective of statistics is to enable the learner to express the given data of a larger population in a precise form - e.g., Average intellectual level of the class is 100 I.Q.

Average span life in India is 35 years. Average income of a person in India is Rs. 5 and 29 paise per day. Average height of a man in India is 5' - 3" etc.

Let us also go through some more definitions of statistics which are as follows -

A.L. Baddington - "Statistics is the science of estimates and probabilities."

According to **R.A. Fisher**, "Science of statistics is essentially a branch of applied mathematics and may be regarded as mathematics applied to observational data."

When one goes through all the definitions, one may come to understand that definition given by Fisher seems to be quite exact because it covers all aspects and field of statistics. However, as far as the latest developments in the field of statistics are concerned, statistics has been taken up as a science of decision-making, under uncertainty, with or without data. It is also essential to note that the field of statistics in the twentieth century has undergone lot of changes.

Let us see still two more definitions of Statistics given by the eminent people. These are by **Croxton** and **Cowden**. "Statistics may be defined as the collection, presentation, analysis and interpretation of numerical data." This definition is considered to be proper as it explains the utility of statistics. The four procedures mentioned in the definition can be examined in brief as follows :

Collection : The data may be collected from various published as well as unpublished sources. Collecting first hand information, is, however, a very difficult task. Usefulness of the data collected depends to a great extent upon the manner in which they are collected.

Presentation : Collected data has to be presented in a suitable form. Just a given mass of figures will signify nothing; but will lead to a sort of confusion to the reader. Therefore, they ought to be presented in a tabular form and represented by diagrams.

Analysis : The data that is presented in a tabular form is an elementary step in the analysis of collected data. If the learner wants to study some characteristic of a big group, exhaustive study will not be possible. Learner has to take a sample, study it and then draw the inferences on the basis of sample studies. Forecasting is also essential sometimes. For example, the management of a firm may be wanting to know about the future sales. For this, management must analyse the past data.

Interpretation : This is the final step of the investigation. Certain conclusions are drawn through the analysis of the collected data; and while drawing the conclusion, the nature of the original data has to be taken into consideration. Final interpretation will have to be made by the experts.

The statistical methods are not as exact as experimental methods. Hence, an expert of that particular field has to be consulted e.g., to interpret the analysis of the data connected with psychological problems, a psychologist is the right person to be called for consultation.

Wallis and Roberts : "Statistics may rightly be regarded as a body of methods for making wise decisions in the face of uncertainty."

Kendall : "Statistics is the branch of scientific methods that deals with the data obtained by counting or measuring the properties of population of natural phenomena". But this definition does not give the idea about the functions of statistics. It is rather vague.

Seligman : "Statistics is that science which deals with the methods of collecting, classifying, presenting, comparing and interpreting numerical data collected to throw some light on any sphere of inquiry".

After having gone through all these definitions, we arrive at one important conclusion and that is, 'Statistics' is the scientific study of handling quantitative information. It embodies a methodology of collection, classification, description and interpretation of data obtained through the conduct of surveys and experiments.

IMPORTANCE OF STATISTICS

From the above said facts, it can be said that statistical thinking and operations in behavioural sciences research are important from many angles. Let us therefore peep through the importance of the study of statistics one by one which is given below -

(1) Statistics permits the use of a descriptive language which is more efficient and exact in communication. It disallows any vague conclusions and emphasizes arriving at definite ones. Such techniques enables one to present his/her results in a summarised, more meaningful and conventional form and thus bring order out of chaos.

(2) Statistics is not studied for its own sake. It is employed as a tool to study the problems in various natural and social sciences; and the analysis of data is used ultimately for forecasting, controlling and exploring.

(3) Statistics enables one to draw generalizations and make predictions.

(4) People in business can study post data and forecast the conditions of their business, so that they can be ready to handle the situation in future. Today, a businessman has to face the problems of his thousands of employees; and only by using statistical methods, he can control their problems or performances e.g., he can set up certain standards and see whether the final product conforms to them. He also can find out the average production per worker and see whether any one is giving less.

(5) Complex and bewildering events can be analysed and casual factors identified with the knowledge of statistics.

(6) Leaving aside a few soliditary fields, research in behavioural sciences will be definitely poorer without the use of statistical analysis. While exploring new theories the validity of the theory has to be tested only by using statistical methods. Even in business, many new methods are introduced. Whether they are really an improvement over the previous ones can be tested by using statistical techniques.

(7) Lastly, study of statistics is gaining further impetus because of the following facts —

(i) Professional literature is replete with statistical symbols, concepts and ideas.

(ii) All advanced courses of study require a formal course work in statistics.

(iii) The professional training of behavioural scientists includes the requirements of the study of statistics.

(iv) There is a wide use of statistics in research in all fields of human knowledge.

USES OF STATISTICS

The various uses of statistics are summarised as follows :

(1) Knowledge of statistics enables the researcher to present his/her facts in a definite form.

(2) It helps in understanding the modern literature in these subjects. Most books and articles in research journals in these subjects use statistical terminology and present the results in a statistical form, which cannot otherwise be understood without adequate knowledge of statistics.

(3) It simplifies unwieldy and complex mass of data and presents them in such a manner that they at once become intelligible.

(4) Statistics helps in conducting research investigations for which sample survey or experimental approach has to be used. Knowledge of sample survey methods, design of experiments and statistical method of data analysis is essential for the advanced students who have to conduct their own investigations.

(5) It helps the professional psychologists, whether counsellors, guidance workers or clinical psychologists, in doing their work efficiently, since in the course of their work they have to administer tests, interpret test scores and maintain a record of number of cases (which constitute data requiring statistical analysis for proper interpretation). For all these purposes, statistics becomes very much helpful.

(6) It helps the teachers and school administrators in evaluating the performance of students and schools. The knowledge of statistics becomes very much helpful to them in order to deal with examination data, test scores of pupils and quantitative data used for different types of evaluation.

(7) It is useful to the teachers in determining the level of the class or group, e.g., he/she may know answers to the questions like 'How is this group like?' - Average, below average or above average? What is the typical level of the performance of the group? etc.

(8) Statistics forms the basis of scientific approach to problems, in which inductive inference is commonly used. Students of psychology and education cannot afford to remain ignorant of the scientific method of approach to problem-solving in their disciplines.

(9) It is useful to the teacher to know the general pattern of the set of scores.

(10) It is also useful to the teacher to determine the extent to which the scores spread out from the average value; e.g., he/she may get an answer to such question like "can I make use of the same material and procedure which can be suitable for all pupils? If not, how widely should they be spread out on a given test?"

(11) It is useful to the teacher to compare one class or group with the same or with other classes.

(12) Statistics provides basic tools of data analysis to educationists who are engaged in planning and administration of educational system. They need to know statistics in order to study past trends of enrollment, to estimate teacher requirements, to plan for new schools and many other such purposes.

(13) Statistics helps the teachers to know about the standing of a particular student, e.g., teacher can easily get answers to such questions like "Has Ram done well or poorly in science?" "Has Ram done better in mathematics or science?"

(14) Statistics is of very much use because it presents facts in a definite form.

(15) It helps the teachers in drawing statistical group of data.

(16) Statistis serves as a foundation for the planning of instructional activities and the basis for altering teaching technique.

(17) It helps the teachers to find out whether groups are homogeneous or heterogeneous by comparing the performance of all groups.

(18) Statistics also helps the teachers to understand and appreciate educational problems in a correct perspective.

(19) In psychology as well as in education, the quantitative methods being increasingly used to study various phenomena, for which statistical techniques are indispensable. In psychophysics one studies relationship between measurements obtained by instruments

and by human judgement. Attempts are made to measure ability (e.g., intelligence, scholastic aptitude, creativity, personality, interest attitude, etc.) by tests. Then there is the theory of learning, almost entirely based on statistical principles.

(20) It gives proper insight into the interpretation of marks.

(21) It develops in teachers the ability for description, and prediction.

(22) It helps teachers in finding discriminating value, and difficulty value of the item.

(23) Statistics is of high value in the administration of classroom instructional programme.

(24) It helps in finding out the objectivity, validity and reliability of a test.

(25) It helps in finding correlation between different subjects.

(26) According to Bowley, statistics helps in research work by guiding the researcher in the selection of representative sample.

In a nutshell, it may be stated, that, knowledge of statistical techniques is required for understanding and problem-solving all such situations, that are quite common in the fields of psychology and education.

FUNCTIONS OF STATISTICS

The statistical methods or techniques are applied only when some data are available irrespective of the method of data collection. The collected data may be quantitative as well as qualitative. If the data are qualitative, they are quantified by using techniques like ranking, scoring, scaling or coding, etc. The data are collected either by experiments or by survey methods and they are tabulated and analysed statistically. Whatever may be the resulting values obtained from analysis, proper and correct inferences have to be drawn from these numerical values. These inferences lead to the final decision.

On the basis of these ideas, the following functions of statistics are drawn out :

(a) Collection of data,

(b) Tabulation of data,

(c) Analysis of data,

(d) Interpretation of results.

Collection of data is done by two sources - Primary and Secondary. Then, researcher has also to see whether the data are suitable for study. In case, data are based on a sample, researcher should see the sample is a proper representative of the population.

Tabulation enables one to come to certain conclusion and make certain comparison.

However, such a brief way of saying about the functions of statistics will not be sufficient. One needs a detailed information regarding the functions of statistics, which is given below :

(1) Statistics presents the data in a numerical form : Numbers give the exact idea about any phenomenan. If we want to compare the speed of two workmen, working in the same factory, then, we have to see the numbers of units they turn out every day with the same type of machine. Only then, we can express the facts with the help of numbers.

(2) It simplifies the complex data : Usually the data that is collected is complex in nature. Therefore, just by looking at the figures, no one can know the real nature of the problem under consideration. But the statistical methods make the data easy to understand.

(3) **It facilitates comparison :** If we want to compare the wage conditions in two factories, we can do it by comparing the average wages and corresponding increase in price level during that period. Such comparisons are very useful in many social sciences.

(4) **It studies relationship between two factors :** The relationship between two factors like height and weight, food habits and health, smoking and occurence of cancer can be studied using statistical techniques. Estimation of one factor can be done if other is at hand and the relationship between two factors can be established.

(5) **It forecasts :** By making use of the past data, forecasting is done; e.g., a shopkeeper usually forecasts the demand for the goods from the public and stores them. He can also store only the required amount. So too, a baker can easily estimate the daily demand for bread.

(6) **It helps the formation of policies :** By studying the effect of policies employed so far by analysing them, using statistical methods, the future policies can be formulated. So too, the requirements can be studied and policies can be determined accordingly.

AIMS OF STATISTICS

Knowledge of statistics is like a knowledge of foreign language. It may prove of use at any time under any circumstances. This fact becomes clear by knowing the aims of statistics which are as stated below :

(1) To master the vocabulary of statistics.

(2) To acquire, to revive and to extend skill in computation.

(3) To learn to interpret statistical results correctly.

(4) To learn proper application of statistics.

(5) To grasp the logic of statistics.

SOME IMPORTANT TERMS USED IN STATISTICS POPULATION

Statistical methods help in describing the numerical properties of and drawing inferences about the number of population from which data are obtained. Word 'population' is commonly used to denote a group or an aggregate of people. It means all the people or object from whom or from which the sample is selected are called as 'POPULATION'. For example, if one wants to study discipline problems in the schools of Maharashtra, then, all the schools of Maharashtra are called as 'population'. But, it is very difficult to visit all the schools of Maharashtra, therefore a very few of them are selected, and these few as called a 'SAMPLE'.

There are two types of population - finite and infinite. In a finite population, the number of individual number is finite. Pupils attending primary classes in the city of NASIK, illiterate adults living in the rural areas of ANDHRA PRADESH, the computers produced by manufacturing companies in a given year are all the examples of a finite population. However, the possible tosses of a coin or the possible observations that can be taken in an experiment constitute infinite populations, since there is no limit to their number; and at least theoretically, any number of tosses can be made and any number of observations can be taken.

SAMPLE

Very often, as said earlier, for the study of a large population, one resorts to sampling. It means, the portions or group under actual study that is selected for actual study is called as sample. In the example quoted above, few schools from Mumbai, few from Kolhapur, few from Pune, few from Satara, few from Aurangabad, few from Sangli, etc., are selected, and they become a sample for the study. A sample is thus a fraction of a population drawn by using a suitable method so that it can be regarded as representative of the entire population. Thus, if we want to study the attitude of teachers towards the profession that they have chosen, then it would be not only expensive but time-consuming too, to measure the attitude of all the teachers. Hence, it becomes necessary to collect the data only from the selected sample. However, it is also necessary to know the method of selecting a sample. There are different Method of Sampling *viz.* random, stratified or quota, incidental and purposive.

SCORE

The marks assigned to a student after assessing his/her test paper in any test is called score. Suppose we want to know our student's performance in Evaluation, we would administer a test in Evaluation, and assign them marks. These marks are scores. Thus, the measurement of individual performance by means of a test is usually expressed as a score.

A score is a numerical summary of pupil's test or performance.

SERIES – CONTINUOUS OR DISCRETE

A series is formed after arranging raw scores in a definite order. Therefore, we can say that :

"A series is a systematic arrangement of items". The arrangement may be -

(1) according to magnitude i.e., the item may be arranged in ascending or descending order,

(2) according to time (time of occurance),

(3) according to their geographical location.

When the arrangement is on the basis of magnitude, the series takes the form of frequency distribution.

According to H. E. Garret, there are two types of series. They are :

(a) Continuous series and

(b) Discrete series.

(a) A continuous series is one which is capable of any degree of sub-division, though in practice, divisions smaller than some convenient unit are rarely met. For example, time, length, age, I.Q. etc. Now, I.Qs, for instance, are usually thought of as increasing by increments of one unit along an ability continuum which runs from idiot to genius. However, with more refined methods of measurement, it is conceivable that we might get I.Qs of 100.8 or even 100.83. Thus, physical measures as well as mental test scores fall into continuous series : within the given range any "score" - integral or functional - may exist and have meaning.

Thus, scores in a continuous series are continuous and are represented by the same number.

(b) Series that exhibit real gaps are called as discrete series. A salary scale in a department store, for example, may run from Rs. 8000/- to Rs. 9000/- per month in units of Re 1 : no one receives. For instance, Rs. 8009.53 per month. So too, the average number of members in a particular family may be reported to consist of 2.59 children though there is obviously a real gap between two children and three children. Fortunately, most of the variables dealt with in psychology as well as education are continuous or may be profitably treated as continuous. (A variable is an attribute or quality which may exhibit differences in magnitude, and which vary along the same dimension).

PARAMETERS AND ESTIMATES

Measurement of samples generate some numerical values like an arithmetical average. These values are termed as *estimates.* Values that are discriptive of the population are called as *parameters.* Parameters are generally estimated from sample statistics.

Thus, the numerical quantities which characterise a population (in respect of any variable) are called parameters of the population. For example, if the variable is height and the measurement of height are taken for a large population of male adults of a tribe, the mean height can be regarded as a parameter. Similarly, we can think of a parameter which gives a measure of variability in the heights of the persons belonging to the population. Usually all the important characteristics of a population can be specified in terms of a few parameters. Statistical methods help in describing the properties of a population in terms of its parameters, by providing suitable estimates of the parameters from sample observations.

DISCRIPTIVE AND INFERENTIAL STATISTICS

Discriptive statistics refers to procedures for organizing, summarizing and describing quantitative data about the samples or about the population where complete population data are available. It does not involve the drawing of an inference from a sample to its population. For example, measures of central tendency - mean, mode, median, and measures of variability - standard deviation, average deviation and range - are descriptive statistical techniques.

Statistical procedures used for drawing of inferences about the properties of populations from sample data are generally referred to as *sampling* or *inferential* techniques. Inferences about population drawn from sample measures may involve some error or discrepancy, the magnitude of which can be estimated on the basis of the probability theory. Hence, mere description of the numerical properties of samples is within the realm of descriptive statistics while making inferences from small to large group of subjects or events on the basis of probability theory in the province of inferential statistics.

VARIABLES AND CONSTANT

The term variable is used for some characteristic of a population on which the units, (that is, individual numbers) of the population differ from one another. For example, age, sex, height, intelligence, ability to perform a given task, attitude towards something, etc., are variables on which individuals differ. One can be interested in any of these variables. While some variables are amenable to measurement on a scale (e.g., height, weight), others are such that only differentiation in respect of a qualitative trait (e.g., skin colour, occupation, etc.) is possible. Therefore, we get two types of variables quantitative and qualitative.

However, opposed to the term variable is the term 'CONSTANT' satisfying the condition that the members of a group do not differ among themselves on this property. But, it must be noted that, a particular property, may be a variable in a specific situation and a constant is another situation. The property of sex, in a mixed group of boys and girls is a variable, whereas in a group of boys only, is a constant. The particular values of a variable are referred to as variates or variate values.

Variables may be continuous or discrete (discontinuous). A continuous variable may take an infinite number of values between any two points on the scale. Height, weight and chronological time are examples of continuous variables. A discrete variable can assume only a finite number of values between any two points on the scales. Size of family is a discrete variable.

Further, variables may also be classified into independent and dependent categories, if their functional relationship is of interest. The expression Y = F (X) signifies that the given value Y is some unspecified function of another variable X. It shows that given a value of X and a knowledge of a functional relationship, Y can be predicted. In experiments, the independent variable is the stimulus variable in whose effect the experimenter is interested. The dependent or criterian variable appears, disappears or varies as the independent variable is introduced, withdrawn or given in different quantities.

MEASUREMENT SCALES

Measurement can be defined as the assignment of numbers to objects and events according to the logically accepted rules. Measurement of individual performance by means of tests is usually expressed as a 'score'; and scores may be in terms of time taken to complete a task or amount done in a given time. Less often scored as expressed in terms of difficulty of task or excellence of results.

In fact, quantitative variables are classified in altogether another way in respect of scale of measurement.

(i) Internal scale and

(ii) Ratio scale

When scores are expressed in equal, units, they constitute an 'interval scale'. Thus, the scale of equal intervals denotes that the magnitude of the attribute represented by a unit of measurement on the scale is regardless of where on the scale the unit falls.

A difference in heights between 60 inches and 65 inches is equal to the difference in height between 67 inches and 72 inches. However, when working with psychological phenomena, it may not be possible to interpret the equality of units of different points of the measurement scale. For example, a difference of IQ's between 170 and 190 may not be considered to be equal to the difference between, IQ's of 100 and 120. Hence, the IQ scale does not possess equal intervals, and another immediate attribute of a measurement scale is an 'absolute zero point'.

An 'absolute zero point' is that value which indicates that a zero.quantity of the attribute exists at that point or nothing at all of the attribute being measured exists. For example, a zero height indicates "no height" at all and a zero weight "no weight" at all. However, in case of intelligence and aggressivess one may assign zero score to a person but it does not mean a point of an absolute absence of all intelligence or aggressiveness in the person.

"Ratio Scales" are those scales where the absolute zero point is known. These measures are expressed in equal units. The scale of measurement which has all the three attributes - magnitude, equal intervals and an absolute zero point - is called a ratio scale. Now, interval scale has no absolute zero point but, it is on additional characteristic of ratio scale which means, exactly nothing of the quantity being measured whether it is a physical or a psychological variable that is concerned. Ratio scales are almost non-existent in psychology and other social sciences, except in the area of psychological judgement.

Ratio scales allow for mathematical manipulation of multiplication, division and taking of square roots, etc. and permit us to arrive at sensible results that can be verified.

RANGE

Difference between the highest and the lowest score is termed as 'range'.

MISUSE OF STATISTICS / DISTRUST IN STATISTICS

Some people are of the opinion that the inferences based on statistical data are very reliable, as the numbers cannot be false; whereas, there are few people who do not trust statistical results at all. Those who are the non-believers say that numberals are the tissues of falsehood.

The statement made by HULL while expressing his distrust in statistics is given below -

"The secret language of statistics, so appealing in a fact minded culture, is employed to sensationalise, inflate, confuse and over simplify".

All such confusion is emerged due to the fact that it is not easy to differentiate between fictitious data and the data collected and tabulated in a well planned manner.

Statistics is misused either deliberately or often due to lack of knowledge. As defined earlier, statistics is a tool, technique or an approach to deal with the data to arrive at correct conclusion or decision.

In fact, if intelligently used, statistics gives wonderfully good results and if misused, it can be disastrous. This is well supported by the statement :

"Figures won't lie but liars figure".

Another statement in support of the misuse of statistics is -

"Statistics is like clay, of which, you can make a god or a devil!"

Statistics thus supports many mistaken things including statisticians! Therefore, it must be admitted that statistics in the hands of a beginner is an uncertain tool and in the hands of a propogandist, a dangerous one.

The conclusion one comes to is that, at present times statistics is a highly developed science with a deep rooted mathematical base. It is applicable to large number of social economic and business phenomena. Statistics is the backbone of industrial research, basic research and planning.

❑❑❑

CHAPTER II

CLASSIFICATION OR ORGANISATION OF DATA

We have already seen that the collected material is called data. In a true sense, the dictionary meaning of the term 'data' is facts (plural of datum, meaning fact). Thus, in wider sense, the term data designates the facts or evidence for describing a group or a situation, but in a particular sense, it is generally used for numerical facts such as heights, weights, scores on achievement tests or intelligence tests, etc.

Today, thousands of students are examined at the same time. If all, the marks secured and scored by the students are put down, without any proper organization, then, it will not be possible for us to measure the ability as well as the aptitude of the students. Further, this unwieldy, unorganised and shapeless mass of collected data is not capable of being rapidly or easily assimilated or interpreted. Now, consider, for example, the marks listed in TABLE A obtained by the students of Std. IX in the subject of mathematics.

TABLE A – DATA AS ORIGINALLY COLLECTED

Marks obtained in Mathematics by 36 students of Std. IX

55	57	55	63	64	88
65	68	59	61	63	77
85	88	88	71	76	88
70	77	75	65	69	67
58	63	88	64	71	73
80	85	63	88	56	57

Without reorganizing the above data, a cursory survey yields a general impression that most of the students obtained marks between 60 and 75.

A more laborious examination shows the lowest marks to be 55 and the heighest 88, so that, the range may be stated as 33 (88 – 55 = 33). Beyond this, it is difficult to go with the data in their present form. However, if the same marks of the students are put down in the minimum possible groups or classes, then it becomes possible to know the ability of the students at the earliest. Hence, it becomes very necessary to organize as well as systematize the data that is obtained from tests of experiments. Therefore, this task of organizing and systematizing of the data has to be done for understanding the meanings and also for arriving at some useful conclusions. Now, in order to make the data easily understandable, the first task is to condense and simplify them in such a way that irrelevant details are eliminated and their significant features stand out prominently. The procedure adopted for this process is known as the method of classification and tabulation.

CLASSIFICATION & TABULATION

The data which are not arranged according to any order and is placed in a haphazard manner is known as raw data or ungrouped data. For example, if we say that the scores of 30 students in mathematics out of 100 marks are :

35, 15, 40, 30, 10, 30, 20, 3, 14, 30, 75, 60, 15, 30, 40, 15, 36, 37, 70, 71, 38, 33, 78, 87, 16, 45, 43, 28, 20, 75.

It will be a raw or ungrouped data.

The raw data should be arranged according to either ascending or descending order. We can arrange the above data as –

3, 10, 14, 15, 15, 15, 16, 20, 20, 28, 30, 30, 30, 33, 35, 36, 37, 38, 40, 40, 43, 45, 60, 70, 71, 75, 75, 78, 80, 87.

Such a type of arrangement in an ascending order is known as ARRAY.

METHODS OF ARRANGING THE RAW DATA

(1) By Inspection : The raw data can be arranged by inspection. First we take the smallest number, then the next greater and next greater and so on. This method is useful only when the number of items is very small.

(2) By Preparing Cards : The second method is that we write down individual items on separate pieces of papers or cards and then arrange those cards in order. From those arranged cards, we can re-write the data in an arranged manner. This method is very convenient and there are less chances of making mistakes; but this involves a lot of labour.

(3) By Writing The Scores in Groups : The third method is by writing the scores or numbers under separate groups, e.g., groups of 1 to 10, 11 to 20, 21 to 30 and so on.

Before proposing to form the groups, it is advisable to find out the highest and lowest scores of the given data. This will avoid writing unnecessary groups.

This method is also very useful and can be applied easily.

Note : After the data has been arranged, number of items should be counted; and we have to be sure that the total number of items remains the same. This will enable us to find out the mistake, if there is any.

Example : Form an 'ARRAY' of the following series of 50 items.

84	46	72	74	96	65	77	47	55	80
75	67	75	57	50	44	41	86	60	86
65	69	80	55	57	90	57	71	71	76
71	70	64	61	61	63	66	68	92	78
79	72	72	87	72	73	77	83	82	71

Solution : Here we may use any of the three methods explained above. The method of inspection will be a bit difficult here.

The lowest score here is 41 and highest is 96. If we apply the third method, we can easily propose groups like 41-50, 51-60, 61-70, 71-80, 81-90, 91-100.

Group	Scores
41 – 50	46, 47, 50, 44, 41
51 – 60	55, 57, 60, 55, 57, 57
61 – 70	65, 67, 65, 69, 70, 64 61, 61, 63, 66, 68
71 – 80	72, 74, 77, 80, 75, 75, 80, 71 71, 76, 71, 78, 79, 72, 72, 72, 73, 77, 71
81 – 90	84, 86, 86, 90, 87, 83, 82
91 – 100	96, 92

After writing down the scores in groups, it is easy to apply the method of inspection and to write the data in an array.

The desired arrangement in ascending order is thus :

41	44	46	47	50
55	55	57	57	57
60	61	61	63	64
65	65	66	67	68
69	70	71	71	71
71	72	72	72	72
73	74	75	75	76
77	77	78	79	80
80	82	83	84	86
86	87	90	92	96

After writing the data in the arranged order, on counting the number of items, we see that there are 50 items.

Example 2 : Arrange the following data showing the marks obtained by 25 students out of a maximum of 100 in mathematics.

39	46	41	39	38
33	35	38	43	41
38	42	36	36	39
35	38	44	35	47
37	36	45	42	40

Solution : Here the lowest score is 33 and highest is 47. As the number of scores is limited and the difference between lowest and highest is very less, we can use the method of inspection.

Thus, the arranged data will be as under :

33	33	35	35	35
36	36	37	38	38
38	38	38	39	39
40	41	41	42	42
43	44	45	46	47

Example 3 : Arrange the following 25 scores in the descending order and then put them in term of frequencies :

171	174	176	166	171
180	177	164	185	172
166	181	175	175	169
182	176	162	171	171
160	166	183	168	163

Solution : Here the highest score is 185 and lowest is 160. Thus, we can safely make the following groups 190-180, 179-170, 169-160.

Group	Scores
180 – 189	180, 185, 181, 182, 183
170 – 179	171, 174, 176, 171, 177, 172, 175, 175, 176, 171, 171
160 – 169	166, 164, 166, 169, 162, 160, 166, 168, 163

Now, the scores can be arranged within the groups in required manner.

185	183	182	181	180
177	176	176	175	175
174	172	171	171	171
171	169	168	166	166
166	164	163	162	160

The number of items remains 25.

Let us now arrange the above scores in term of frequences :

Scores	Frequencies	Scores	Frequencies
185	1	172	1
183	1	171	4
182	1	169	1
181	1	168	1
180	1	166	3
177	1	164	1
176	2	163	1
175	2	162	1
174	1	160	1
			N = 25

CLASS INTERVALS

When the total number of scores is very great and there is a wide gap between the lowest and highest scores, we select suitable class intervals to arrange the given data. The length of each interval is usually kept as 3, 5 or 10 units. All scores lying in a particular class - interval are put together, and, it is presumed that each score concentrates round the middle point of that class interval. To find the middle point, we take the mean of the lower and upper limit of that class interval.

This type of classification gives the grouped data.

Before we count, in order to accumulate useful information, we must know what it is that we count. We do not count indiscriminately. The frequency that we record refers to a particular class of objects or events, and this involves the process of classification. Classification is a basic psychological process which can be seen in rudimentary form even in the simplest conditioned response. Wherever discriminations are made, along with generalizations, classification of a sort occurs.

To define still more clearly, it may be said then, that, Classification is the process of arranging things (either actually or notionally) in groups or classes according to their resemblances and affinities, and gives expression to the unity of attributes that may subsist amongst a diversity of individuals. It serves the following purposes :

(1) eliminates unnecessary details,

(2) brings out clearly the points of similarity and dissimilarity,

(3) allows comparisons and drawing of inferences.

Now, the question is how exactly are we to organise and systematize the disorganised and unsystematic statistical data. Let us take the same example of the marks obtained in Mathematics by 36 students of Std. IX.

In order to group these statistics or figures, into proper form, we will have to take the following steps :

(i) Finding out the Range

(ii) Dividing them into convenient Groups

(iii) Finding out their Frequency.

Let us go in details now -

(i) Finding out the Range : First of all, we have to find out which is the smallest figure in the statistical data available with us. Then we also have to know the highest figures as well. After this, let us try to find out the difference between the highest and the lowest figures. This difference is called as Range. In our example of the marks obtained in mathematics by 36 students of Std. IX, 55 is the lowest figure and 88 is the highest. In this case, Range is 33 (88 - 55 = 33). This indicates that there are about 33 figures in our statistics.

(ii) Division or Classification of the Statistics (Collected data) into Convenient Groups : After finding out the range, we have to put down the statistics into group or classes. The question is, how many groups should be formed and how many figures should be put under one group.

The law in this regard is that, there should be group ranging from 10 to 20. They should not be less than 10 or more than 20. If we shall put out 33 figures into 11 groups, then each group shall have

$33 \div 11 = 3$ figures. In other words, there will be class interval of 3. The statistics or collected data will now be written in groups or classes in the following manner :

86	–	88
83	–	85
80	–	82
77	–	79
74	–	76
71	–	73
68	–	70
65	–	67
62	–	64
59	–	61
56	–	58
53	–	55

It is not necessary to begin the classification or grouping of the statistics or data from the lowest figure. The only thing that is to be kept in mind is that the lowest figure must be included in the first group. In the above list, the classification of groups have started with figure 53 instead of 55.

Notes: (a) The lowest figure of each group is called *Lower Limit,* while the highest figure is called *Upper Limit.* In the list given above, 53 is the Lower Limit, while 55 is the Upper Limit.

(b) In statistics, 53 does not mean 53 only, 52.5 to 53.5 is taken as 53. Therefore, in the first group, we have the figures from 52.5 to 55.5.

(iii) Finding out the Frequency : After classification of the statistics under various convenient groups, we now have to find out the frequency.

After we have classified the statistics or data into various groups, we have to see which figures of our list, are included in each group and how many of the figures are there. We shall have to see about each figure of the disorganized list and its position in each group. A perpendicular line shall be drawn against the group in which a particular figure of the disorganised group find a place. This perpendicular line is called Talley. If against one group, we have put 4 Tallies and again we have to put fifth against it, we shall draw it in such a way that it runs across four straight lines. It may be drawn like this - //// (4 Tallies). ~~////~~ (5 Tallies).

Suppose we have to put 13 Tallies against one group, we shall put them as shown below –

~~////~~ ~~////~~ ///

Let us try to draw Tallies against the group that we have already drawn. This is shown as below :

Class Interval	Tallies	Frequency
86 – 88	~~////~~ /	6
83 – 85	//	2
80 – 82	/	1
77 – 79	//	2
74 – 76	//	2
71 – 73	///	3
68 – 70	//	2
65 – 67	//	2
62 – 64	~~////~~ /	6
59 – 61	//	2
56 – 58	~~////~~ /	6
53 – 55	//	2
		Total : 36

This means, after completing the tallying, the next step is to count the tallies and write down in the column of frequency. The total No. of tallies in each class interval are written in numerical form. In this way we get, the required frequency distribution table.

After putting tallies against each group, they are added up and written out, and in the end, total of the frequencies is found out. This total is denoted as (Σf).

Illustration :

Preparation of frequency distribution table is illustrated below :

The following is the record of marks obtained by 50 students in an examination. Prepare a frequency distribution table using 10 as a size of class interval and let the first class interval be 10 – 19.

63	72	53	25	39	53	17	19	64	24
58	70	89	76	42	31	55	77	68	86
50	82	54	34	75	93	64	40	36	42
31	55	21	59	49	71	61	63	29	34
83	93	66	55	45	95	47	88	49	92

Highest Score = 95

Lowest Score = 17

Range = 95 – 17 = 78

Size of class interval = 10

$$\text{Number of Class Interval} = \frac{\text{Range}}{\text{Size of class interval}} + 1$$

$$= \frac{78}{10} + 1$$

$$= 7.8 + 1$$

$$= 8.8 \text{ or } 9$$

Frequency Distribution Table

Class interval	Tallies	Frequency
90 - 99	////	4
80 - 89	~~////~~	5
70 - 79	~~////~~ /	6
60 - 69	~~////~~ //	7
50 - 59	~~////~~ ////	9
40 - 49	~~////~~ //	7
30 - 39	~~////~~ /	6
20 - 29	////	4
10 - 19	//	2
		N = 50

EXACT LIMITS AND MID POINTS OF CLASS INTERVALS

Scores as discrete values like 10, 11, 12, 13 etc., is based on the assumption that the value recorded represents a value falling within certain limits. These limits are usually taken as one-half or .5 unit above and below the value reported. A score of 51 on a test of general intelligence would imply that if a more accurate form of measurement has been used, this value would fall within the limits 50.5 and 51.5. In more precise terms, these limits are 50.5 to 51.5. In more precise terms, these limits are 50.5 to 51.499, in which the later value has a recurring decimal, but for convenience, we write the limits as 50.5 to 51.5. If the measuring process allows for a higher level of accuracy like measurement to the nearest thousandth of a second (As in psychophysical experiments), an observation of say, .285 seconds would fall within the limits of .2845 and .2855 seconds. These limits are often known as exact limits of the class interval. The terms, 'real limits', 'class boundaries' or 'end values' are also used for the purpose.

In the case of discrete variable* the class intervals themselves as given, represent the exact limits and no subtraction or addition of one half unit is required to arrive at the exact limits. For instance, the lowest class interval of 100 – 109 has the exact limits of 99.5 – 109.5. Now 99.5 is the lowest exact limit of the score 100 and is therefore the low exact limit of the class interval. Similarly, 109.5, the upper exact limit of the score 109, becomes the upper exact limit of the same class interval.

The mid points of the class intervals are required in the calculation of further statistics like mean, median, standard deviation, etc., for which the frequency distributions are generally constructed. Moreover, all the individual scores in a class interval lose their identify and take over the value of the mid point of the class interval to which they belong.

It is not difficult to determine the mid points of the class interval. The mid point of any class interval can be obtained by adding one half of the range of the class interval to the lower exact limit of that interval.

* The term variable refers to a property or characteristics on which the members of a group or set differ from one another. These properties can be sex, age, height, weight, intelligence, attitude, socio-economic status and a host of other such factors.

To illustrate see the following table :

TABLE

Exact Limits and Midpoints of Class Intervals

Class Interval	Exact Limits (Lower-Upper)	Midpoints of Intervals	Frequency f
190 – 199	189.5 – 199.5	194.5	2
180 – 189	179.5 – 189.5	184.5	4
170 – 179	169.5 – 179.5	174.5	15
160 – 169	159.5 – 169.5	164.5	11
150 – 159	149.5 – 159.5	154.5	38
140 – 149	139.5 – 149.5	144.5	8
130 – 139	129.5 – 139.5	134.5	6
120 – 129	119.5 – 129.5	124.5	2
110 – 119	109.5 – 119.5	114.5	7
100 – 109	99.5 – 109.5	104.5	7

$\Sigma f = 100$

Let us refer to the two lowest class intervals of the frequency distribution in the above table.

The class interval has a size of 10 units.

Class Interval	Lower exact Limit		One half of range	Midpoint
110 – 119	109.5	+	5	114.5
100 – 109	99.5	+	5	104.5

The important point is to take the lower exact limit and not the stated limit.

Generally, the mid point of a class interval can also be obtained by using the formula.

$$\text{Mid point} = \frac{\text{Lower Limit} + \text{Upper Limit}}{2}$$

This applies to both the stated as well as the exact limits. In our case,

$$\text{Mid point of class interval } 110 - 119 = \frac{110 + 119}{2} = 114.5$$

$$\text{Mid point of class interval } 100 - 109 = \frac{100 + 109}{2} = 104.5$$

Using the exact limits also, we obtain the same values.

$$\text{Mid point of class interval } 110 - 119 = \frac{109.5 + 119.5}{2} = 114.5$$

$$\text{Mid point of class interval } 100 - 109 = \frac{99.5 + 109.5}{2} = 104.5$$

The concepts of size, exact limits and mid points of a class interval are illustrated in the following figure.

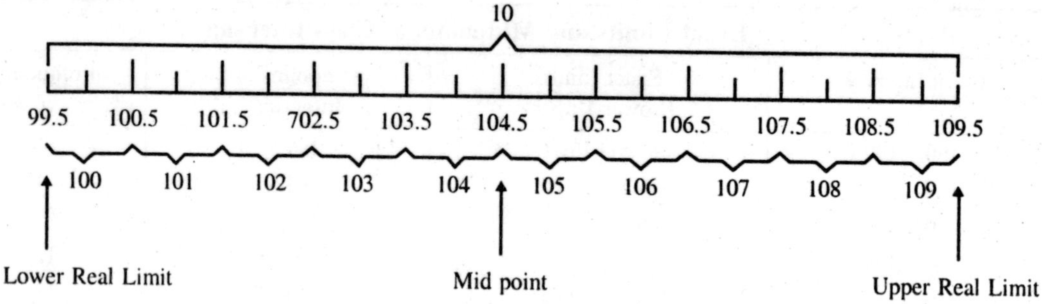

Fig. 1 Illustration of Size, Lower and Upper exact Limits and Mid point of the Interval 100 – 109.

It may seem a bit baffling that the size of the class interval 100 – 109 is 10 and not 9 as it might initially appear. But if all the scores contained in the class interval 100 – 109 are listed. (100, 101, 102, 103, 104, 105, 106, 107, 108 and 109), these are clearly 10 and not 9 of them. Moreover, it may be kept in mind that we do not calculate the size of the class interval simply by subtracting the stated lower limit from the stated upper limit of the interval. It would mean a size deficient by one unit. However, if the lower and upper exact limits are used for the purpose, the answer will be correct as in the case of the class interval 100 – 109.

Size of the class interval = 109.5 – 99.5 = 10

(1) **(A) Inclusive Method :** In this method, both scores (lower and upper) of class-interval are included.

For example : (10 – 19) means that this interval begins with score 10 and ends with score 19; but, the exact limit of the class interval are not given. In fact, score 10 means the interval 9.5 to 10.5.

(2) **(B) Exact Method :** The intervals in group (B) covers the same distance as in (A); but the upper and lower limits of each interval are defined more exactly. Therefore, to express more exactly we may write (9 – 10) as (9.5 – 10.5) and so on.

(3) **(C) Exclusive Method :** If the upper limit of a class interval is the lower limit of next class interval and the score of upper limit is not included in that class-interval, then, this type of grouping is called an exclusive method of grouping frequency distribution. In group (C) the interval (10 – 20) means that all scores from 10 upto 19 but not including 20 fall in this group. Thus, for score 20 tally will be put in class interval (20 – 30) and not in (10 – 20). Similarly, 30 will go to interval (30 – 40) and not in (20 – 30).

For rapid tabulation of scores within proper class-interval, method (A) as mentioned above should be used.

MID POINT OF CLASS INTERVAL

Mid point of a class interval is found by adding the upper and lower limits and dividing by two i.e.,

$$\text{Mid point} = \frac{\text{Lowest Limit + Highest Limit}}{2}$$

(A) $\frac{10 + 19}{2} = 14.5$ (B) $\frac{9.5 + 10.5}{2} = 14.5$ (C) $\frac{10 + 19}{2} = 14.5$

In (C) upper limit is 19 as 20 is not included in that interval.

Advantages of Frequency Distribution

Presentation of scores in the form of a frequency distribution table is very important and useful because –

(1) It makes data easier to interpret.
(2) It provides a clear visual and mental picture of the group.
(3) It enables brief and compact presentation of the data.
(4) If forms the basiș for the graphical representation of the data.
(5) It increases the clarity of the form of the distribution of scores.
(6) It helps us in comparing the performance of groups.
(7) It is essential for computing different statistics.
(8) It makes easier the detection of errors and omission.

Limitations of Frequency Distribution

With all the above advantages, frequency distribution has some limitations too. These are :

(1) Scores lose their individual importance, i.e., in class-interval (30 – 39) there are 6 scores, but we cannot say which are they – 31, 34, 35 or 36; they may be any one from 30 to 39.
(2) It is not possible to find out the scores of a particular student from it.
(3) For further calculation, it is assumed that mid-point will be representative score for the class-interval which may not be true in all cases.

Çertain Solved Examples

Example (1) : Write a frequency distribution from the following data.

39	33	38	35	37
46	35	42	38	36
41	38	36	44	45
39	43	33	35	42
38	41	39	47	40

Solution : Here the lowest score is 33 and highest is 47. Gap between the highest and lowest is 14 (47 – 33 = 14). We can have a class interval of 3 units of length; and thus we shall have 5 class-intervals.

Class Interval	Tallies	Frequencies
33 – 35	𝍸	5
36 – 38	𝍸 //	7
39 – 41	𝍸 /	6
42 – 44	////	4
45 – 47	///	3
		N = 25

Example (2) : Tabulate the following data in a frequency distribution.

3	30	49	21	29	9
5	16	40	23	32	11
8	7	30	22	15	14
15	35	15	25	1	32
25	40	14	27	8	43

Solution :

The lowest score = 1

Highest score = 49

There can be 10 suitable class intervals with the length of each interval as 5.

Class Interval	Tallies	Frequencies
1 – 5	///	3
6 – 10	////	4
11 – 15	𝍸 /	6
16 – 20	/	1
21 – 25	𝍸	5
26 – 30	////	4
31 – 35	///	3
36 – 40	//	2
41 – 45	/	1
46 – 50	/	1
		N = 30

Example (3) : Prepare a frequency distribution for the following scores using a suitable class interval.

214	258	261	232	342	215
233	244	190	195	214	224
237	274	308	221	194	244
326	257	372	236	307	285
192	239	247	243	184	200
300	267	192	242	228	231
248	219	244	301	266	311
219	306	184			

Solution : There are 45 items in all. The lowest score is 184 and highest is 372.

Gap between highest and lowest is 372 – 184 = 188.

If we take 15 as the class interval starting from 180, the total number of intervals will be 13.

Class Interval	Tallies	Frequencies
180 – 194	卌 /	6
195 – 209	//	2
210 – 224	卌 /	6
225 – 239	卌 //	7
240 – 254	卌 //	7
255 – 269	卌	5
270 – 284	/	1
285 – 299	/	1
300 – 314	卌 /	6
315 – 329	/	1
330 – 344	//	2
345 – 359	–	0
360 – 374	/	1
		N = 45

Note : You will see in all the above solved examples, the fifth tally mark has been drawn to cross the first four tally marks. This facilitates the counting of tally marks because it is in group of five.

❑❑❑

CHAPTER III
MEASURES OF CENTRAL TENDENCY

INTRODUCTION

The grouping of test scores into frequency tables is one step in the process of condensing them, so that they can be analysed as well as interpreted. Thus, after tabulating the scores or the data, it becomes necessary to interpret it; and to compare the performance of the group as a whole. Now, see, for example, if we take the achievement score of the students of a class and then arrange them in a frequency distribution, we can easily find that there are very few students who either score very high or score very low. The marks of most of the students lie somewhere between the highest and the lowest score of the whole class. In such a case, if one is asked to state one value that would best "capture" and communicate the distribution as a whole, which value will be chosen? One way to answer this question is to find out that score value which is a good "bet" about any randomly selected case for the distribution. Such a score may not be exactly correct for any given case but it should be a fairly good guess about the obtained score for that case. However, there are three different ways to specify what we mean by a "good bet" about any case :

(i) The Arithmetic Average of the Distribution.

(ii) The point exactly mid-way between the top and bottom halves of the distribution.

(iii) The most frequently occurring score or the mid point of the most frequent measurement class.

Now, such a tendency of finding out the exact value score from amongst the distributed score is called as CENTRAL TENDENCY. Such a tendency of the group of distribution that is named as Central Tendency is the typical score lying between the extremes and shared by most of the students. In this way, a measure of central tendency as Tate defines, "is a sort of average or typical value of the items in the series and its function is to summarise the series in terms of this average value".

Class Interval	Tallies	Frequencies
180 – 194	𝍸 /	6
195 – 209	//	2
210 – 224	𝍸 /	6
225 – 239	𝍸 //	7
240 – 254	𝍸 //	7
255 – 269	𝍸	5
270 – 284	/	1
285 – 299	/	1
300 – 314	𝍸 /	6
315 – 329	/	1
330 – 344	//	2
345 – 359	–	0
360 – 374	/	1
		N = 45

The discussion in earlier paragraph has already made us clear that the Arithmetic Average of the distribution is one of the different ways to specify the correct value of the whole distribution. Thus, the first of these ways of defining the Central Tendency leads to the familiar measure known as the average or the MEAN; the second leads to the MEDIAN i.e., the point exactly lying mid-way between the top and between halves of the distribution; and the third is known as MODE – the most frequently occurring score or midpoint of the most frequent measurement class.

MEAN, MEDIAN and MODE, all these three, as a class are known as Measures of Central Tendency. We do know, Frequency Distribution Table and its Graphic Representation, does give us a picture of scores of the group. But what we need is to have a performance of the group in concise form and we also want to know the level of performance of the group; hence, we must have to find out the central tendency of the group. We have already seen the definition given by Tate. Let us also go through another definition of Central Tendency that is given by Freeman. According to Freeman, "A Measure of Central Tendency is a single value interpreted to represent one of the main characteristics of the group studies." Thus, measures of central tendency indicates the central position of the performance of the group or the average performance. It indicates how the performance of the group on the average is.

Mean, Median and Mode, each of them, in its own way can be called a representative of the characteristics of the whole group and thus the performance of the group as a whole can be described by the single value which of these measures give. Since, all these values - Mean, Median and Mode - which may be taken to represent an entire distribution of scores are usually found near the centre of the data when arranged in order of size, they are commonly called 'Measures of Central Tendency'.

WHY SHOULD WE HAVE A MEASURE OF CENTRAL TENDENCY?

As an answer to the question - 'Why should we have a measure of central tendency?' We have to first of all know the importance of Central Tendency; and it is here, we automatically get an answer to the question. Hence, let us find out the Importance of Central Tendency.

The importance (or uses) of Central Tendency may be listed as follows :

(1) Central tendency is an average which represents all of the scores made by the group.

(2) Central tendency gives a concised description of the performance of the group as a whole.

(3) Central tendency enables us to compare two or more groups in terms of typical performance.

(4) Central tendency helps us in the calculation of higher statistics such as Standard deviation, Correlation, etc.

(5) Central tendency gives a true significance of the aggregate of facts on measurements on hand.

Yet, Central tendency has its own limitations too. Limitations of Central Tendency are as follows :

(i) Central tendency does not indicate any characteristics of individual scores as it represents the whole group.

(ii) Central tendency will not be a true representative of the group if the group is heterogeneous.

(iii) In a statistical analysis, if one uses different averages (mean, median, mode) he or she will get difference in results.

Let us now go in detail of each of these measures of central tendency –

MEAN

Mean is also sometimes called as Arithmetic Mean. It is the simplest and most useful measure of Central Tendency; and is nothing but the 'average' and therefore can be easily defined as the sum of all the values of the items in a series divided by the number of items. It is designated by the symbol M. or A.M.

In fact, an average is a number indicating the central value of observations or of individuals. To the question 'How good is the 6th standard in mathematics?', the most reliable and meaningful kind of answer would be the mean or median in some acceptable test of mathematical achievement. To the question, 'What is the weakest tone to which this dog will respond?' The best kind of answer is to state the average result from a number of trials. In either case, a single score or a single measurement of the threshold stimulus would be highly unreliable; for, not all measurements even from repeated observations of the same thing, have the same value. To answer those questions by reciting the long list of individual measurements, would be highly uneconomical in the reporting and therefore not very enlightening to the questioner.

The average, whether it be mean, median or mode, serves two important purposes. These are –

(i) Firstly, it is a short hand description of a mass of qualitative data obtained from a sample. It is surely more meaningful and economical to let one number stand for a group than to try to note and remember all the particular numbers.

(ii) Secondly, it also describes indirectly but with some accuracy the population from which the sample was drawn. If the sample of 6th standard children is representative of all the 6th standard children in the same school, in the same city or even in the same country, then, the average of their scores tells us much about the average that would be made by the population that they represent, be it school-wise city-wise or country-wise.

An average is therefore descriptive of a sample obtained at a particular time in a particular way. In fact, MEAN is the term for an arithmetic average. Every one who has ever computed an 'average' has computed a mean. Very simply, the Mean is the sum of the scores divided by the number of cases. Suppose that we have the

Scores : $X_1 = 10$, $X_2 = 12$, $X_3 = 15$, $X_4 = 18$ and $X_5 = 20$;

then, the mean would be –

$$M = \frac{X_1 + X_2 + X_3 + X_4 + X_5}{N}$$

$$= \frac{10+12+15+18+20}{5}$$

$$= \frac{75}{5}$$

$$= 15$$

Now, instead of the above, we just write equation for the Mean as follows –

$$M = \frac{\Sigma x}{N}$$

where, M = mean

Σx = the sum of the scores; (Σ is the capital sigma in the Greek alphabet and is customarily used as an abbreviation for sum.)

N = the number of cases.

Thus, the Arithmetic Mean or the Mean is the sum of the separate scores divided by their number. The 'average' is the popular term for the arithmetic mean. But in statistical work, 'average' is the general term for any measure of Central Tendency. However, there arise now two situations while computing mean.

These two situations are :

(1) When data are not grouped, and

(2) When data are grouped into frequency distribution table.

Let us now therefore find out the method of calculating Mean when data are not grouped.

CALCULATION OF MEAN WHEN DATA ARE NOT GROUPED

To find out the arithmetic mean, popularly called the average, we make total of measurements and then divide this total by the number of measurements or scores in terms of the following formula–

$$M = \frac{\Sigma x}{N}$$

Where M = Mean / Arithmetic Mean

Σ = "the sum of"

X = each of the measurements or series in turn

N = number of measurements of scores.

Let us take one example.

In a Mathematics Unit Test, 20 students scored the following marks out of 25 –

13,17, 15, 11, 18, 20, 11, 16, 12, 15, 18, 20, 21, 17, 12, 11, 14, 16, 15, 18

Now, the sum of these marks is 310. Therefore, by the application of the formula, we can get the mean –

$$M = \frac{\Sigma x}{N}$$

$$M = \frac{310}{20}$$

$$M = 15.5.$$

Thus, in the above example, the Mean score of the 20 students' marks in Mathematics Unit Test is 15.5.

Let us take one more example which is as follows :

Example : Find the Mean of the scores of 30 students in an examination in English.

The scores are –

10	20	30	35	40	15
7	20	35	10	15	9
11	13	17	20	40	8
15	12	11	10	9	22
24	26	28	25	35	38

Solution : $\Sigma x = 67 + 81 + 121 + 100 + 139 + 92 = 600$

$$M = \frac{\Sigma x}{N}$$

$$M = \frac{600}{30}$$

$$M = 20.$$

So far, we have solved two examples of calculating the M by the formula $M = \frac{\Sigma x}{N}$. But this method will not be useful when the data is too big or data is in the form of frequency table or when the series is too lengthy for comfortable addition.

A Mean is never an abstract number; it is always a mean of something and is always in terms of unit of measurement.

So far, we have now understood to calculate the Mean of the data that is not grouped. Now, let us know the method of calculating M of Grouped Data.

CALCULATION OF MEAN WHEN DATA ARE GROUPED

When the collected data are too lengthy for comfortable addition, it is more convenient to apply another formula for the Mean – This is as follows :

$$M = \frac{\Sigma fx'}{N} \text{ (Arithmetic M from Grouped Data)}$$

Symbol, M and Σ have the same meaning as before; x' means the midpoint of the class interval and f means the number of cases within the interval. It means, when measures have been grouped into a frequency distribution, the M is calculated by a slightly different method. Let us illustrate now, using the following example.

Example : Calculate the mean of the following distribution:

Scores X	10-14	15-19	20-24	25-29	30-34	35-39	40-44	45-49	50-54	55-59
frequency '*f*'	2	8	6	12	7	6	4	3	1	1

Solution : **Table : Calculation of the M in a Grouped Data**

Scores X	Midpoint of class interval x'	Frequency f	f.x'
55 – 59	57	1	57
50 – 54	52	1	52
45 – 49	47	3	141
40 – 44	42	4	168
35 – 39	37	6	222
30 – 34	32	7	224
25 – 29	27	12	324
20 – 24	22	6	132
15 – 19	17	8	136
10 – 14	12	2	24
		N = 50	Σfx' = 1480

$$M = \frac{\Sigma fx'}{N} = \frac{1480}{50} = 29.60$$

With the help of this method let us solve another example.

Example : Calculate the mean from the following grouped data:

Class-Interval	Frequency f	Mid point x'	fx'
90 – 94	2	92	184
85 – 89	2	87	174
80 – 84	4	82	328
75 – 79	8	77	616
70 – 74	8	72	576
65 – 69	12	67	804
60 – 64	9	62	558
55 – 59	7	57	399
50 – 54	5	52	260
45 – 49	1	47	47
40 – 44	2	42	84
		N = 60	Σfx' = 4030

In finding mean, we will first of all find the mid point of various class intervals. The method adopted for finding midpoints will be this :

$$x' = L + \frac{U - L}{2}$$

Where x' = mid point

L = Lower limit of class interval.

U = Upper limit of class interval.

The mid point of the class interval 40–44

$$= 39.5 + \frac{44.5 - 39.5}{2}$$

$$= 39.5 + 2.5$$

$$= 42$$

By applying the above formula, we find out the mid points of all the other class intervals. In the foregoing Table, we have put these in the column marked x'.

After finding x' we find the product of f and x' and put it in the next column.

We then add all the products of f x' which is represented by $\Sigma fx'$.

$$\text{Therefore, Mean} = \frac{\Sigma fx'}{N} = \frac{4030}{60}$$

$$= 67.16$$

This is known as the **long method** of finding the mean.

Let us go in for one more example of finding out the M by long method.

Example : Students of a class have secured the following marks in Mathematics. Find out the Mean of their marks by the Long Method :

97, 94, 92, 33, 47, 19, 28, 87, 9, 37, 54, 77, 5, 1, 69, 41, 70, 35, 59, 84, 30, 16, 85, 33, 34, 49, 72, 91, 2, 48, 79, 21, 7, 26, 51, 14. 81, 45, 75, 47, 83, 69, 12, 66, 36, 64, 25, 43, 68, 32, 67, 24, 15, 62, 11.

Class Interval	Midpoint of class interval x'	Frequency f	fx'
90 – 99	94.5	4	378.0
80 – 89	84.5	5	422.5
70 – 79	74.5	5	372.5
60 – 69	64.5	7	451.5
50 – 59	54.5	3	163.5
40 – 49	44.5	7	311.5
30 – 39	34.5	8	276.0
20 – 29	24.5	5	122.5
10 – 19	14.5	6	87.0
0 – 09	4.5	5	22.5
		N = 55	Σfx' = 2607.5

$$\text{Mean} = \frac{\Sigma fx'}{N} = \frac{2607.5}{55} = 47.4$$

Answer : M = 47.4

Example : Find out the mean from the following frequency table.

Class Interval	Midpoint (x')	Frequency (f)	Frequency x Midpoint (f × x')
45 – 49	47	2	94
40 – 44	42	3	126
35 – 39	37	2	74
30 – 34	32	6	192
25 – 29	27	8	216
20 – 24	22	8	176
15 – 19	17	7	119
10 – 14	12	5	60
5 – 09	7	9	63
		N = 50	Σfx' = 1120

Formula :

$$\text{Mean} = \frac{\Sigma fx'}{N}$$

Substituting the values in the formula :

$$\therefore \text{Mean} = \frac{1120}{50} = 22.40$$

Example : Calculate mean by long method of the following data :

Class interval	156-164	147-155	138-146	129-137	120-128	111-119	102-110	93-101	84-92	75-83
frequency	2	3	6	6	7	5	4	2	2	3

Solution :

Class interval	f	x'	fx'
156 – 164	2	160	320
147 – 155	3	151	453
138 – 146	6	142	852
129 – 137	6	133	798
120 – 128	7	124	868
111 – 119	5	115	875
102 – 110	4	106	424
93 – 101	2	97	194
84 – 92	2	88	176
75 – 83	3	79	237
		N = 40	Σfx' = 4897

$$M = \frac{\Sigma fx'}{N}$$

$$= \frac{4897}{40}$$

$$= 122.425$$

In the method of finding out the Mean given above, there is a good deal of calculation. In the column fx, there are huge figures that run into more digits. This makes the work difficult. Then there is a Short Method, which is more is use. In this method the Mean is assumed. This is called Assumed Mean. With the help of this Assumed Mean the real Mean is found out.

CALCULATION OF MEAN OF GROUPED DATA BY SHORT METHOD

The long method of finding mean does give us accurate results but often requires the handling of large numbers and entails tedious calculation. Because of this said fact, 'Assumed Mean' method or simply the 'Short Method' has been devised for computing the mean. The most important fact to remember in calculating the mean by the Short Method is that one 'guesses' or 'assumes' a mean at the outset and later apply a correction to this assumed value (AM) in order to obtain the actual mean (M).

Calculation of the mean of a grouped data can be computed easily with the help of the following formula :

$$M = AM + \frac{\Sigma fx'}{N} \times i \quad \text{or} \quad M = A.M + Ci \quad \left(\text{where } C = \frac{\Sigma fx'}{N}\right)$$

and AM stands for Assumed Mean, i for size of class-interval, f for the representative frequency and x' for $\frac{X - AM}{i}$ (the quotient obtained after division of the difference between the mid-values of the class and assumed mean by *i*)

The use of the above quoted formula can be easily understood through the following illustration :

Scores	f	x	$x' = \frac{X - AM}{i}$	fx'
65 – 69	1	67	5	5
60 – 64	3	62	4	12
55 – 59	4	57	3	12
50 – 54	7	52	2	14
45 – 49	9	47	1	9
40 – 44	11	42	0	0
35 – 39	8	37	– 1	– 8
30 – 34	4	32	– 2	– 8
25 – 29	2	27	– 3	– 6
20 – 24	1	22	– 4	– 4
				$\Sigma fx' = 26$

Let Assumed Mean = 42.

$$M = AM + \frac{\Sigma fx'}{N} \times i$$

$$= 42 + \frac{26}{50} \times 5$$

$$= 42 + 2.6 = 44.6$$

Let us see one more example of finding M by a short method.

Example : Find out the mean in the following frequency distribution.

Class Interval	Frequency
84 – 86	2
81 – 83	3
78 – 80	1
75 – 77	3
72 – 74	5
69 – 71	3
66 – 68	4
63 – 65	3
60 – 62	1

Solution :

Let the assumed mean be 73 which is the middle point of the class-interval 72 – 74.

Class Interval	Midpoint	f	x'	fx'	
84 – 86	85	2	4	8	+ 22
81 – 83	82	3	3	9	
78 – 80	79	1	2	2	
75 – 77	76	3	1	3	
72 – 74	73	5	0	0	
69 – 71	70	3	– 1	– 3	– 24
66 – 68	67	4	– 2	– 8	
63 – 65	64	3	– 3	– 9	
60 – 62	61	1	– 4	4	
		N = 25		Σfx' = – 2	

Sum of fx' = + 22 – 24 = – 2

$$C = \frac{\Sigma fx'}{N}$$

$$M = AM + \frac{\Sigma fx'}{N} \times i$$

$$= \frac{-2}{25}$$

$$M = 73 + \frac{-2}{25} \times 3$$

$$M = 73 + (-0.8) \times 3$$

$$M = 73 + (-0.24)$$

$$M = 73 - 0.24$$

$$M = 72.76$$

$$\therefore \quad C = -0.8$$

$$Ci = -0.8 \times 3$$

$$= -0.24$$

So far, we have known the method of finding mean by Long Method. The example that we have just solved is of finding the mean through the Short Method. Following are the steps that we have followed –

(i) We first assumed the value for the mean by choosing the midpoint of that class interval which is near to the middle of the distribution.

(ii) We now call this Assumed Mean (AM) as zero and denote it in x' column. In this column, we lay off the deviations from the assumed mean by intervals. Thus 76, the midpoint of the class interval 75 – 77 deviates from 73, the AM, by one interval and hence '1' is placed in the x' column opposite 7.3. In the like manner, 79, the mid point of the class interval 78 – 80 deviates from 73, the AM, by two interval and hence '2' goes in the x' column opposite 79. Note that the values of the deviations from the all the mid points having values greater than the assumed mean will be positive and less than that of assumed mean will be negative.

(iii) Now, multiply the x' (deviation) values by their corresponding frequencies and enter the products in the fx' column. All fx' on intervals above (greater than) AM are positive and all fx' on intervals below (smaller than) AM are negative. Now determine the algebraic sum of the deviation of the score in the fx' column. This sum comes out to be 2 in the table.

(iv) Now divide the algebraic sum of the deviations by N. This gives the correction C (–0.8) in units of class interval. If we multiply this C by i (the size of class interval), result is the correction (–.24) in score units. Add this Ci to 73 the assumed mean; the result is the actual mean 72.76

The correction may sometimes come out to be zero. In that case, it would mean that the assumed mean is the same as the true mean. This method is sometimes called as the 'coding method' since X' units really are coded values of the mid points of the class interval. One should remember that we can select the new origin (AM) anywhere in the distribution, though in order to obtain the greater benefit from the coding method, it is good to choose the origin near the centre of the distribution.

Let us have one more example :

Example : Calculate the Mean by Short Method from the following grouped Data :

Class Interval	90-94	85-89	80-84	75-79	70-74	65-69	60-64	55-59	50-54	45-49	40-44
Frequency	2	2	4	8	8	12	9	7	5	1	2

Solution :

Class Interval	Midpoint of class interval	Frequency f	x'	fx'	
90 – 94	92	2	5	10	
85 – 89	87	2	4	8	
80 – 84	82	4	3	12	
75 – 79	77	8	2	16	
70 – 74	72	8	1	8	+ 54
65 – 69	67	12	0	0	
60 – 64	62	9	– 1	– 9	
55 – 59	57	7	– 2	– 14	
50 – 54	52	5	– 3	– 15	
45 – 49	47	1	– 4	– 4	
40 – 44	42	2	– 5	– 10	– 52
		N = 60		$\Sigma fx' = +2$	

$$\text{Mean} = Am + Ci$$

$$= 67 + \frac{2}{60} \times 5$$

$$= 67 + 0.16$$

$$M = 67.16$$

$$C = \frac{\Sigma fx'}{N}$$

$$= \frac{2}{60}$$

$$= \frac{1}{30}$$

$$\therefore Cxi = \frac{1}{30} \times 5 = \frac{1}{6}$$

$$= 0.16$$

Example : Calculate Mean from the following data using Assumed Mean Method (on short method) :

Scores	49.5-51.5	51.5-53.5	53.5-55.5	55.5-57.5	57.5-59.5	59.5-61.5	61.5-63.5	63.5-65.5	65.5-67.5	67.5-69.5	69.5-71.5
f	1	3	3	4	5	7	6	4	3	2	2

Solution :

Table : Calculation of Mean from Data grouped into frequency distribution.

Scores	Midpoint	f	x	fx'	
69.5 – 71.5	70.5	2	5	10	
67.5 – 69.5	68.5	2	4	8	
65.5 – 67.5	66.5	3	3	9	
63.5 – 65.5	64.5	4	2	8	
61.5 – 63.5	62.5	6	1	6	+ 41
59.5 – 61.5	60.5 (AM)	7	0	0	
57.5 – 59.5	58.5	5	– 1	– 5	
55.5 – 57.5	56.5	4	– 2	– 8	
53.5 – 55.5	54.5	3	– 3	– 9	
51.5 – 53.5	52.5	3	– 4	– 12	
49.5 – 51.5	50.5	1	– 5	– 5	– 39
		N = 40		Σfx' = 2	

AM = 60.5

$$M = AM + Ci$$

$$= 60.5 + .10$$

$$= 60.60$$

$$C = \frac{\Sigma fx'}{N} \qquad i = 2$$

$$C = \frac{2}{40}$$

$$C = \frac{1}{20}$$

$$C = .5$$

$$Ci = .5 \times 2$$

$$= .10$$

MEAN FROM COMBINED SAMPLES OR GROUPS

Sometimes the question arises 'what will be the mean when two groups are combined ?' So, if the mean of two or more groups are known, then, the mean of a combined group can be calculated from the following formula –

$$M_{comb.} = \frac{M_1N_1 + M_2N_2 + M_3N_3 + \ldots\ldots\ldots M_nN_n}{N_1 + N_2 + N_3 \ldots\ldots\ldots N_n}$$

Where,

M_1 = Mean of the first sample.

M_2 = Mean of the second sample.

M_3 = Mean of the third sample and so on.

N_1 = Total number of cases first sample.

N_2 = Total number of cases second sample.

N_3 = Total number of cases third sample and so on.

Combined Mean is also known as Weighted Mean

Illustration : Find the combined mean of the following three groups of which the total number and mean response time is given below :

Group	N	Mean Response Time
A	20	2.6
B	25	1.7
C	25	0.8

Solution :

$$M_{comb.} = \frac{M_1 \times N_1 + M_2 \times N_2 + M_3 \times N_3}{N_1 + N_2 + N_3}$$

$$= \frac{2.6 \times 20 + 1.7 \times 25 + 0.8 \times 25}{20 + 25 + 25}$$

$$= \frac{52 + 42.5 + 20.0}{70}$$

$$= \frac{114.5}{70}$$

$$= 1.635$$

$$= 1.64 \text{ Approx.}$$

Let us have one more example.

Example : There are 5 sections for Std. X class. Number of pupils in these sections respectively are 40, 40, 45, 50 and 50. The mean score of students in mathematics test are 30.2, 32.1, 29.6, 28 and 21.2. Find the mean score of all 225 pupils ?

$$M_{comb.} = \frac{40 \times 30.2 + 40 \times 32.1 + 45 \times 29.6 + 50 \times 28 + 50 \times 21.2}{225}$$

$$= \frac{1208 + 1284 + 1227 + 1400 + 1060}{225}$$

$$= \frac{6584}{225}$$

$$= 29.2 \text{ Approx.}$$

CHARACTERISTICS OF THE ARITHMETIC MEAN

(1) Each item of the distribution matters. If we change one item, the mean will change.

(2) Arithmetical mean is greatly affected by the extreme values.

(3) The sum of the deviations about this mean is zero. That is, if we find differences between each score and the arithmetic mean and add these differences the sum will be zero.

ADVANTAGES

(a) Arithmetic mean is the most commonly used average.

(b) Arithmetic mean is easily computed and understood.

(c) If the means of sub-groups are known, the mean of the total group can be easily computed. Similarly, if the mean of the total group is known and that of one part, the mean of the second part can be easily found.

DISADVANTAGE

Its value can be greatly distorted by extreme values.

THE MEDIAN

The median is that point on the scale of scores below which one half of the scores lie and above which one of the scores lie. According to H.E. Garrent, "When the ungrouped scores or other measures are arranged in ascending or descending order of magnitude, the median is the midpoint in the series." Our readers should note that median is defined as a point and not as a score or any particular measurement. This conception has to be clearly kept in mind.

The median is symbolically written as Md or Mdn.

In an ungrouped series, the term 'midscore' or mid-measure' is used; whereas, the term 'median' is a point on the scale. It does not show any individual's actual score. When the items in the series are either in ascending or descending order of magnitude, the value or the measure of the central item in the series is median. Accordingly, Bloomers and Lindquist have defined the term as follows :

"The Median of a distribution is that point on the score scale below which one-half or 50 percent of the scores fall."

Thus, median is the score or value of that central item which divides the series into two equal parts. In this connection it should be clearly understood that central item itself is not the median. It is only the measure or value of the central item that is known as median. For example, if we arrange in ascending or descending order the marks of 5 students, then the marks obtained by the third student from either side will be termed as the median of the score of the group of students under consideration.

Now, let us see the method of computing the Median.

METHODS OF COMPUTATION OF MEDIAN

There are different methods of computation of Median. We can compute the median –

(A) When data is ungrouped and odd in number.

(B) When data is ungrouped and even in number.

(C) When data is grouped.

From the above different methods of computation, one can easily note that there are two cases in an ungrouped data (i) When the number of scores is odd and (ii) When the number of scores is even. Let us first try to solve an example when the data is ungrouped and odd in number.

Example : Find the median of the following scores –

20 18 22 27 25 12 15

Solution : First of all, arrange all the scores in ascending order –

viz., 12 15 18 20 22 25 27

Formula for finding the value of median in an ungrouped data with odd scores is Mdn $= \left(\frac{N+1}{2}\right)^{th}$ term.

$$\text{Mdn} = \left(\frac{N+1}{2}\right)^{th} \text{term} = \frac{7+1}{2} = \text{4th term} = 20.$$

Let us have another example –

Example : In an arithmetic test, 7 students scored

17 47 15 35 25 39 44 in an Arithmetic Test. Compute the Median.

Solution : First of all, for calculating the Median, the scores are to be arranged in ascending or descending order like 15, 17, 25, 35, 39, 44, 46. Here N = 7 which is odd number and therefore the score of the

$\left(\frac{N+1}{2}\right)^{th} = \left(\frac{7+1}{2}\right)^{th} = 4$. So, the student score is 35 which is the median of the given scores.

Let us have one more example

Example : Calculate the median from the following scores :

18, 20, 12, 8, 9, 22, 24, 28, 30, 34, 40.

Solution : Number of scores here is odd. First of all we shall arrange the scores in ascending or descending or magnitude such as :

8, 9, 12, 18, 20, 22, 24, 28, 30, 34, 40

Here evidently we see that median is 22 because 5 scores are on the left of it and 5 scores on the right of it. In this way we can find the median when the scores are odd. However, by applying the formula Mdn $= \left(\frac{N+1}{2}\right)^{th}$ score, we do get the some answer –

$$\text{Mdn} = \left(\frac{N+1}{2}\right)^{th} \text{ score}$$

$$= \left(\frac{11+1}{2}\right)^{th} \text{ score}$$

$$= \left(\frac{12}{2}\right)^{th} \text{ score}$$

= 6th score in the series and,

6th score in the series is 22. Hence, Mdn = 22.

Let us now put our attention on the calculation of median *when the scores are even* in number in an ungrouped data.

Example : The group of 8 students had the following scores in English Test –

8, 2, 4, 12, 4, 3, 4, 4, 9, 8, 3, 4

Solution : Let us first arrange all scores in an ascending order –

2, 3, 3, 4, 4, 4, 4, 4, 8, 8, 9, 12

Next step is of finding out the middle term – Here 4 and 4 are both the middle terms and average of them will be $\frac{4+4}{2} = 4$. Hence, Median = 4.

If the number of scores are even in an ungrouped data, we have also the formula Mdn $= \left(\frac{N+1}{2}\right)$ the measure in order of size, where N is the total number of scores.

Example : Find out the median from the following scores :

16 18 12 9 30 20 25 6 10 40

Solution : First we arrange all scores in ascending order of the magnitude –

6 9 10 12 <u>16 18</u> 20 25 30 40

We take the middle two scores and divide their sum by 2, we get $\frac{16+18}{2} = \frac{34}{2} = 17$ is the median –

By application of formula Mdn $= \left(\frac{N+1}{2}\right)^{th}$ measure in order of size

$$= \left(\frac{10+1}{2}\right)^{th} = \left(\frac{11}{2}\right)^{th}$$

$= 5.5^{th}$

Now, in the series 5.5^{th} measure in order of size is 17.

METHOD OF COMPUTATION OF MEDIAN WHEN DATA IS GROUPED

The median in grouped scores is said to be the point of distribution below which and above which lie 50% of the scores.

The formula of finding the Median of a grouped data is as follows :

$$\text{Median} = L + \frac{\frac{N}{2} - F}{f} \times i$$

where

(a) L is the lower limit of that class interval in which median lies.

(b) $\frac{N}{2}$ is half of the total of the scores

(c) i is length of class interval

(d) F is the sum of all scores below that interval in which median lies

(e) f is frequency that lies in the interval in which the median lies

Example : Compute the median from the following Grouped Data.

Scores	130-139	120-129	110-119	100-109	90-99	80-89	70-79	60-69
f	3	6	9	16	20	16	7	3

Solution :

Scores	Frequency f	Cumulative frequency
130 – 139	3	80
120 – 129	6	77
110 – 119	9	71
100 – 109	16	62
90 – 99	20	46
80 – 89	16	26
70 – 79	7	10
60 – 69	3	3

N = 80

N/2 = 40

Median falls in the interval 90 – 99. Lower limit of the interval is 89.5, Number of cases below the median interval, F = 26, Size of class interval i = 10, Frequency within the median interval, f = 20.

$$\text{Mdn} = L + \frac{\frac{N}{2} - F}{f} \times i$$

$$= 89.5 + \left(\frac{40 - 26}{20}\right) \times 10$$

$$= 89.5 + \left(\frac{14}{20}\right) \times 10$$

$$= 89.5 + 7 = 96.5$$

When scores in a continuous series are grouped into frequency distributions, the median by definition is the 50% point in the distribution. To locate the median, therefore, we take 50% $\left(\text{i.e., } \frac{N}{2}\right)$ of our scores and count into the distribution until the 50% point is reached. In the above solved example, there are 80 cases and so, the median is that point on the measuring scale above which there are 40 cases and below which there are 40. Starting with the lowest score, we count up until we have the necessary 40 cases. The above table i.e., table shows the cumulative frequencies as well as the frequency in each interval. Cumulative Frequency shows the total number having a score equal to or less than the highest score in that interval. Thus, there are 10 cases scoring at or below 79.5 and 26 cases scoring at or below 89.5. As indicated, we wish to identify the point below which 50% of the cases fall. Since 50% of 80 is 40 (N = 80), we must identify the point below which 40 pupils fall. We note that 26 pupils have scores below 89.5. We need to include 14 more cases to make up the required 40 cases. Hence, the median lies somewhere within the interval 90 – 99, whose exact limits are 89.5 – 99.5. We assume for the sake of computation that the 20 cases within this interval are evenly spread over distance from 89.5 to 99.5. In order to get the 14 extra scores needed to make exactly 40, we must go 14/20 of the way, for 14 is the number we require and 20 is the total number in the interval. The size of the interval is 10 units and so on the scale of measurement we go 14/20 × 10 or 7 units and add this to 89.5, the lower limit of the median interval. This puts the median at 89.5 + 7.0 = 96.5.

STEPS INVOLVED IN INTERPOLATING THE MEDIAN –

(i) Find N/2 or half the number of cases in the distribution.

(ii) Count up from the lower and until the interval containing the median is located (F).

(iii) Determine how many cases are needed out of this interval to make $\frac{N}{2}$ cases $\left(\frac{N}{2} = F\right)$

(iv) Divide the number needed, by the frequency (f) within the interval and multiply this by the size of the interval, (f).

(v) Add this to the exact lower limit (L) of the interval containing the median.

$$\text{Mdn} = L + \left(\frac{\frac{N}{2} - f}{f}\right) \times i.$$

Let us have one more example :

Example : Calculate median from the following grouped data :

Class interval	Frequency	Cumulative frequency
70 – 71	2	40
68 – 69	2	38
66 – 67	3	36
64 – 65	4	33
62 – 63	6	29
60 – 61	7	23
58 – 59	5	16
56 – 57	4	11
54 – 55	2	7
52 – 53	3	5
50 – 51	2	2
	N = 40	

Solution : $\frac{N}{2} = 20.$

Let us now find out in which class interval 20 lies. For this we will count the frequencies from the bottom and will proceed upwards. In the class-interval in which 20 lies, its lowest limit will be taken. Then we will find out the value of F and f and substitute them in the formula.

In the present example,

$$\text{Mdn} = 59.5 + \frac{20-16}{7} \times 2$$

$$= 59.5 + \frac{4}{7} \times 2$$

$$= 59.5 + 1.14$$

$$= 60.14$$

We have taken i 59.5 because N/2 or 20 lies in the class interval 60–61. Its lowest limit is 59.5. The cumulative frequency below this class interval is 16 and frequency which lies in this interval is 7. The length of class interval i = 2.

CHARACTERISTICS OF MEDIAN

(1) It is the middle position of the distribution.

(2) It is affected by the number of the cases, not by the size of the cases i.e., values.

(3) It is appropriate for ordinal level.

(4) Standard Error of Median is more than Mean but less than Mode.

(5) It gives the best results in a study of direct qualitative measurements such as intelligence, honesty, virtue etc.

ADVANTAGES OF MEDIAN

(1) It is easily calculated and understood.

(2) It is not affected by unusual items at extremes.

(3) It can be obtained without measuring all the objects, if objects can be arranged in order of magnitude.

(4) It can be determined by mere inspections in a frequency graph.

(5) The size of median can never be changed greatly by the addition of few more items.

(6) Median can be calculated in the case of open end distribution also, where the values of the extremes are not known.

(7) It is also useful in qualitative measurements where scores are expressed as Grades, Ranks or order of students.

DISADVANTAGES OF MEDIAN

(1) The items have to be arranged in size before median can be computed which is sometimes very tedious.

(2) The median cannot be added algebrically, therefore it is not useful for finding combined median.

(3) In a discrete series it may become indefinite.

(4) It cannot be used for computing other statistical measures such as standard deviation correlation etc.

(5) It is not useful in the cases where greater importance is to be given to extreme items as it treats all frequencies alike.

It may be concluded that median is the proper measure of Central Tendency when there is a danger that the extreme value or some abnormal value of the distribution would affect the value of the mean.

WHEN TO USE MEDIAN

We have the necessity of using median –

(i) When the exact midpoint of the distribution is required.

(ii) When it is desired that certain scores should influence the Central Tendency, but all that is known about them is that they are above or below the median.

(iii) When there are extreme scores which may affect the mean significantly.

(iv) Median is the exact midpoint of a series as 50% cases lie below and above it. Hence, when the exact midpoint of the distribution is desired, median is to be computed.

(v) Median is not affected by the extreme scores in the series. Hence, when the series contains extreme scores, median is perhaps the most representative central measure.

(vi) In case of an open end distribution (incomplete distribution '80 and above' or '20 and below' etc.) mean is impossible to be calculated. In such cases, median is the most reliable measure that can be computed.

(vii) Mean cannot be calculated graphically. But in case of median we can compute it graphically. Hence, when we have suitable graphs like Frequency Curve, Polygon, etc., we should try to compute median.

(viii) The median is specifically useful for the data, the items of which cannot precisey be measured quantitatively, e.g., qualities like health, çulture, honesty, intelligence, etc.

THE MODE

The score in a given set of data that appears most frequently is called Mode. For example in the following series –

2 3 8 6 8 9 12 8 15 16.

We say 8 is the mode because it appears most frequently.

Thus, the mode is the most often recurring score. Mode may therefore be defined as the item that occurs most frequently in a statistical series. When a particular type of dress is worn more frequently than other type in a particular season, that particular type of dress is referred to as the mode for that season.

In the frequency distribution, the frequency that is maximum in a particular class interval, the mid point of that class-interval is taken as a mode. Thus, a mode is that point on the score scale that corresponds to the maximum frequency of the distribution.

TRUE MODE AND CRUDE MODE

When data are grouped into a frequency distribution, we disinguish between a "True Mode" and a "Crude Mode".

Mode obtained by mere inspection is called the Crude empirical, apparent or inspectional mode. When data are grouped into a frequency distribution, the midpoint of the interval which contains the largest frequency is taken to be the 'Crude' or the emperical mode.

The "True Mode" is also known as estimated, computed or refined mode. The true mode is the point of the greatest concentration in the distribution i.e., the point at which more scores fall than at any other point. The true mode cannot actually be determined. A formula for approximating the true mode is as follows :

Mode = 3 median – 2 mean.

UNIMODAL, BIMODAL AND MULTIMODAL DISTRIBUTION

The mode that is obtained by mere inspection, as discussed earlier is called the crude, empirical, apparent or inspectional mode. It is almost instantaneously obtainable and it frequently serves as a good typical value of the thing measured. But, a distribution may have more than one mode. If there are two intervals with the same maximum frequency, and if they are separated by more than one intervening interval of lower frequency, we say that the distribution is BIMODAL. For example, here in the table given below, we see that in this group there are two outstanding frequencies and it has two modal values. Such a situation usually occurs when a class consists of two distinct types of pupils such as very bright and very dull students.

80 – 84	...	2
75 – 79	...	2
70 – 74	...	15
65 – 69	...	2
60 – 64	...	6
55 – 59	...	6
50 – 54	...	6
45 – 49	...	15
40 – 44	...	4
35 – 39	...	3

Now let us have a look at the following table :

80 – 84	...	2
75 – 79	...	4
70 – 74	...	6
65 – 69	...	12
60 – 64	...	12
55 – 59	...	4
50 – 54	...	3
45 – 49	...	0
40 – 44	...	3
35 – 39	...	2

Here we find that two maximum frequencies occur in adjacent class intervals. There are not two distinct groups in this class; the distribution is therefore probably really unimodal and the crude mode will be the dividing between these intervals which is 64.5. That this distribution is unimodal, can also be seen if we increase the size of the class interval from 5 to 10 units.

Sometimes, a distribution possesses several modes and none of them is prominent enough to justify one single modal value; e.g., let us have a look at the following table :

80 – 84	...	2
75 – 79	...	10
70 – 74	...	6
65 – 69	...	10
60 – 64	...	4
55 – 59	...	5
50 – 54	...	3
45 – 49	...	1
40 – 44	...	5
35 – 39	...	1

Here in this group, there are more than two outstanding frequencies and it appears that the distribution has several modal values. We are therefore, justified in saying that the distribution is multimodal. Such a situation arises when a class consists of pupils of varying abilities and when they cluster at about 3 or 4 different levels.

In grouped data, we can also find the Mode by the following method :

Mode = 3 (Median) – 2 (Mean).

The formula will give us only the approximates Mode.

Example 6 : Calculate Mode from the following grouped scores :

	Frequency	d	Df
15	1	5	5
14	2	4	8
13	3	3	9
12	6	2	12
11	12	1	12
			Total : 40
10	15	– 0	– 0
9	20	– 1	– 20
8	30	– 2	– 60
7	16	– 3	– 48
6	2	– 4	– 8
5	1	– 5	– 5
4	2	– 6	– 12
			Total : 153

N = 110 Efu = 107

First we will find out the Mean and the Median of this frequency distribution. We will find out Mean by short method.

$$\text{Mean} = \text{Am} + \text{Ci}$$

$$= 10 + \left(\frac{-107}{110}\right) \times 1$$

$$= 10 + (-9.7)$$

$$= 9.03 \text{ or Approx. } 9$$

$$\text{Median} = E + \frac{\frac{N}{2} - F}{1} \times 1$$

$$= 8.5 + \frac{55 - 51}{20} \times 1$$

$$= 8.5 + \frac{4}{20} \times 1$$

$$= 8.5 + 1/5$$

$$= 8.5 + .2$$

$$= 8.7$$

$$\text{Mode} = 3 \text{ Median} - 2 \text{ Mean}$$

$$= 2 \times 8.7 - 2 \times 9$$

$$= 26.1 - 18 = 8.1$$

CHARACTERISTICS OF MODE

(1) Mode is entirely independent of the extreme values.

(2) Mode is an average of position.

(3) Mode is that value of the items in the series which occurs most frequently.

WHEN TO USE MODE

Usually we make use of mode –

(1) When we wish to know what is the most typical case i.e., when information regarding the most typical case, such as the style of dress or shoes is all that is wanted.

(2) When highest and lowest scores are not to be given much importance, provided they are not in the model class, we require to make use of mode.

(3) In many cases crude mode can be computed by just having a look at the data. It gives the quickest, although approximate, measure of central tendency. Therefore, in cases where a quick and approximate measure of central tendency is all that is desired, we compute mode.

(4) Mode is that value of the item which occurs most frequently or is repeated maximum number of times in a given series. Therefore, when we need to know the most often recurring score or value of the item in a series, we compute mode. On account of this characteristic, mode has unique importance in the large scale manufacturing of consumption goods.

(5) Mode can be computed from the histogram and other frequency curves. Therefore, when we already have a graphical representation of the distribution in the form of such figures it is appropriate to compute mode instead of mean.

(6) The aspect of 'when to use mode' can be determined with considerable accuracy from the well selected sample data.

MODE IS USEFUL

(1) When a quick measure is all what is wanted.

(2) When an approximate measure of central tendency would do.

(3) When only the most typical value is required. For example the most typical size of the shirt or shoes worn by an average man.

ADVANTAGE OF MODE

(1) It is easily understood.

(2) In smaller number of cases it can be a calculated observation.

(3) It is capable for further algebric treatment.

(4) It can be very easily determined from the graph.

(5) It is the most descriptive average.

(6) The values need not be arranged in order of size.

DISADVANTAGES OF MODE

(1) A clearly defined mode does not always exist.

(2) Sometimes it is difficult to calculate mode.

(3) It does not help us for further statistical treatment.

(4) As it is not based on all the observation of the series, it may also be unrepresentative in many cases.

(5) Its significance is very limited.

(6) In small number of cases, there may be no mode at all; because, no value may be repeated.

(7) As compared to mean, it is very much affected by fluctuations of sampling.

COMPARISON OF MEAN, MEDIAN AND MODE

When we want to make a comparison between Mean, Median and Mode, means, we have to find out certain emperical relationships that exist between mean, median and mode.

The Mean, Median and Mode are sensitive to different aspects of a group of scores; generally they are not the same in a given distribution. Their relative positions from the following figures.

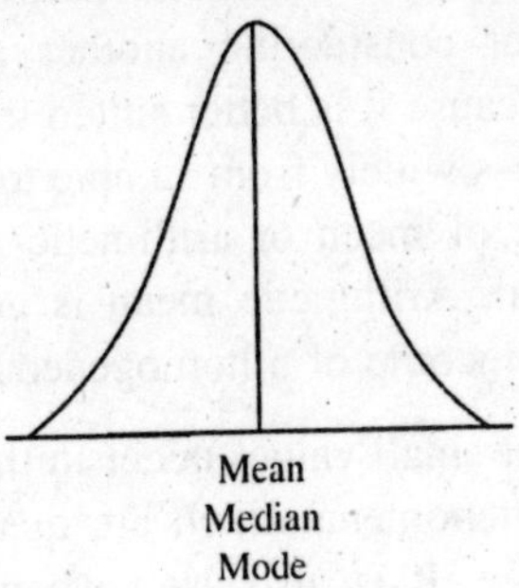

(A)

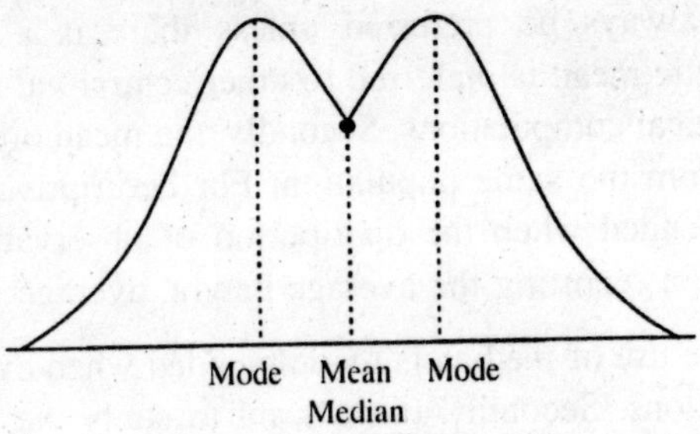

(B)

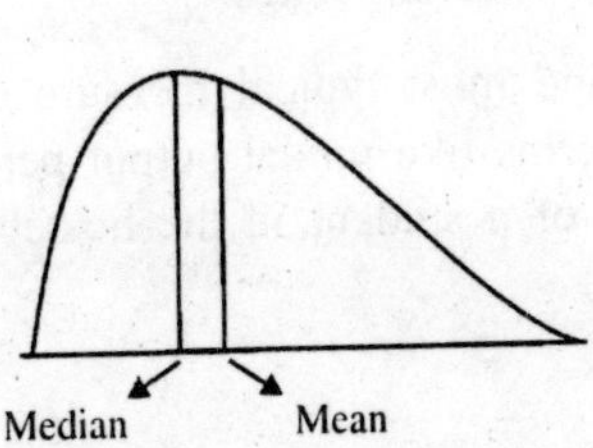

(C)

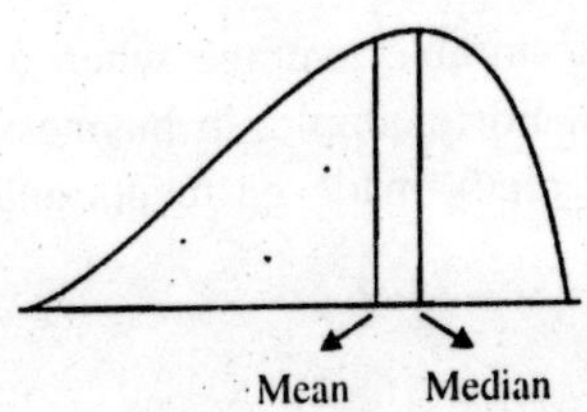

(D)

(i) If the distribution is symmetrical and unimodal (having one mode only), the mean, mode and median fall at the same point, i.e., they have the same value (See figure A). Thus, in case of such a perfectly symmetrical distribution, mean, median and mode are equal.

(ii) If the distribution is symmetrical but bimodal (having two modes, the mean and the median fall at the same point but the values of the modes are different. (See figure B)

(iii) For moderately, asymmetrical distributions, the locations of mean, median and mode are shown in the figure C. Here the scores are bunched on the lower side of the mean. It is a positively skewed curve where mean has higher value than that of median and mode the lowest.

(iv) On the other hand, in case of the figure D, we see a negatively skewed curve. Here the scores are bunched on the higher side of mean; and value of median is now higher than that of mean; and the mode the largest.

LIMITATIONS OF THE AVERAGES

As defined earlier, an average is a single representative value which possesses not only the convenience of compactness, but also the inconvenience of brevity. Due to this fact, there is no all purpose average which can be universally used. Moreover, it is not always easy to decide which average is most suitable for a particular statistical analysis. The characterstics of different averages are listed in terms of merits and demerits. But these terms too have no fixed meaning. For example, arithmetic mean is suitable as its computation is based on all the variates. But we cannot use it even if a single variate or observation is missing in some investigation. Median or mode may then be used for calculating the central value of the given variates. Thus, while using averages, their inherent limitations should always be kept in mind and it is not always easy to decide about a suitable average in a given field of investigation. We shall consider few examples to illustrate the selection of an average.

It is generally believed that arithmetic mean is the best average for all general purposes and should always be preferred unless there is a definite reason for considering another average. Arithmetic mean is preferred to other central value in most cases because it is better suited to further arithmetical computations. Secondly, the mean ordinarily fluctuate less widely from sample to sample taken from the same population. For descriptive purposes, the use of mean or arithmetic mean is recommended when the distribution of observations is symmetrical. Arithmetic mean is generally suitable in reporting the average height, average score and average income of a homogeneous class.

The use of median is recommended when exceptionally large or small values occur in the given observations. Secondly, if we want to study the average of such phenomena which are qualitative, e.g., intelligence, honesty etc., median is the most suitable average. It is also used when one is reporting the average performance of students on several tests in different states.

Mode is a suitable average when a quick, approximate and most typical measure of central value is desired. For example, in business and commerce, the terms like modal output per machine average size of ready-made garments and average expenditure of a student in the hostel refers to mode.

CHAPTER IV

MEASURES OF VARIABILITY

Measure of central tendency - mean, median and modeprovide central value or typical representative of a set of scores as a whole. Through these measures we can represent a characteristic or quality of the whole group by a single number. By comparing such typical representative of the different sets of scores we can compare the achievement of the two groups. But these representative numbers give us merely an idea of the general achievement of the group as a whole, and does not show how the individual scores and spread out. Therefore, through measures of central tendency we are unable to know much about the distribution of scores in a series or characteristics on items in a group. Hence, measures of central tendency provide insufficient base for the comparison of two or more frequency distribution or sets of scores. It can be made more clear from the following example.

The scores of two groups of students may be as

Group A					Group B				
19,	16,	20,	26	21,	18,	17,	18,	22,	18,
12,	16,	18,	11,	50,	10,	15,	20,	25,	19,
6,	12,	5,	40,	8.	27,	16,	17,	14,	15

In both these groups, the number of students is 15 and total number of scores is 270 for each group. Thus, the average for each group is 18. But in the first group, the difference between the lowest and highest score is 50 – 2 = 48, while in the second group it is 27 – 10 = 17 only. The variability of the two groups is obviously different.

Looking in this way, there is a great need of paying consideration to the variability or dispersion of the scores in the sets of scores or series if we want to describe and compare them.

DIFFERENT MEASURES OF VARIABILITY OR DISPERSION

These are chiefly, four measures of indicating variability or dispersion within the set of scores. They are :

(a) The Range (R)

(b) The Quartile Deviation (Q)

(c) The Average Deviation (AD) or The Mean Deviation (MD)

(d) The Standard Deviation (SD)

Each of the above measures of variability gives us the degree of variability or dispersion by the use of a single number and tells us how the individual scores are scattered or spred over throughtout the distribution or gives data.

1. THE RANGE

It is very simple and quick measure of variability. It is calculated by subtracting the lowest score from the highest score of the group.

(i) Range of Group A = Highest score - Lowest score
= 50 − 2
= 48

(ii) Range of Group B = Highest score - Lowest score
= 27 − 10
= 17

Merits of Range :

(1) It is very easily determined and understood.

(2) It is very useful as a supplementary meausre. In addition to other measures it helps in the description of data.

(3) It is a moderately reliable measure in large unimodal samples

(4) It is a very simple measure of variability.

Shortcomings of Range :

(1) It is not a representative measure of variability.

(2) It is based only on two extreme scores and tells nothing about the variation among other Intermediate scores. If we change the middle scores keeping highest and lowest score same, the range may not change. This it is not the sensitive measure of variability.

(3) It has poor applicability in Psychology and Education.

2. THE QUARTILE DEVIATION

The measure of variability (Q) is an improvement over the range. The quartile deviation in its procedure does not consider the highest 25 per cent and lowest 25 per cent scores. It consideres the middle 50 per cent scores. The fact is evident by its formula.

$$Q = \frac{Q_3 - Q_1}{2} = \frac{P_{75} - P_{25}}{2}$$

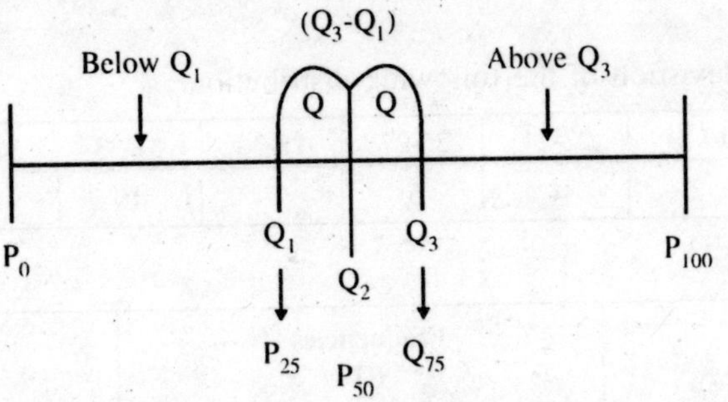

The one half of the range from Q_1 to Q_3 is sometimes used as an index of variability. This index is also known as the semi-interquartile range (Q) is defined by the formula

$$Q = \frac{Q_3 - Q_1}{2} = \frac{P_{75} - P_{25}}{2}$$

Another way to define the sami-interquartile (Q) is the mean of distance of Q_3 and Q_1 from the median. The type of distance value which is indicative of variability is the average of the distances of certain score values from some central point. Suppose we determine the mean of the distance of Q_3 and Q_1, from the median. This can be shown repectively -

$$(Mdn - Q_1) \text{ and } (Q_3 - Mdn)$$

By adding these distances from the median point and dividing by two, to find their mean the following formula is used, and Q is obtained by the following expressions.

$$Q = \frac{(Q_3 - Mdn) + (Mdn - Q_1)}{2}$$

$$= \frac{Q_3 - Q_1}{2} = \frac{P_{75} - P_{25}}{2}$$

Actually any point between Q_1 and Q_3 would serve as well as the median. The quartile deviation is useful only in the situations in which a crude measure is sufficient or required for the purpose of the paricular analysis. It is alos used along the *medion* in skewed distribution of data.

The quartile-deviation is one half of difference $(Q_3 - Q_1)$ or $(P_{75} - P_{25})$ which is one half of middle 50 percent of the distribution. Therefore it is known as quartile-deviation, because middle one half of 50 percent is one quarter of the distribution. The formula for calculating quartile deviation has been devised in this expression -

$$Q = \frac{(Q_3 - Q_1)}{2} \text{ or } \frac{(P_{75} - P_{25})}{2}$$

It is also known as semi-inter-quartile range of a distribution. It is the range of middle one half of the distribution.

METHOD FOR CALCULATING QUARTILE DEVIATION

Consider the following example :

Example :

Calculate quartile devistion of the following distribution :

Class Interval	19-21	22-24	25-27	28-30	31-33	34-36	37-39	40-42
Frequencies	2	4	5	7	10	9	8	5

Solution :

Class-interval (x)	Frequencies (f)	Cumulative frequencies (cd)
40-42	5	50
37-39	8	45
34-36	9	37
31-33	10	28
28-30	7	18
25-27	4	11
22-24	4	6
19-21	2	2
Total	**N = 50**	**Upward**

Solution :

Q_1 or P_{25} is calculated by using the following formula

$$Q_1 \text{ or } P_{25} = L_1 + \left(\frac{N/4 - fb}{fa}\right) i \qquad \text{... (i)}$$

Where : Q_1 = First-quartile i.e. P_{25}

L = Lower limit of class-interval in which Q_1 or P_{25} falls.

N = Size of the group

fa = Actual frequency of the C. I.

fb = Frequency below the C.I

i = Size of the class-interval.

Putting the values in the formula for Q_1

$$Q_1 = 27.5 + \left(\frac{12.5 - 11}{7}\right) \times 3$$

$$= 27.5 + 0.64 = 28.14$$

Similarly Q_3 or P_{75} is calculated by employing the following formula –

$$Q_3 \text{ or } P_{75} = L_3 + \left(\frac{(3N/4 - fb)}{fa}\, i\right) \quad \text{... (2)}$$

Where : Q_3 = Third quartile or P_{75}

L_3 = Lower limit of the class-interval in which Q_3 or P_{75} falls.

N = Size of sample

fa = Actual frequency of the C.I.

fb = frequency below the C.I.

i = Size of the class-interval

Putting the values in this formula for Q_3

$$Q_3 = 36.50 + \left(\frac{37.5 - 37}{8}\right) \times 3$$

$$= 36.50 + 0.19 = 36.69$$

Now the values are put in the formula of Q.

$$Q_3 = \frac{Q_3 - Q_1}{2} \text{ or } \frac{P_{75} - P_{25}}{2}$$

$$= \frac{(36.69 - 28.14)}{2} = \frac{8.55}{2} = 4.28$$

The quartile deivation is 4.28

Example : Caculate quartile deviation of the following distribution :

Class Interval	45-49	40-44	35-39	30-34	25-29	20-24	15-19
Frequencies	2	3	5	9	6	4	1

Solution :

Class-Interval	**frequencies (f)**	**Cumulative frequencies (cf)**
45 – 49	2	30
40 – 44	3	28
35 – 39	5	25
30 –34	9	20
25 – 29	6	11
20 – 24	4	5
15 – 19	1	1
	N = 30	

$$Q_1 = L_1 + \frac{(N/4 - f_b)}{f_a} \times i$$

$$= 24.5 + \frac{7.5 - 5}{6} \times 5$$

$$= 24.5 + \frac{2.5 \times 5}{6}$$

$$= 24.5 + \frac{12.5}{6}$$

$$= 24.5 + 2.83$$

$$= \mathbf{27.33.}$$

$$Q_3 = L_3 + \frac{(3N/4 - f_b)}{f_a} \times i$$

$$= 34.5 + \frac{22.5 - 20}{9} \times 5$$

$$= 34.5 + \frac{2.5 \times 5}{9}$$

$$= 34.5 + \frac{12.5}{9}$$

$$= 34.5 + 1.39$$

$$= \mathbf{35.89.}$$

$$Q = \frac{Q_3 - Q_1}{2}$$

$$= \frac{35.89 - 27.33}{2}$$

$$= \frac{8.56}{2}$$

$$= \mathbf{4.28.}$$

Merits of Quartile Deviation :

(1) Q is not dependent on the values of the exterme items and, therefore, it is more representative than the range.

(2) It is very easy to compute, to understand and to interpret.

(3) It is the most useful measure of variability in which median has been used as a measure of variability.

(4) It is applicable even to those frequency distribution which have unequal class-intervals.

(5) It is quite useful in small samples and when there are extreme meaures in the distribution.

Shortcomings of Quartile Deviation :

(1) Twenty-five per cent of scores fall below the first quartile, and 25% above the Q_3. The Q, therefore, is a measure of only 50% of the middle scores.

(2) It is a non-algebraic property and so is less reliable then the S.D.

3. THE AVERAGE DEVIATION OR MEAN DEVIATION

The quartile deviation does not provide the awarness about the variability of total distribution. It represents the variation of middle 50 percent scores. Therefore, mean deviation and standard deviation are the improvement over the quartile and range measures of variability. All the scores are considered in calculating mean deviation and standard deviation.

Definition of Mean Deviation : "The mean deviation or average deviation is the arithmetic mean of all the deviations from the mean we do not consider the plus, *minus signs.*"

The mean deviation of ungrouped data is calculated by using the following formula –

$$\text{M.D.} = \frac{\Sigma(|X-M|)}{N} = \frac{E|x|}{N}$$

Where; X = Score

M = Mean

$|X - M|$ = Modulus values regardless of sign or $|x|$

Σ = Sum

N = Size of sample

The sum of deviation from the mean is always zero, hence moduls values are considered. It means, that the difference is taken not arithmeticasl subtration. All the deviations of scores from mean are added without considering the signs of the deviation.

(i) Compulation of Average Deviation (AD) from ungrouped data :

Example : Find out the Average Deviation of the scores 15, 10, 6, 8, 11 of a series.

Solution : The mean of given series = 15 + 10 + 6 + 8 + 11 = 10

Scores X	*Deviation from the mean (X - M) = x*	$\|x\|$
15	5	5
10	0	0
6	-4	4
8	-2	2
11	1	1
N = 5		$\Sigma \|x\| = 12$

$$\text{Average Deviation} = \frac{\Sigma|x|}{N}$$

$$= \frac{12}{5}$$

$$= 2.4$$

(ii) Computation of Average Deviation from grouped data :

From grouped data AD can be computed by formula -

$$\text{Average Deviation} = \frac{\Sigma(x)}{N}$$

Consider the following example.

Example :

Calculated Mean Deviation from the following grouped data :

Class Interval	45-49	40-44	35-39	30-34	25-29	20-24	15-19
Frequency	2	3	5	9	6	4	1

Solution :

Class-Interval	*f*	*Mid-Point X*	*fX*	*Deviation x'*	*fx'*	$\|fx'\|$
45–49	2	47	94	15	30	30
40–44	3	42	126	10	30	30
35–39	5	37	185	5	25	25
30–34	9	32	288	0	0	0
25–29	6	27	162	–5	– 30	30
20–24	4	22	88	–10	– 40	40
15–19	1	17	17	–15	–15	15
	N = 30		$\Sigma fx = 960$			$\Sigma \|fx'\|$

Steps :

(1) First of all mean is calculated.

(2) Values of deviations from mean (x') are calculated using the formula.

Deviation (x') = Mid-point of the class interval – Mean

(3) Deviations are multiplied by the respective class freguencies to get fx'

(4) Corresponding values of $|fx'|$ are found with no regard to sings.

(5) $\Sigma |fx'|$ is computed.

(6) Formula is applied to get the value of Average Deviation

$$\text{Average Deviation} = \frac{\Sigma |fx'|}{N}$$

In this example

$$\text{Mean} = \frac{\Sigma fx}{N} = \frac{960}{30} = 32$$

and

$$\text{Mean Deviation or Average Deviation} = \frac{\Sigma |fx'|}{N} = \frac{170}{30} = 5.66$$

Example :

Calculate Mean Deivation of the following data :

Class Internal	29-31	26-28	23-25	20-22	17-19	14-16
Frequency	2	3	4	3	2	1

Solution :

Class-Interval	*f*	*Mid Point X*	*fX*	*Deviation x'*	*fx'*	*|fx'|*
29-31	2	30	60	6.6	13.2	13.2
26-28	3	27	81	3.6	10.8	10.8
23-25	4	24	96	0.6	2.4	2.4
20-22	3	21	63	–2.4	–7.2	7.2
17-19	2	18	36	–5.4	–10.8	10.8
14-16	1	15	15	–8.4	–8.4	8.4
	N = 15		ΣfX = 351			Σ |fx'| = 52.8

$$\text{Mean} = \frac{\Sigma fx}{N} = \frac{351}{15} = 23.4$$

$$\text{Mean Deviation} = \frac{\Sigma|fx'|}{N}$$

$$= \frac{52.8}{15}$$

$$= 3.52$$

Merits of Mean Deviation :

(1) It is a very simple measure of variability and is eaily understood

(2) It is also very meaningful, even to persons not rained in statistical procedures.

(3) It is not based on extreme measures alone, but into account the fluctuations of all the items, or values in a given series.

(4) It is a very reliable measure even in small samples, and where it is desirable o give due importance to all the deviations.

Shortcomings of Mean Deviation :

(1) Being based on all the deviations it may be inflated or depressed by a single extreme value, which is very high or very low.

(2) Since signs are disregarded and only absolute values are taken, it is not an algebraic measure and so canot be reliably used in mathematical operations.

Standard Deviation :

Standard Deviation of a set of a scores is defined as the square root of the average of the quares of the deviation of each from the mean.

Symbolically we can saya that

$SD = \sqrt{\sum(X-M)^2 N} = \sqrt{\frac{\sum x^2}{N}}$ Where X stands for individual score, M for mean of the given set of scores. N for total number of the scores and x for the deviation of each score from the mean.

The *standard deivation* is by far the most important and most widely used index of variability. It makes complete use of information on variability contained in the data, and is much more meaningful. The standard deviation is most stable index of variability and it is used in research work.

The standard deviation differes differes from the mean deviation in several respects. In computing standard deviation. The signs are disregarded and all deviations are treated as positive, where as in computing standard deviatio, the problem of signs is avoided by squaring the deviations. The squared deviations used in computing the standard deviaton are always taken from mean, never from the median or mode.

Standard Deviation is regarded as a most stable and reliable measure of variability as it employs mean for its computation. It is often called as Root - mean square deviation and is denoted by the Greek letter sigma (σ).

Computation of Standard Deviation (SD) from ungrouped data :

SD can be, computed from the ungrouped scores by the following formula -

$$\sigma = \sqrt{\frac{\sum x^2}{N}}$$

Below we illustrate the use of this formula by taking a particular example.

Example : Calculate SD for the following set of test scores : 52, 50, 56, 68, 57, 70

Solution : Mean of the given scores = 480/8 = 60

Scores *X*	*Deviation from the mean* *(X - M) = x*	*Squares of Deviations* x^2
52	-8	64
50	-10	100
56	-4	16
68	8	64
65	5	25
62	2	4
57	-3	9
70	10	100
		$\Sigma x^2 = 382$

$$\text{Now } \sigma = \sqrt{\frac{\sum x^2}{N}} = \sqrt{\frac{382}{8}} = \sqrt{47.75} = 6.91$$

Example :

Calculate standard deviation of the following scores :

5, 7, 9, 12, 15, 17 and 19.

Solution :

$$\text{Mean of the scores (M)} = \frac{5+7+9+12+15+17+19}{7}$$

$$= \frac{84}{7}$$

$$= 12$$

Scores *X*	*Deviation from the mean* *(X – M) or x*	*Square of Deviation* x^2
5	-7	49
7	-5	25
9	-3	9
12	0	0
15	3	9
17	5	25
19	7	49
N = 7		$\Sigma x^2 = 166$

$$\sigma = \sqrt{\frac{\sum x^2}{N}}$$

$$= \sqrt{\frac{166}{7}}$$

$$= \sqrt{23.714}$$

$$= 4.87$$

Compultation of SD from the grouped data :

The method of calcualtion of S.D. from grouped data into a frequency distribution has been illustrated with the help of following examples.

Long Method of Computing Standard Deviation :

Compute SD of the following grouped data :

Class Interval	45-49	40-44	35-39	30-34	25-29	20-24	15-19	10-14	5-9
frequency	2	3	4	6	8	7	5	3	2

Solution :

Class Interval	*f*	*X*	*fX*	x^2	fx^2	fx^2
45-49	2	47	94	20.37	40-74	829-8738
40-44	3	42	126	15.37	46-71	708-7101
35-39	4	37	148	10.87	41-48	430-1476
30-34	6	32	192	5.37	32.22	173-0214
25-29	8	27	216	.37	2.96	1.0952
20-24	7	22	154	-4.63	-32.41	150.0583
15-19	5	17	85	-9.63	-48.15	463.6845
10-14	3	12	36	-14.63	-43.89	642.1107
5-9	2	7	14	-19.63	-39.26	770.6738
	N = 40		1065			4169.3760

Solution :

$$\text{Mean} = \frac{\Sigma fX}{N}$$

$$= \frac{1065}{40} = \mathbf{26.63}$$

$$\text{SD} = \sqrt{\frac{\Sigma fx'^2}{N}}$$

$$= \sqrt{\frac{4169.3760}{40}}$$

$$= \sqrt{104.2344}$$

$$= 10.209 = \mathbf{10.21}$$

This method of computing standard deviation is known as long method or actual mean method. This is a method which takes quite long time and due to decimal figures the possibility of committing error is also higher. These limitations are removed in calculating S.D. by another method known as short method or assumed mean method. The anser always remains the same irrespective of the method used. An example of calculating S.D. by short method is given here.

Short Method of Computing Standard Deviation :

Example : Calculate Standard Deveation of the following grouped data :

Class Interval	45-49	40-44	35-39	30-34	25-29	20-24	15-19	10-14	5-9
Frequency	2	3	4	6	8	7	5	3	2

Solution :

Class Interval	*f*	*x*	*fx*	*fx²*
45 – 49	2	4	8	32
40 – 44	3	3	9	27
35 – 39	4	2	8	16
30 – 34	6	1	6	6
25 – 29	8	0	0	0
20 – 24	7	– 1	– 7	7
15 – 19	5	– 2	– 10	20
10 – 14	3	– 3	– 9	27
5 – 9	2	– 4	– 8	32
	40		– 3	167

In computing SD by the short or assumed mean method, first of all mid point of any class-interval is taken as the assumed mean and then deviations (*x*) from it are taken as +1, +2, +3 in the ascending side and –1, –2, –3 in the descending side. The 'class-interval' near the centre of the whole

frequency distribution is generally chosen. It is 25–29 in the above case. Now the frequency (f) column is multiplied with the deviation (x) column to obtain fx^2. The fx^2 may again be multiplied with x^2 to obtain fx^2, the fx and fx^2 columns may be totalled to get Σfx and Σfx^2 respectively. SD may then be calculated by the formula given.

Example :

Compute SD for the frequency distribution given below. The mean of this distribution is 115.

I.Q. Scores	127-129	124-126	121-123	118-120	115-117	112-114	109-111	106-108	103-105	100-102
Frequency	1	2	3	1	6	4	3	2	1	1

Solution :

I.Q. Scores	*f*	*X*	*M*	*X-M (x)*	x^2	fx^2
127-129	1	128	115	13	169	169
124-126	2	125	115	10	100	200
121-123	3	122	115	7	49	147
118-120	1	119	115	4	16	16
115-117	6	116	115	1	1	6
112-114	4	113	115	-2	4	16
109-111	3	110	115	-5	25	75
106-108	2	107	115	-8	64	128
103-105	1	114	115	-11	121	121
100-102	1	101	115	-14	196	196
	N = 24					$\Sigma fx^2 = 1074$

$$\text{Now } \sigma = \sqrt{\frac{\sum fx^2}{N}} = \sqrt{\frac{1074}{25}} = \sqrt{47.75} = 6.69$$

In the above computation work we have made/use of M, the mean of the distribution If not given in the example, it can be computed in the following way :

Calculation of Mean. Let Assumed Mean be 116.

Scores	*f*	*x (mid-value)*	$x' = \frac{x - A}{i}$	*fx'*
127-129	1	128	4	4
124-126	2	125	3	6
121-123	3	122	2	6
118-120	1	119	1	1
115-117	6	116	0	0
112-114	4	113	-1	-4
109-111	3	110	-2	-6
106-108	2	107	-3	-6
103-105	1	104	-4	-4
100-102	1	101	-5	-5
	N = 24			$\Sigma fx' = 8$

Formula

$$M = A + \sqrt{\frac{\sum fx'}{N}} \times i = 116 - \frac{8}{24} \times 3 = 116 - 1 = 115$$

Mean = 115

Computation of SD from grouped data by Short-cut Method :

SD from grouped data can also be computed by the following formula -

$$\sigma = i\sqrt{\frac{\sum fx'^2}{N} - \left(\frac{\sum fx'}{N}\right)^2}$$

Where the notation have the same meaning as desired earlier. The use of this formula can be explained by solving the example given above.

I.Q. Scores	*f*	*X*	$x' = \frac{x-A}{i}$	*fx*	fx^2
127-129	1	128	4	4	16
124-126	2	125	3	6	18
121-123	3	122	2	6	12
11-120	1	119	1	1	1
115117	6	116	0	0	0
112-114	4	113	-1	-4	4
109-111	3	110	-2	-6	12
106-108	2	107	-3	-6	18
103-105	1	104	-4	-4	16
100-102	1	101	-5	-5	25
	N = 24			Σfx = -8	Σfx^2 = 122

Formula $\sigma = i\sqrt{\frac{\sum fx^2}{N} - \left(\frac{\sum fx}{N}\right)^2}$

$$= \sqrt[3]{\frac{122}{4}\left(\frac{-8}{24}\right)^2}$$

$$= 3 \times \sqrt{\frac{122}{4} - \left(\frac{64}{24 \times 24}\right)} = \frac{3}{24}\sqrt{122 \times 24 \times -34}$$

$$= \frac{1}{8}\sqrt{2864} = \frac{53.51}{8}$$

Standard Deviation = 6.69

Merits of Standard Deviation :

(1) It is the most reliable measure of variability and is useful in further statistical operations and in making inferences.

(2) It is most useful in those cases when Mean ha sbeen taken as a measure of central tendency.

(3) The greater the value of S.D. the more would scores scatter from the Mean. S.Ds. can be shown on distribution curves. 1 S.D. distance includes 68.3% cases, 2 S.D. distance 95.4% cases and so on.

(4) It is an algebraic measure and does not suffer from the mathematical fallacy of the M.D., in which signs are disregarded.

(5) It can be reliably used in those cases when extreme deviations exercise greater incluence than other deviations.

Shortcomings of Standard Deviation :

(1) S.D.is easily understood. Persons not trained in statistical Procedures find it interpret.

(2) It is sensitive to extreme values. If majority of scores are of moderate values and there are few very extreme scores, the S.D.would be unduly deflected.

PERCENTILES, DECLES AND PERCNTILE RANKS

Q_1 and Q_3 represent 25% and 75% scores respectively. They can also be written as P_{25} and P_{75}. Median is a point dividing the scale of score by 50%. So it can also be written as P_{50} or Q_2. Similarly, other points in the distribution can also be marked, such as P_5, P_8, P_{10}, P_{15}, P_{20}, P_{30}, P_{40}, P_{50}, P_{90}, etc. These are called percentiles. The Pth percentile is that point below which p per cent of the items. scores or values lie. Percentile can be calculated in the same way as quartiles or median. Percentiles in the units of 10 are called deciles, as P_{10}, P_{20}, P_{30}, P_{40}, P_{50} etc. P_{10} is first decile, P_{20} is second decile and so on.

Formula for percentiles is

$$Pp = l + \left(\frac{pN - F}{fp}\right) \times i$$

in which,

P = percentage in the distribution required to be computed.

I = lower limit of the C–I in which the percentile lies.

N = frequency counted from below up the distribution to obtain the required percentage.

F = sum of the frequencies below the C–I in which the percentile lies.

i = size of the class-interval.

fp = number of frequencies in the C–I in which the percentile lies.

Some of the actual calculations for various percentiles in the following distributions are given below :

Class-Interval	f	Cumulative frequency
60–64	2	40
55–59	4	38
50–54	7	34
45–49	5	27
40–44	9	22
35–39	7	13
30–34	6	6 → F
	N = 40	

$$P_{20} = l + \left(\frac{pN - F}{fp}\right) i$$

$$= l + \left(\frac{\frac{20 \times 40}{100} - F}{fp}\right) i$$

$$= 34.5 + \left(\frac{8-6}{7}\right) 5$$

$$= 34.5 + \frac{2}{7} \times 5$$

$$= 34.5 + \frac{10}{7}$$

$$= 34.5 + 1.428$$

$$= \mathbf{35.928}$$

$$P_{80} = l + \left(\frac{\frac{80 \times 40}{100} - 27}{5}\right) \times 5$$

$$= 49.5 + \left(\frac{32-27}{7}\right) \times 5$$

$$= 49.5 + \frac{5}{7} \times 5 = 49.5 + \frac{25}{7}$$

$$= 49.5 + 3.57$$

$$= \mathbf{53.07.}$$

Besides percentiles and deciles, percentile ranks can also be calculated. The percentile rank of a gien point is the percentage of measures in the distribution which are below the oint given. It can be computed by the formula :

$$PR = \frac{100}{N}\left\{\frac{F\times(X-L)}{i}f\right\}$$

in which, X = score of the percentile rank.

N = number of scores in the distribution.

F = cumulative frequency upto the C–I in which the X lies.

L = lower limit of the C–I in which the X lies.

f = frequency of the class-interval in which X lies.

i = size of the class-interval.

Percentile ranks are very useful in comparing distributions of similar scors in expressing an individual's position in the given group in terms of the percentage of individuals which are below him. Through percentiles the measures of an individual in two or more abilities may be reduced to a common base. But they are not subject to algebraic operations. The units of a percentile scale are not proportionate to units on the scales of scores.

❑❑❑

CHAPTER V

NORMAL PROBABILITY CURVE

INTRODUCTION

Consider the following situations :

(1) A stone is thrown in the air.

(2) A nail is put over surface of water.

(3) Kerosene is poured over fire.

(4) A pinch of salt is put in water.

(5) A coin in tossed.

(6) A six faced die is thrown.

(7) A card is drawn from a well shuffled pack of cards.

(8) A blind folded person draws out one marble from a box containing 10 red, 20 white and 25 blue marbles.

In the first four cases, the result of the action is certain. A stone is certain to fall, a nail is sure to sink, kerosene is sure to burn, salt is sure to dissolve in water. In the rest of the cases, we cannot state with certainty the result of action. We can enumerate all the possible results of action but cannot state which one of them will definitely occur. When a coin is tossed there are two possible results, either the 'head' or the 'tail' but we cannot say which one will definitely appear. When a six faced die is thrown, the possible outcome is either 1, 2, 3, 4, 5 or 6. But it is not certain which one will appear. Similarly, when a card is drawn from well shuffled pack of cards there are 52 different possible results.

In practical life the actual results of such actions are sometimes of much importance. For example, when two cricket teams play cricket, which team should bat first is decided by tossing a coin. Fortunes are won or lost on particular cards turning up at draws. In all such situations, we say in ordinary language that there is an element of chance.

These are the origins of the theory of probability. In fact, probability theory had its origin in games of chance. However, it is no longer confined to the gambling dens or casinos but has very important and wide applications in all sciences where a statistical approach is sought. The probability theory incorporating different probability models helps the scientists to interpret the relationship between deductive consequences of theory and the observed data. Several theoretical models such as binomial, normal, poisson, hypergeometric etc., are in vogue. However, the first two are more frequently used in educational research. It is so because of their suitability to the data based on educational phenomena.

The probability of an event may be stated mathematically as a ratio. The probability of an unbiased coin falling head is $^1/_2$; and the probability of a die showing two-spot is $^1/_6$. "Probability can be regarded as the ratio of the favourable cases to the total number of equally likely cases."

Thus, the probability of the appearance of any face on a six-faced cube can be obtained by using the following ratio :

$$\text{Probability} = \frac{\text{desired outcome}}{\text{total number of outcome}} = \frac{1}{6}$$

It should be noted,

(i) A probability ratio always falls between the limits 0.00 (impossibility of occurrence) and 1.00 (certainty of occurrence). Thus, the probability that a stone will dissolve in water is 0.00; that an individual now living will some day die is 1.00. Between these limits are all possible degrees of likelihood, which may be expressed by appropriate ratio.

(ii) The total probability for all the possible events is always unity or 1.00 and can be obtained by adding up the probabilities of the individual events. The following examples will make this clear.

Example :

Suppose a coin is tossed then

	No. of desired outcomes	Total number of outcomes	Probability
One Head	1	2	$^1/_2$
One Tail	1	2	$^1/_2$
			Total : 1

Example :

Suppose a regular cubic die is thrown. It has six faces, with number 1, 2, 3, 4, 5 and 6. The probability of occurrence of each one of these number is $^1/_6$.

Face with No.	No. of desired outcome	Total number of outcomes	Probability
1	1	6	$^1/_6$
2	1	6	$^1/_6$
3	1	6	$^1/_6$
4	1	6	$^1/_6$
5	1	6	$^1/_6$
6	1	6	$^1/_6$
			Total : 1

Binomial Distribution :

This is also known as Bernoulli distribution, in the honour of Jakob Bernoulli a Swiss Mathematician.

We may consider tossing of a coin which is unbiased. There are two possible outcomes, head (H) and tail (T). Expressed as ratio, the probability of H is $^1/_2$; of T is $^1/_2$.

If two coins (a) and (b) are tossed at the same time, there are four possible arrangements of the coins.

Arrangements	1		2		3		4	
Coins	a	b	a	b	a	b	a	b
H/T	H	H	H	T	T	H	T	T

Expressed as ratios

(i) the probability of two Heads (H) = $^1/_4$.

(ii) the probability of two Tails (T) = $^1/_4$

(iii) the probability of one Head and one Tail (HT or TH) = $^1/_4$ + $^1/_4$ = $^1/_2$

The sum of probability ratios is $^1/_4$ + $^1/_4$ + $^1/_2$ = 1.

If three coins (a), (b) and (c) are tossed simultaneously then there are eight possible outcomes.

Outcomes	1			2			3			4			5			6			7			8		
Coins	a	b	c	a	b	c	a	b	c	a	b	c	a	b	c	a	b	c	a	b	c	a	b	c
H/T	H	H	H	H	H	T	H	T	H	T	H	H	H	T	T	T	H	T	T	T	H	T	T	T

Expressed as ratios the probability of

(i) three heads = $^1/_8$

(ii) two heads and one tail = $^3/_8$

(iii) one head and two tails = $^3/_8$

(iv) three tails = $^1/_8$

The sum of probability ratios = $^1/_8$ + $^3/_8$ + $^3/_8$ + $^1/_8$ = 1

By exactly the same method used above for two and for three coins, we can determine the probability of different combinations of heads and tails, when we have 4, 5 or any number of coins.

If there are 'n' independent factors, the probability of the presence or absence of each being the same, the "compound" probabilities of various combinations will be expressed by expansion of the binomial $(p + q)^n$ where

p = the probability that a given event will happen

q = the probability that the event will not happen

n = number of factors operating to produce the final result.

If we substitute H for p (occurrence of Head) and T for q (non-occurrence of Head i.e., occurrence of tails). We have for two coins $(H + T)^2$.

Expansion of the binomial gives

$$(H+T)^2 = H^2 + 2HT + T^2$$

Illustration

Terms	Meaning	Probability Ratio
1 H^2	1 chance in 4 of 2 heads	$^1/_4$
2 HT	2 chances in 4 of one H and One T	$^2/_4$ (i.e. $^1/_2$)
1 T^2	1 chance in 4 of 2 tails	$^1/_4$
		Total : 4

These outcomes are identical with those obtained above by listing the three different combinations possible when two coins are tossed.

If three independent factors are operating (e.g., three coins) the expression for three coins becomes $(H + T)^3$.

$$\text{Now } (H + T)^3 = H^3 + T^3 + 3HT\,(H+T)$$

$$= H^3 + T^3 + 3H^2T + 3HT^2$$

$$= H^3 + 3H^2T + 3HT^2 + T^3$$

which may be written.

Terms	Meaning	Probability Ratio
1 H^3	1 chance in 8 of 3 heads	$^1/_8$
3 H^2T	3 chances in 8 of 2 heads and 1 tail	$^3/_8$
3 HT^2	3 chances in 8 of 1 head and 2 tails	$^3/_8$
1 T^3	1 chance in 8 of 3 tails	$^1/_8$
		Total : 8

Again these results are identical with those got by listing the four different combinations possible when three coins are tossed.

If we have n repeated trials each having two outcomes then the different probabilities of getting success with probability 'p' and failure with probability 'q' are given by the terms in the expansion of

$$(p+q)^n = p^n + {}^nC_1\, p^{n-1}\, q^1 + \ldots\ldots\ldots + {}^nCr\, p^{n-r}\, q^r + \ldots\ldots\ldots + q^n.$$

This is called Binomial probability distribution or Binomial distribution.

THE NORMAL DISTRIBUTION

The normal distribution is a special case of the binomial distribution with probability (p) = 0.5 and a sufficiently large N. As N grows infinitely large, the normal and binomial probabilities become identical for any interval.

The normal distribution, mathematically is an approximation of the type of distribution generated by tossing coins. If 12 coins are tossed simultaneously a large number of times,

(i) The most frequently occurring combination of the results would be 6 heads and 6 tails.

(ii) Other combinations would be fewer as compared to that mentioned in (i).

(iii) As one proceeds towards 12 heads and no tails, or 12 tails and no heads, the frequencies will go on decreasing.

(iv) The occurrence of extreme combinations (12 H and OT or 12T and OH) would be very rare.

The frequencies with which each combination appears can be worked out as follows :

$$(H+T)^{12} = {}^{12}C_0H^{12} + {}^{12}C_1H^{11}T + {}^{12}C_2H^{10}T^2 + {}^{12}C_3H^9T^3 + {}^{12}C_4H^8T^4 +$$
$${}^{12}C_5H^7T^5 + {}^{12}C_6H^6T^6 + {}^{12}C_7H^5T^7 + {}^{12}C_8H^4T^8 + {}^{12}C_9H^3T^9 +$$
$${}^{12}C_{10}H^2T^{10} + {}^{12}C_{11}HT^{11} + {}^{12}C_{12}T^{12}$$

the general formula to work out is $^{n}C_r = \dfrac{n!}{r!\,(n-r)\,!}$

$$*(1)\quad {}^{12}C_0H^{12} = \frac{12\,!}{0\,!\times(12-0)\,!}H^{12} = \frac{12\,!}{0\,!\times 12\,!}H^{12}$$
$$= H^{12}$$

(*)

4 ! is read as 4 factorial or factorial 4

$4\,! = 4\times3\times2\times1$

$6\,! = 6\times5\times4\times3\times2\times1$

It is customary to consider 0 ! = 1

(2) $$^{12}C_1H^{11}T = \frac{12!}{1! \times (12-1)!} H^{11}T = \frac{12 \times 11!\ H^{11}T}{11!} = 12\ H^{11}T$$

(3) $$^{12}C_2H^{10}T^2 = \frac{12!}{2! \times (12-2)!} H^{10}T^2 = \frac{12 \times 11 \times 10!}{2! \times 10!} H^{10}T^2$$

$$= 66\ H^{10}T^2$$

(4) $$^{12}C_3H^9T^3 = \frac{12!}{3! \times (12-3)!} H^9T^3 = \frac{12 \times 11 \times 10 \times 91}{3 \times 2 \times 9!} H^9T^3$$

$$= 220\ H^9T^3$$

(5) $$^{12}C_4H^8T^4 = \frac{12!}{4!(12-4)!} H^8T^4 = \frac{12 \times 11 \times 10 \times 9 \times 8!}{4 \times 3 \times 2 \times 8!} H^8T^4$$

$$= \frac{12 \times 11 \times 10 \times 9}{4 \times 3 \times 2} H^8T^4$$

$$= 495\ H^8T^4$$

(6) $$^{12}C_5H^7T^5 = \frac{12!}{5!(12-5)!} H^7T^5 = \frac{12 \times 11 \times 10 \times 9 \times 8 \times 7!}{5 \times 4 \times 3 \times 2 \times 7!} H^7T^5$$

$$= 792\ H^7T^5$$

(7) $$^{12}C_6H^6T^6 = \frac{12!}{6!(12-6)!} H^6T^6 = \frac{12 \times 11 \times 10 \times 9 \times 8 \times 7 \times 6!}{6 \times 5 \times 4 \times 3 \times 2 \times 6!} H^6T^6$$

$$= \frac{12 \times 11 \times 10 \times 9 \times 8 \times 7}{6 \times 5 \times 4 \times 3 \times 2} H^6T^6$$

$$= 924\ H^6T^6$$

(8) $$^{12}C_7H^5T^7 = \frac{12!}{7!(12-7)!} H^5T^7 = \frac{12 \times 11 \times 10 \times 9 \times 8 \times 7!}{7! \times 5!} H^5T^7$$

$$= \frac{12 \times 11 \times 10 \times 9 \times 8}{5 \times 4 \times 3 \times 2} H^5T^7$$

$$= 792\ H^5T^7$$

$$(9)\quad {}^{12}C_8H^4T^8 = \frac{12\,!}{8\,!\,(12-8)\,!}\,H^4T^8 = \frac{12\times 11\times 10\times 9\times 8\,!}{8\,!\times 4\,!}\,H^4T^8$$

$$= \frac{12\times 11\times 10\times 9}{4\times 3\times 2}\,H^4T^8$$

$$= 495\,H^4T^8$$

$$(10)\quad {}^{12}C_9H^3T^9 = \frac{12\,!}{9\,!\times(12-9)\,!}\,H^3T^9 = \frac{12\times 11\times 10\times 9\,!}{9\,!\times 3\,!}\,H^3T^9$$

$$= \frac{12\times 11\times 10}{3\times 2}\,H^3T^9$$

$$= 220\,H^3T^9$$

$$(11)\quad {}^{12}C_{10}H^2T^{10} = \frac{12\,!}{10\,!\,(12-10)\,!}\,H^2T^{10} = \frac{12\times 11\times 10\,!}{10\,!\times 2\,!}\,H^2T^{10}$$

$$= \frac{12\times 11}{2\times 1}\,H^2T^{10}$$

$$= 66\,H^2T^{10}$$

$$(12)\quad {}^{12}C_{11}HT^{11} = \frac{12\,!}{11\,!\,(12-11)\,!}\,HT^{11} = \frac{12\times 11\,!}{11\,!\times 1\,!}\,HT^{11}$$

$$= 12\,HT^{11}$$

$$(13)\quad {}^{12}C_{12}T^{12} = \frac{12\,!}{12\,!\times(12-12)\,!}\,T^{12} = \frac{12\,!}{12\,!\times 0\,!}\,T^{12}$$

$$= T^{12}$$

Thus,

$$(H+T)^{12} = H^{12} + 12\,H^{11}T + 66\,H^{10}T^2 + 220\,H^9T^3 + 495\,H^8T^4 + 792\,H^7T^5 + 924\,H^6T^6 +$$

$$792\,H^5T^7 + 495\,H^4T^8 + 220\,H^3T^9 + 66\,H^2T^{10} + 12\,HT^{11} + T^{12}$$

This may be summarized as follows :

Combinations	Interpretation	Probability Ratio
1 H^{12}	1 Chance in 4096 of all coins falling heads.	1/4096
12 $H^{11}T$	12 Chances in 4096 of 11 heads and 1 tail.	12/4096
66 $H^{10}T^2$	66 Chances in 4096 of 10 heads and 2 tails.	66/4096
220 H^9T^3	220 Chances in 4096 of 9 heads and 3 tails.	220/4096
495 H^8T^4	495 Chances in 4096 of 8 heads and 4 tails.	495/4096
792 H^7T^5	792 Chances in 4096 of 7 heads and 5 tails.	792/4096
924 H^6T^6	924 Chances in 4096 of 6 heads and 6 tails.	924/4096
792 H^5T^7	792 Chances in 4096 of 5 heads and 7 tails.	792/4096
495 H^4T^8	495 Chances in 4096 of 4 heads and 8 tails.	495/4096
220 H^3T^9	220 Chances in 4096 of 3 heads and 9 tails.	220/4096
66 H^2T^{10}	66 Chances in 4096 of 2 heads and 10 tails.	66/4096
12 HT^{11}	12 Chances in 4096 of 1 head and 11 tails.	12/4096
1 T^{12}	1 Chance in 4096 of all coins falling tails.	1/4096
Total = 4096		Total = 1

If frequencies with each combination appears are plotted on a graph, an approximately normal distribution is obtained. It appears even upon superficial examination that the measures are concentrated closely around the centre and taper off from this central point or crest to the left and right. There are relatively few measures at the 'low score' end of the scale; an increasing number upto a maximum at the middle position and a progressive falling off towards the 'high score' end of the scale. The bell shaped figure so obtained is called the normal probability curve or simply the normal curve.

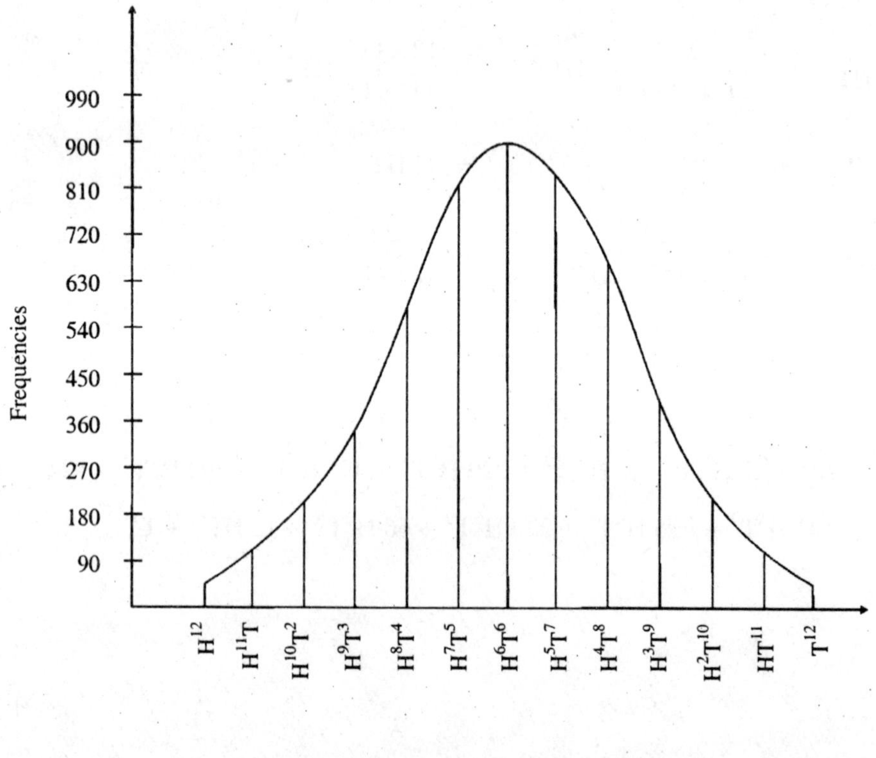

De Moivre (1733) first developed the equation of the curve, this concept was further developed and perfected by Gauss and Laplace.

PROPERTIES OF THE NORMAL PROBABILITY CURVE

(1) It is a bell-shaped curve because of its characteristic roundness at the top and inflections on each side.

(2) Theoretically the curve never touches the base line. As the distance from the mean increases, the curve approaches the baseline (or X axis) but never touches it.

(3) The mean, mode and median in a normal curve fall at the same point. All these coincide exactly in the middle of the normal curve. They have the same numerical values. It means in a normal curve

Mean = Median = Mode.

(4) It is bilaterally symmetrical about the Mean. It means in a normal curve the area below the mean = the area above the mean.

(5) The curve is unimodal.

(6) The points of inflection (the points where the curvature changes its direction) occur at points plus and minus one σ unit above and below the mean i.e. $\pm$ 1SD from the mean ordinate. It means the curve changes from convex to concave in relation to the horizontal axis at + 1SD and – 1SD.

(7) The entire area under the curve represents the total frequency (N) of the distribution.

(8) The maximum ordinate of the curve occurs at the mean or where z = 0. The highest of the ordinate at this point is 0.3989.

(9) The highest of the ordinate at 1σ, 2σ and 3σ are 0.2420, 0.0540 and 0.0044 resp.

(10) In a normal curve

(i) Quartile Deviation (Q) = Probable Error = $0.6745\,\sigma$.

(ii) Mean Deviation or Average Deviation (AD) = $0.7979\,\sigma$

(iii) Skewness = 0 (as mean = Median)

(iv) Kurtosis = 0.263.

(11) In a normal curve the first and third quartiles are equidistant from the median.

(12) The normal curve is defined by the following equation :

$$Y = \frac{N}{\sigma\sqrt{2\pi}}\, e^{(-x^2)/2\sigma^2}$$

THE EQUATION OF THE NORMAL CURVE

The formula for the ordinate or height of the normal curve is

$$Y = \frac{N}{\sigma\sqrt{2\pi}}\, e^{(-x^2)/2\sigma^2}$$

in which Y = the height of the curve above the X-axis i.e., the frequency for any given point of the base line.

N = Number of cases

σ = Standard deviation of the distribution

π = 3.1416 (Approx.) A mathematical constant (the ratio of the circumference of a circle to its diameter).

e = 2.718 (Approx.) A mathematical constant (base of the Napierian system of logarithms).

x = deviation of a score from mean; $(X - \overline{M})$.

FEATURES OF THE CURVE IN THE LIGHT OF THE EQUATION

(1) With N and σ fixed, all elements, except, x are constant.

(2) Since x is squared, the negative or the positive values of x will give the same value of y, hence the curve is bilaterally symmetrical.

(3) Since x^2 has negative sign, as x increases the index or exponent of e decreases and y also decreases.

(4) If x = 0 the index becomes zero, hence $e^0 = 1$ The equation then reduces to $y = \dfrac{N}{\sigma\sqrt{2\pi}}$

The value of y is maximum at this point.

THE POSITION AND SHAPE OF THE NORMAL CURVE

The position and shape of the normal curve depend upon Mean (M), standard deviation (σ) and the number of cases (N).

(a) If σ, and N remain the same and Mean (M) changes, the curve will have the same shape but different positions.

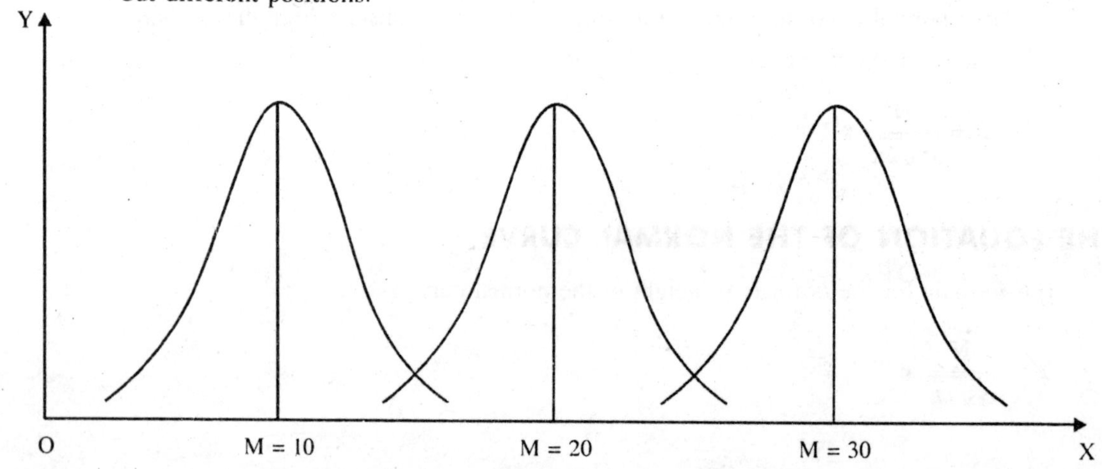

(b) (i) If Mean (M) and N remain the same but σ decreases the curve will contract.

(ii) If Mean (M) and N remain the same but σ increases the curve will expand.

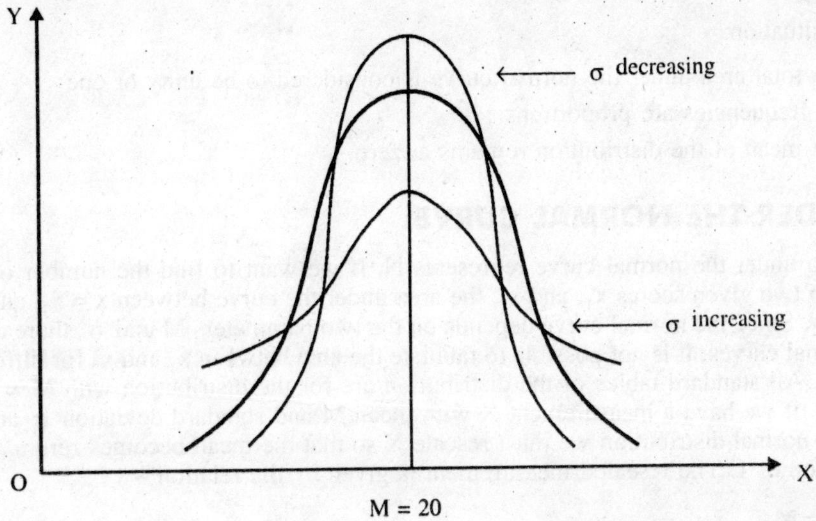

(c) If both Mean (M) and σ change, the curve will change, its positions as well as its shape.

(d) If Mean (M) and σ remain the same but N change, there will be change in shape.

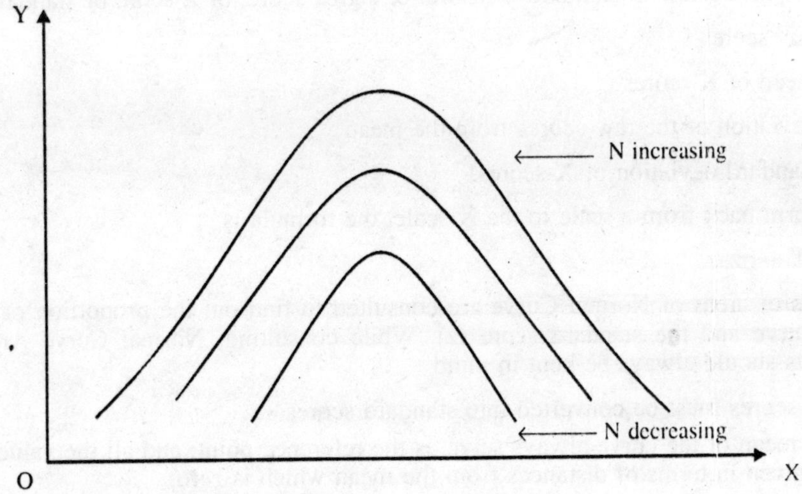

THE UNIT NORMAL CURVE

Table of areas of normal curve have been prepared considering –

(i) N = 1 and

(ii) σ = 1.0

The equation for the normal distribution curve, under these consideration becomes

$$y = \frac{1}{\sqrt{2\pi}} e^{\left(\frac{-z^2}{2}\right)}$$

In this situation.

(a) the total area under the normal curve is considered to be unity or one

(b) all frequencies are proportions

(c) the mean of the distribution remains at zero.

AREA UNDER THE NORMAL CURVE

The area under the normal curve represents N. If we want to find the number of observations lying between two given scores x_1, and x_2, the area under the curve between $x = x_1$, and $x = x_2$ gives that frequency. Since the normal curve depends on the two parameters M and σ, there are great many different normal curves. It is not possible to tabulate the area between x_1 and x_2 for different values of M, σ and N. All standard tables of the distribution are for the distribution with M = 0 and σ = 1. Consequently, if we have a measurement X with mean M and standard deviation σ and wish to use a table of the normal distribution we must rescale X so that the mean becomes zero and the standard deviation becomes 1. The rescaled measurement is given by the relation –

$$z = \frac{X - M}{\sigma} = \frac{x}{\sigma}$$

In which

z = standard normal variate, or standard normal deviate, or standard normal variable, or normal variate in standard measure, or sigma score, or Z score or standard score.

X = raw score

M = mean of X scores

x = deviation of the raw scores from the mean

σ = standard deviation of X-scores.

To transform back from z scale to the X scale, the formula is

$$X = M + \sigma z.$$

The tables of areas of Normal Curve are consulted to find out the proportion of area between mean of the curve and the standard score (z). While consulting, Normal Curve Area tables, the following points should always be kept in mind :

(1) The scores must be converted into standard scores.

(2) The mean of the curve always serve as the reference point, and all the values of the areas are given in terms of distances from the mean which is zero.

(3) The area can be converted into percentage by dividing it with 100 or by simply shifting the decimals two places to the right.

(4) While consulting tables, absolute value of z (ignoring sigma) should be taken.

(5) Normal Curve Area tables show only positive values of z. Since the curve is bilaterally symmetrical, the areas for the positive and negative values of a z score are the same.

The following table (Table A) depicts the fractional parts of the total area (taken as 10,000) under the Normal Probability Curve, corresponding to distances on the baseline between the mean and successive points laid off from the mean in units of standard deviation.

Table A **Fractional parts of the total area (taken as 10,000) under the normal probability curve, corresponding to distances on the baseline between the mean and successive points laid all from the mean in units of standard deviation**

Example : between the mean and a point 1.38σ $\left(\frac{x}{\sigma} = 1.38\right)$ are found 41.62% of the entire area under the curve.

$\frac{x}{\sigma}$	.00	.01	.02	.03	.04	.05	.06	.07	.08	.09
0.0	0000	0040	0080	0120	0160	0199	0239	0279	0319	0359
0.1	0398	0438	0478	0517	0557	0596	0636	0675	0714	0753
0.2	0793	0832	0871	0910	0948	0987	1026	1064	1103	1141
0.3	1179	1217	1255	1293	1331	1368	1406	1443	1480	1517
0.4	1554	1591	1628	1664	1700	1736	1772	1808	1844	1879
0.5	1915	1950	1985	2019	2054	2088	2123	2157	2190	2224
0.6	2257	2291	2324	2357	2389	2422	2454	2486	2517	2549
0.7	2580	2611	2642	2673	2704	2734	2764	2794	2823	2852
0.8	2881	2910	2939	2967	2995	3023	3051	3078	3106	3133
0.9	3159	3186	3212	3238	3264	3290	3315	3340	3365	3389
1.0	3413	3438	3461	3485	3508	3531	3554	3577	3599	3621
1.1	3643	3665	3686	3708	3729	3749	3770	3790	3810	3830
1.2	3849	3869	3888	3907	3925	3944	3962	3980	3997	4015
1.3	4032	4049	4066	4082	4099	4115	4131	4147	4162	4177
1.4	4192	4207	4222	4236	4251	4265	4279	4292	4306	4319
1.5	4332	4345	4357	4370	4383	4394	4406	4418	4429	4441
1.6	4452	4463	4474	4484	4495	4505	4515	4525	4535	4545
1.7	4554	4564	4573	4582	4591	4599	4608	4616	4625	4633
1.8	4641	4649	4656	4664	4671	4678	4686	4693	4699	4706
1.9	4713	4719	4726	4732	4738	4744	4750	4756	4761	4767
2.0	4772	4778	4783	4788	4793	4798	4803	4808	4812	4817
2.1	4821	4826	4830	4834	4838	4842	4846	4850	4854	4857
2.2	4861	4864	4868	4871	4875	4878	4881	4884	4887	4890
2.3	4893	4896	4898	4901	4904	4906	4909	4911	4913	4916
2.4	4918	4920	4922	4925	4927	4929	4931	4932	4934	4936
2.5	4938	4940	4941	4943	4945	4946	4948	4949	4951	4952
2.6	4953	4955	4956	4957	4959	4960	4961	4962	4963	4964
2.7	4965	4966	4967	4968	4969	4970	4971	4972	4973	4974
2.8	4974	4975	4976	4977	4977	4978	4979	4979	4980	4981
2.9	4981	4982	4982	4983	4984	4984	4985	4985	4986	4986
3.0	4986.5	4986.9	4987.4	4987.8	4988.2	4988.6	4988.9	4989.3	4989.7	4990.0
3.1	4990.3	4990.6	4991.0	4991.3	4991.6	4991.8	4992.1	4992.4	4992.6	4992.9
3.2	4993.129									
3.3	4995.166									
3.4	4996.631									
3.5	4997.674									
3.6	4998.409									
3.7	4998.922									
3.8	4999.277									
3.9	4999.519									
4.0	4999.683									
4.5	4999.966									
5.0	4999.997133									

Let us consider the following example to understand the method of consulting the above table.

Example : Find the percentage of the distribution between the mean and 1.57 σ.

Solution : Go down the x/σ column to 1.5 (ignoring σ), then across horizontally to the column headed .07 and take the entry 4418. This means 4418 cases in 10000 lie between mean and 1.57 σ or 44.18% of the total area (N) lies between mean and 1.57 σ

Example : Find the percentage of distribution between the mean and 1 σ.

Solution : Go down the x/σ column until 1.0 is reached, and in the next column under 0.00 take the entry opposite to 1.0 *viz.* 3413. This figure means that 3413 cases in 10000 or 34.13% of the entire area of the curve, lies between the mean and 1 σ. In other words, 34.13% of the cases in a normal distribution fall within the area bounded by the base line of the curve, the ordinate erected at the mean, the ordinate erected at a distance of 1 σ from the mean and the curve itself (see the following fig.)

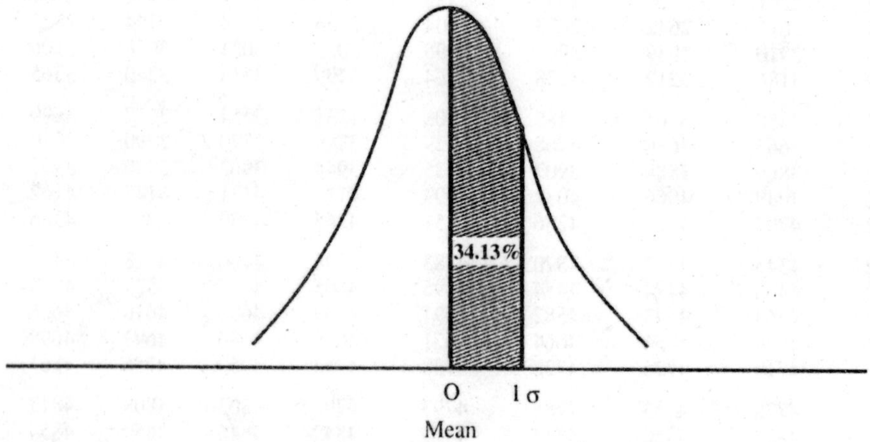

Example : Find the percentage of distribution between the mean and –1.92 σ

Solution : Take the entry in the column headed 0.02, opposite 1.9 in the x/σ column. This entry (4726) means that 47.26% of the cases in the normal distribution fall between the mean and –1.92 σ. (see the following fig.)

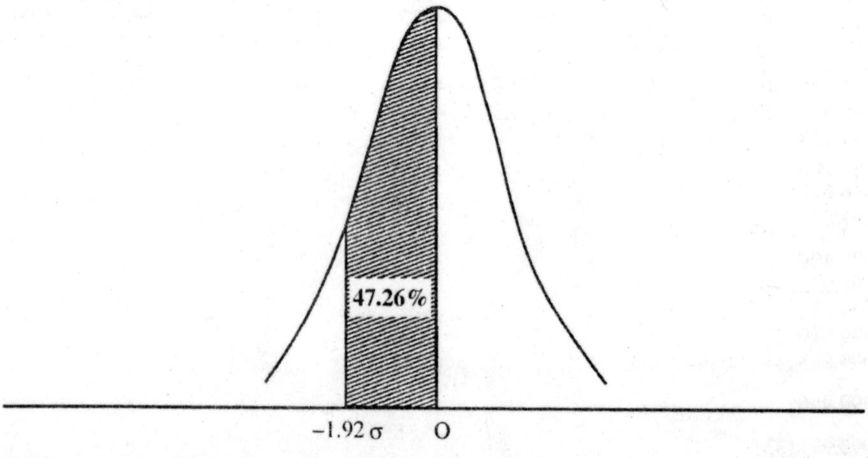

Important ranges under the Normal Probability Curve

(a) Between the mean and $\pm 1\sigma$ lie the middle two third (68.26%) of the cases in the normal distribution. It means that there are about 68 chances in 100 that a case will lie within $\pm 1\sigma$ from the mean in the normal distribution.

(b) Between the mean and $\pm 2\sigma$ are found 95% (approximately) of the distribution. It means that there are 95 chances in 100 that a case will lie within $\pm 2\sigma$ from the mean.

(c) Between the mean and $\pm 3\sigma$ are found 99.7% or very close to 100% of the distribution. In other words there are 99.7 chances in 100 that a case will lie within $\pm 3\sigma$ from the mean.

(d) Instead of σ, the quartile deviation (Q) may be used as the unit of measurement in determining areas within given parts of the normal curve. In the normal curve, the Q is generally called the probable error or PE. The relationship between PE and σ are given below.

$$PE = 0.6745\,\sigma$$

$$\text{or } \sigma = \frac{1}{0.6745}\,PE$$

$$\text{or } \sigma = 1.4826\ PE$$

Thus, σ is always about 50% larger than the P.E. Consulting Table A we find that $\pm 0.6745\ \sigma$ or ± 1 PE includes the 25% just above and 25% just below the mean. This part of the curve, sometimes called the "middle 50" is important because it defines the ranges of normal performance. The upper 25% is somewhat better and the lowest 25% somewhat poorer than the typical middle or average group.

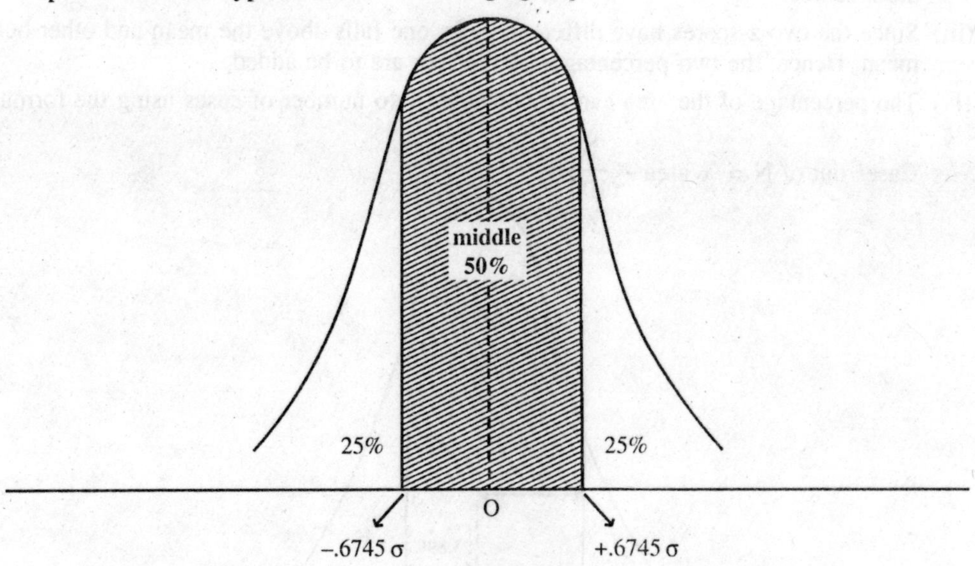

(e) ± 2 PE (or $\pm 1.3490\sigma$) from the mean includes 82.26% of the measures in the normal curve

± 3 PE (or $\pm 2.0235\sigma$) from the mean includes 97.70% of the measures in the normal distribution

± 4 PE (or $\pm 2.6980\sigma$) from the mean covers 99.30% of the measures in the normal curve.

APPLICATIONS OF THE NORMAL PROBABILITY CURVE

Normal distribution has been found very useful in problems involving inferences. The applications of the normal curve are illustrated below, through numerical solution.

(1) To determine the percentage of cases in a normal distribution within given limits of scores :

Generally three types of cases are encountered under this type.

(a) percentage of cases within two score limits.

(b) percentage of cases below a score point.

(c) percentage of cases above a score point.

Example : In a sample of 1000 cases, the mean of a certain test is 14.40 and σ is 2.50. Assuming normality of distribution

(a) What percentage of cases lie between 12 and 16?

(b) How many scores lie below 8?

(c) How many scores lie above 18?

Solution :

(a) Here the z-limits fall on both sides of the Mean.

Steps :

(i) The two score limits are converted into equivalent z-scores.

(ii) Normal curve area tables (Table A) are consulted to find out the readings corresponding to the z-scores.

(iii) Since the two z-scores have different signs, one falls above the mean and other below the mean. Hence, the two percentages of the area are to be added.

(iv) The percentage of the area can be converted into number of cases using the formula

$$\text{Cases out of N} = \%\ \text{area} \times \frac{N}{100}$$

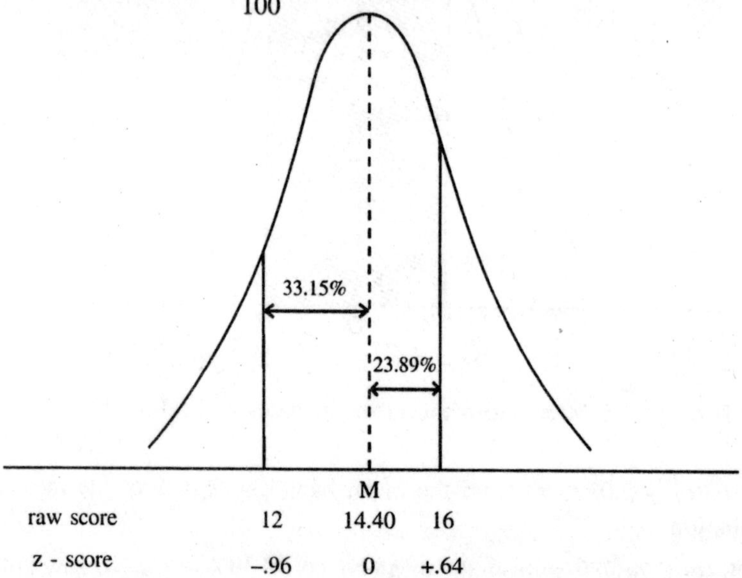

Score limits	Equivalent z-score = $\frac{X - M}{\sigma}$	Normal Curve table reading	% Area or % Cases
12	$\frac{12 - 14.40}{2.50} = \frac{-2.40}{2.50} = -.96$	3315	33.15
16	$\frac{16 - 14.40}{2.50} = \frac{-1.60}{2.50} = +.64$	2389	23.89
		Total :	57.04

$$\text{Cases out of N} = \% \text{ area} \times \frac{N}{100}$$

$$= 57.04 \times \frac{1000}{100}$$

$$= 570.4$$

(b) In this part of the problem the number of cases below 8 is to be worked out, hence the exact lower limit of the raw score 8 i.e., (7.5) is considered.

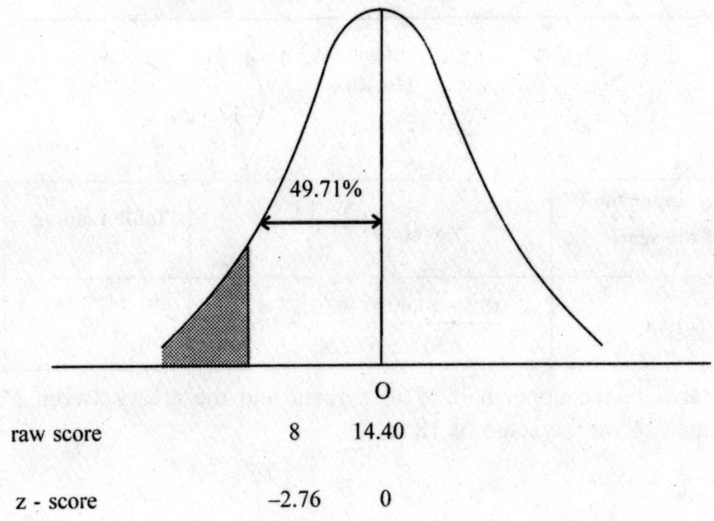

Raw Score	Exact lower limit	z-score = $\frac{X - M}{\sigma}$	Table reading	% Area
8	7.5	$\frac{7.5 - 14.40}{2.50} = \frac{-6.90}{2.50} = -2.76$	4971	49.71

The raw score 8 is below the mean. The area below it will be obtained by subtracting 49.71% from the whole of the lower part of the normal curve i.e., 50%.

$\therefore$ % of Area below 8 $= 50\% - 49.17\%$

$= 0.29\%$

Cases out of 1000 $= 0.29 \times \frac{1000}{100}$

$= 2.9 \div 3$

(c) In this part of the problem the number of cases above 18 is to be found out, hence the exact upper limit of 18 i.e., 18.5 is to be taken into account.

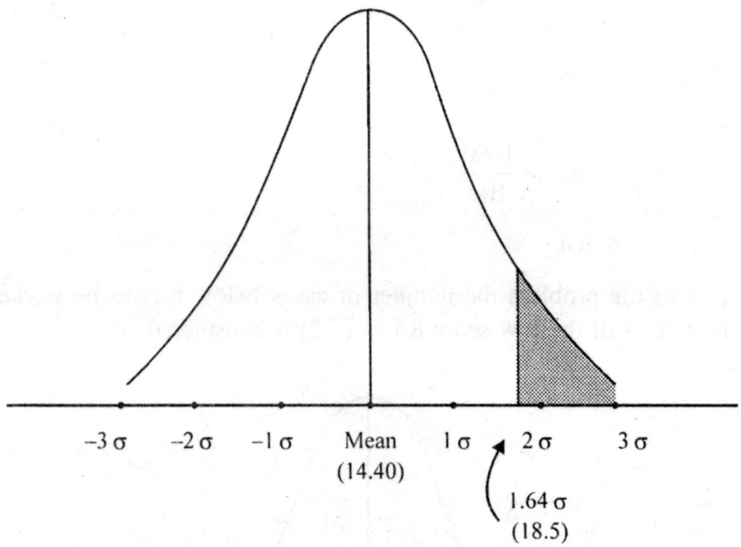

Raw Score	Exact upper limit of the score	z-score $= \frac{X - M}{\sigma}$	Table reading	% Area
18	18.5	$\frac{18.5 - 14.40}{2.50} = \frac{4.10}{2.50} = 1.64$	4495	44.95

Since the total area in the upper half is 50 percent and the area between Mean and 1.64 is 44.95%. Hence, the area above the score of 18 is

$50\% - 44.95\% = 5.05\%$

$\therefore$ Cases out of 1000 $= \%\ \text{area} \times \frac{N}{100}$

$= 5.05 \times \frac{1000}{100}$

$= 50.5$

Example : Given a normal distribution of 500 scores with M = 40 and σ = 8, what percentage of cases lie

(a) between scores of 36 and 42

(b) above a score of 48

(c) below a score of 52.

Solution :

(a)

Score limits	$z = \frac{X - M}{\sigma}$	Normal Curve table reading	% Area
36	$\frac{36-40}{8} = -0.5$	1915	19.15
42	$\frac{42-40}{8} = +0.25$	0987	9.87
		Total :	29.02

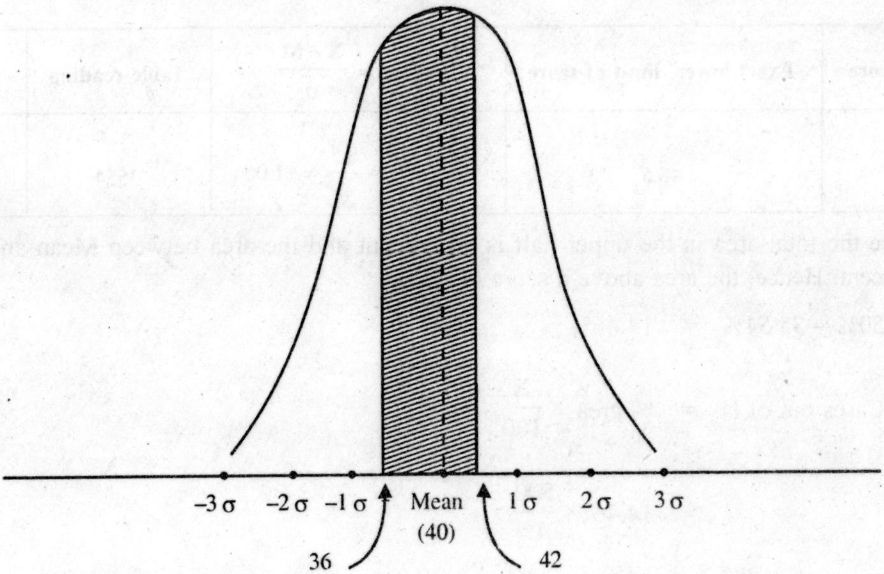

$$\text{Cases out of N} = \% \text{ area} \times \frac{N}{100}$$

$$= 29.02 \times \frac{500}{100}$$

$$= 145.10 \text{ or } 145$$

(b) Percentage of area above a score of 48.

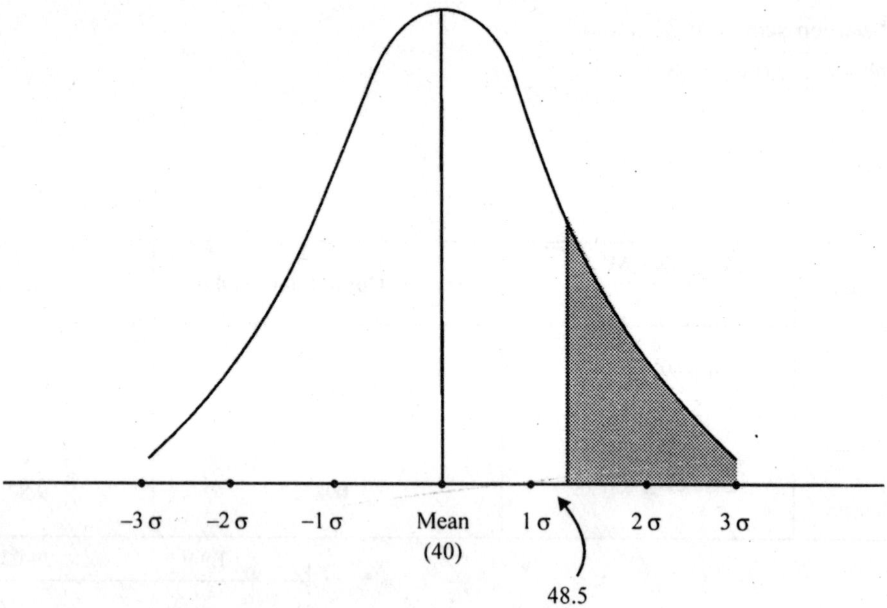

Raw Score	Exact lower limit of score	z-score = $\frac{X-M}{\sigma}$	Table reading	% Area
48	48.5	$\frac{48.5-40}{8} = \frac{8.5}{8} = +1.06$	3554	35.54

Since the total area in the upper half is 50 percent and the area between Mean and + 1.06 is 35.54 percent. Hence, the area above a score of 48 is

$$50\% - 35.54\% = 14.46\%$$

$$\therefore \text{ Cases out of N} = \% \text{ area} \times \frac{N}{100}$$

$$= 14.46 \times \frac{500}{100}$$

$$= 73.30 \text{ or } 72.$$

(c) Percentage of area below a score of 52.

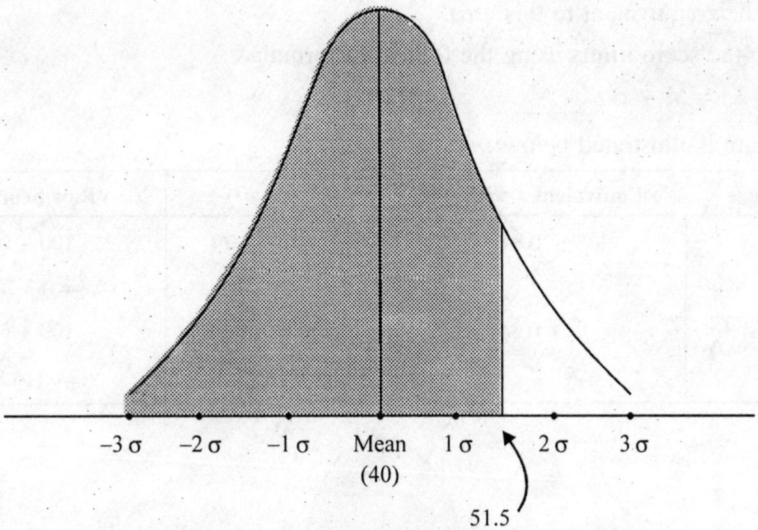

Raw Score	Exact lower limit	z-score = $\frac{X - M}{\sigma}$	Table reading	% Area
52	51.5	$\frac{51.5 - 40}{8} = \frac{11.5}{8} = 1.44$	4251	42.51

The area below z-score of 1.44 would include the whole of the lower half i.e., 50% and 42.51% i.e., from mean to z = 1.44. Hence, percentage of area below a score of 52 is

50 per cent + 42.51 per cent = 92.51 per cent

$$\text{Cases out of N} = \% \text{ area} \times \frac{N}{100}$$

$$= 92.51 \times \frac{500}{100}$$

$$= 462.55 \text{ or } 463 \text{ out of } 500.$$

(2) To determine the limits of scores which include a given limits of scores :

It is the converse of the first application of the Normal curve. The method of determination of the scores is illustrated in the following examples.

Example : In the Army General Classification Test the distribution is essentially normal with a M = 100 and SD = 20. The middle 60% fall between what two points?

Solution : To obtain the middle 60% cases, one has to find out the score limits which combine 30% cases below and 30% cases above the mean. Hence, the normal curve tables are to be consulted in a reverse manner. The following steps are then followed :

(1) Locate the 30% area in table A

(2) Read the z-equivalent to this area.

(3) Obtain the score limits using the following formula.

Raw score (X) = M + σ z

The procedure is illustrated below :

Area Percentage	Equivalent z with sign	$\sigma \times z$	Raw Score = M + σ z
30% below M	– 0.84	– 0.84 × 20	100 + (–16.80)
		= –16.80	= 83.20
30% above M	+ 0.84	+ 0.84 × 20	100 + (+16.80)
		= +16.80	= 116.80

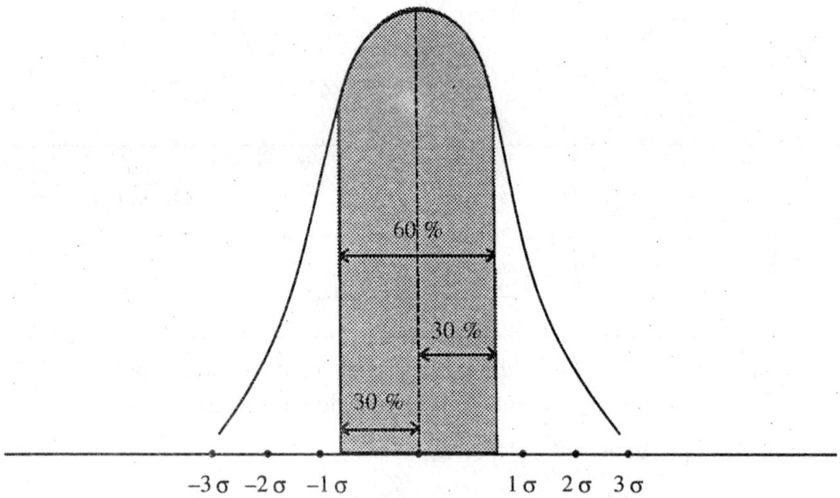

Score limits equivalent to middle 60% cases

The z values below the mean will carry minus sign and that above the mean, plus sign. Thus, the middle 60% of the cases fall between 83.20 to 116.80

Example : In a sample of 400 students the mean of a certain test is 40 and SD is 7. Assuming normality of distribution.

(a) What score limits would include the middle 72% of the cases?

(b) The middle 128 students would fall between what two points?

Solution :

(a) To obtain the middle 72% of the cases, we have to find out the score limits which combine 36% cases below and 36% cases above the mean. Hence, the normal curve tables are to be consulted in a reverse manner to obtain the corresponding values of z equivalents.

The procedure is illustrated below.

Area Percentage	Equivalent z with sign	$\sigma \times z$	Raw Score = M + σz
36% below M	– 1.08	7 × (– 1.08) = – 7.56	40 – 7.56 = 33.44
36% above M	+ 1.08	7 × 1.08 = +7.56	40 + 7.56 = 47.56

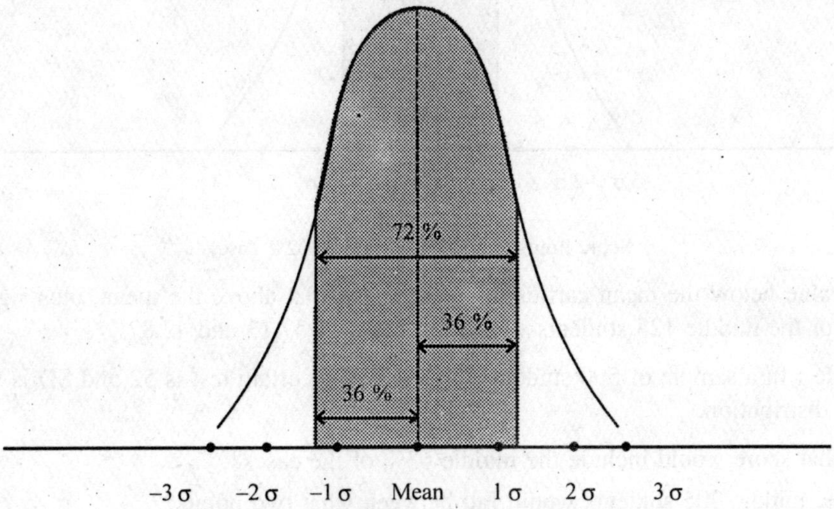

Score limits equivalent to middle 72% cases.

The z value below the mean will carry minus sign and that above the mean, plus sign. Thus, the middle 72% of the cases fall between 33.44 and 47.56.

(b) 128 out of 400 means $\left(\dfrac{128 \times 100}{400}\right)$ % of the total students.

Which is equal to 32% students.

To get the middle 128 students i.e., 32% students we have to find out the score limits which combines 16% below and 16% above the mean. The procedure is explained below.

Area Percentage	Equivalent z with sign	$\sigma \times z$	Raw Score = M + σz
16% below M	– 0.41	7 × (– 0.41) = – 2.87	40 – 2.87 = 37.13
16% above M	+ 0.41	7 × + (0.41) = + 2.87	40 + 2.87 = 42.87

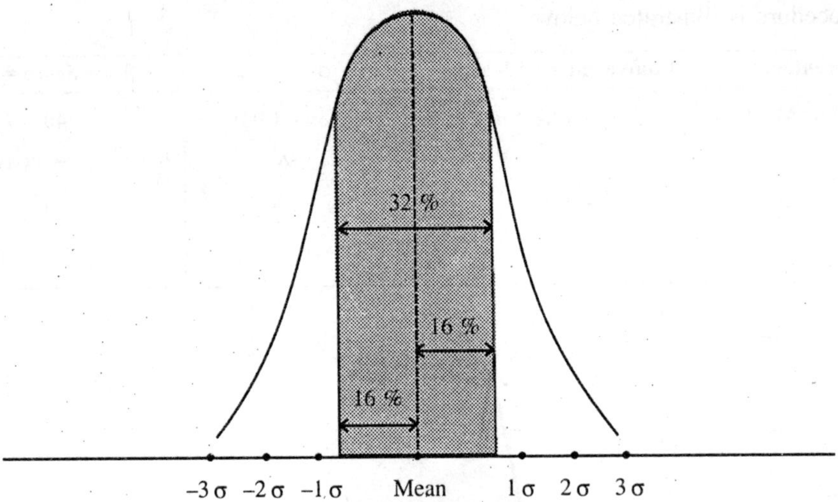

Score limits equivalent to middle 32% cases

The z value below the mean carries minus sign and that above the mean, plus sign. Thus, the middle 30% or the middle 128 students would fall between 37.13 and 42.87.

Example : In a sample of 500 students the mean of a certain test is 52 and SD is 9. Assuming normality of distribution.

(a) What score would include the middle 63% of the cases?

(b) The middle 205 students would fall between what two points?

Solution :

(a) To get the middle 63% of the cases we have to find out the score limits which combine 31.5% cases below and 31.5% cases above the mean. Here the normal curve tables are consulted in a reverse manner to obtain the corresponding value of z scores.

The procedure is as follows :

Area Percentage	**Equivalent z with sign**	**σ × z**	**Raw Score = M + σ z**
31.5% below M	– 0.89	9 × (– 0.89)	52 – 8.01
		= – 8.01	= 43.99
31.5% above M	+ 0.89	9 × (+ 0.89)	52 + 8.01
		= + 8.01	= 60.01

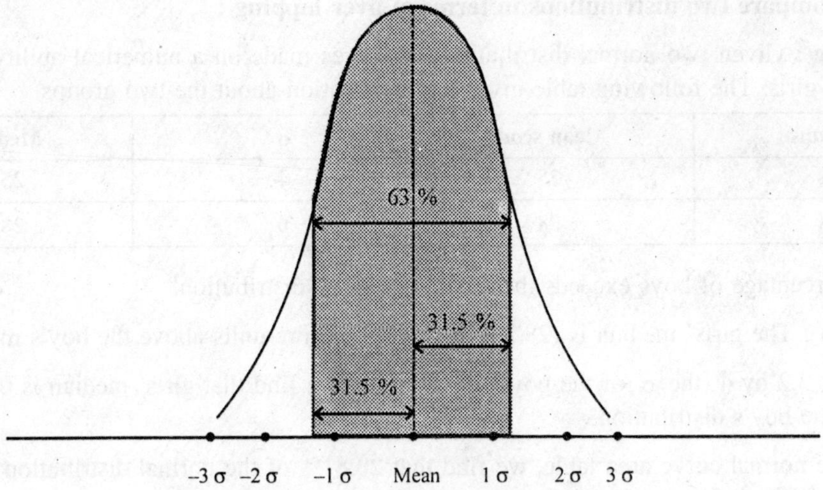

Score limits equivalent to middle 63% cases

The middle 63% of the cases fall between 43.99 and 60.01.

(b) 205 out of 500 means $\left(\frac{205 \times 100}{500}\right)$ % of the total students which is equal to 41% students.

To get the middle 205 students i.e., 41% of the total, we have to find the score limits which combines 20.5% below and 20.5% above the mean. The procedure is illustrated below.

Area Percentage	Equivalent z with sign	$\sigma \times z$	Raw Score = M + σz
20.5% below M	– 0.54	9 × (– 0.54) = – 4.86	52 – 4.86 = 47.14
20.5% above M	+ 0.54	9 × (+ 0.54) = + 4.86	52 + 4.86 = 56.86

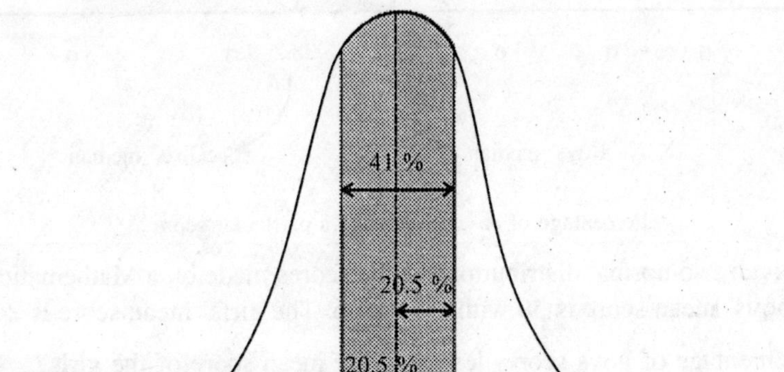

The middle 41% or the middle 205 students would fall between 47.14 and 56.86.

(3) To compare two distributions in terms of over lapping :

Example : Given two normal distributions of scores made on a numerical ability test by 200 boys and 300 girls. The following table gives the information about the two groups.

Groups	Mean score	σ	Median
Boys	25	4	25.2
Girls	28	6	28.2

What percentage of boys exceeds the median of girls' distribution?

Solution : The girls' median is (28.2 – 25.0) or 3.2 score units above the boy's mean.

Dividing 3.2 by 4 (the σ of the boys' distribution) we find that girls' median is 0.80 σ above the mean of the boy's distribution.

From the normal curve area table, we find that 28.81% of the normal distribution lies between the mean and 0.80 σ. Hence, 21.19% of the boys (50% – 28.81%) exceeds the median of the girl's distribution.

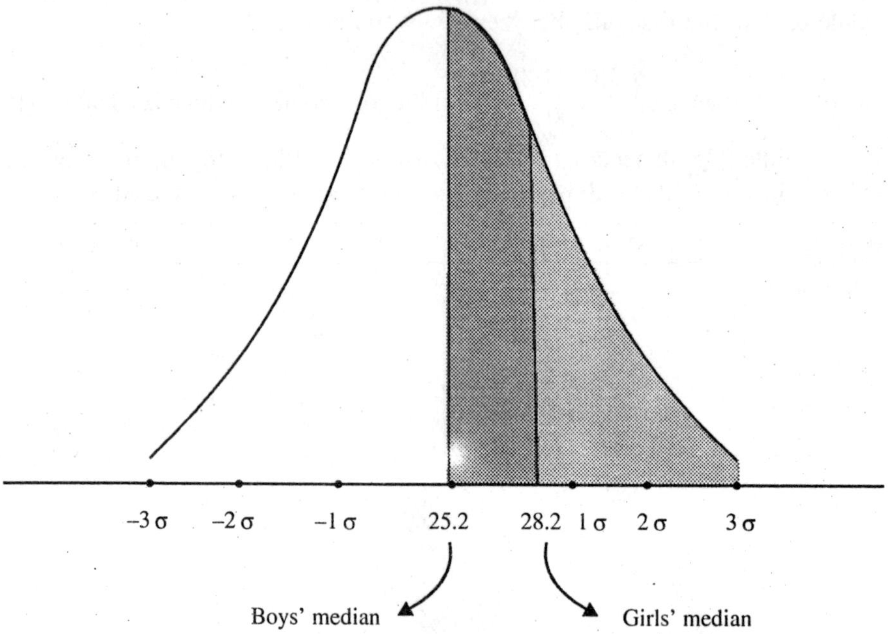

Percentage of cases exceeding a particular score

Example : Given two normal distributions of the scores made on a Mathematics test by 40 boys and 65 girls. The boys' mean score is 30 with a SD of 6. The girls' mean score is 24 with a SD of 5.

(a) What percentage of boys scores less than the mean score of the girls?

(b) What percentage of the girls' exceeds the mean score of the boys' distribution?

Solution :

(a)

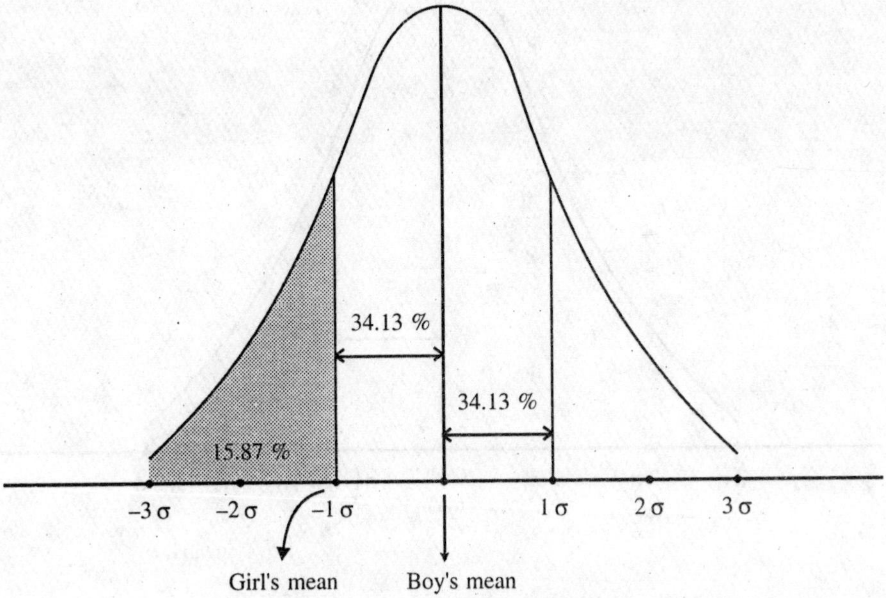

In this part of the example the percentage of the boys scoring less than the mean score of the girls is expected. For this we need (i) Mean score of the boys (ii) SD of the boy's scores (iii) Mean score of the girls.

All other informations are not necessary.

The boy's mean score is (30–24) or 6 scores units above the girls' mean.

Dividing 6 by 6 (the SD for boys distribution) we find that the boy's mean is 1σ above the mean score of the girls' distribution. Table A shows that 34.13% of the cases lie between Mean and 1σ. It is expected to find out the % of the boys scoring $+1\sigma$ below the mean score of the girls'.

Thus, (50% – 34.13%) or 15.87% of the boys score less than the mean score of the girls.

(b) In this part only the following information are needed.

(i) Mean score of the boys

(ii) Mean score of the girls

(iii) SD of the girls' score.

The boy's mean score is (30–24) or 6 score units above the girl's mean score.

Dividing 6 by 5 (the SD of the girls' distribution) we find that boys' mean score is $+ 1.20\ \sigma$ above the girls distribution. From the normal curve area table we find that 38.49% of the normal distribution lies between the mean and $+ 1.20\ \sigma$. Hence, 11.51% of the girls' (50% – 38.49%) i.e., 11.51% exceeds the mean score of the boys.

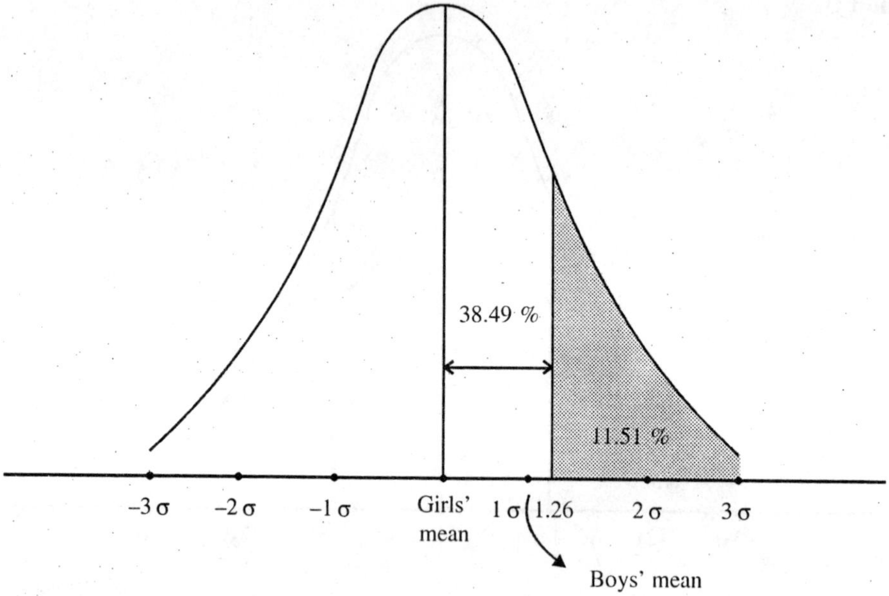

TO DETERMINE THE RELATIVE DIFFICULTY OF TEST QUESTIONS, PROBLEMS AND OTHER TEST ITEMS :

Difficulty level of the problems are indicated either in terms of percentage or σ value. It is suitable to express the difficulty level in term of σ values as we assume the capacity of the measured by the test problems to be distributed normally.

Example : A test question is answered correctly by 10% of a large unselected group, a second test question solved correctly by 20% of the same group; a third test question solved correctly by 30% of the same group. Assuming normal distribution of capacity to solve the test-questions, what is the relative difficulty of the items 1, 2 and 3?

Solution : First of all we shall find out the cut off points of the base line of the Normal Probability Curve which shows

(i) top 10% of the cases

(ii) top 20% of the cases

(iii) top 30% of the cases

Since all the distances are to be taken from the mean, the highest 10% of the cases has 40% of the cases between its lower limit and the mean.

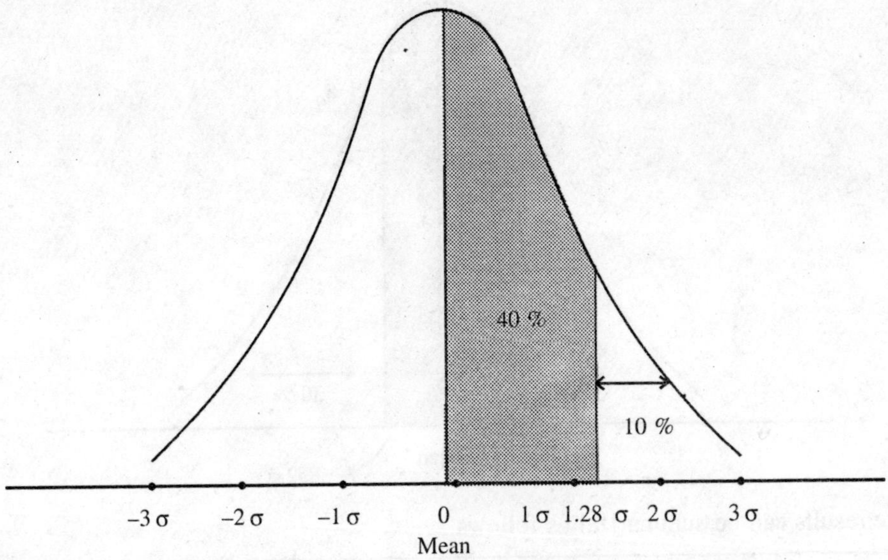

From Table A we find that 39.97% (i.e., 40%) of the normal distribution falls between the mean and 1.28 σ. Thus, 1.28 σ may be set down as the difficulty value of question 1.

Question 2 are attempted correctly by 20% falls at point in the distribution 30% above the mean.

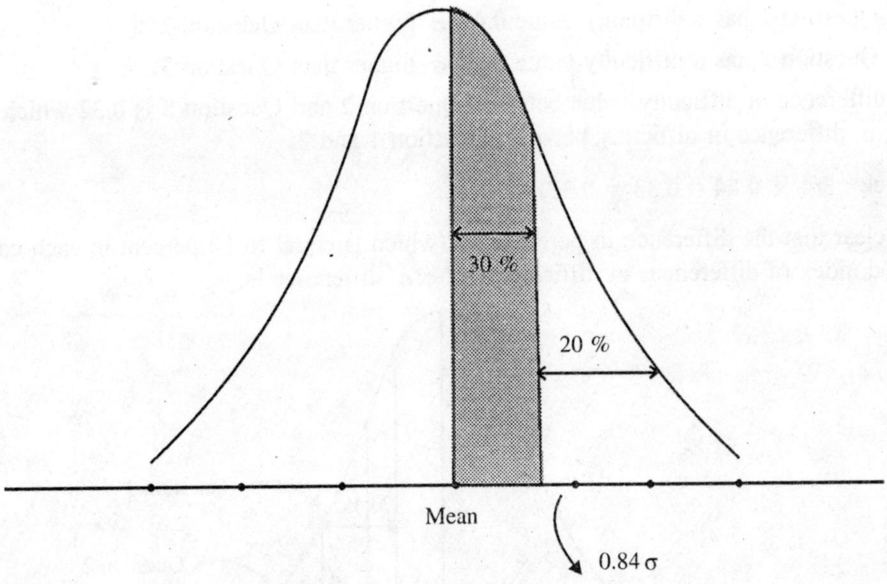

From Table A it is found that 29.95% (i.e., 30%) of the group falls between the mean and 0.84 σ, hence question 2 has a difficulty value of 0.84 σ.

Question 3, passed by 30% of the group falls at a point in the distribution 20% above the mean. From Table A it is found that 19.85% of the distribution falls between the mean and 0.52 σ.

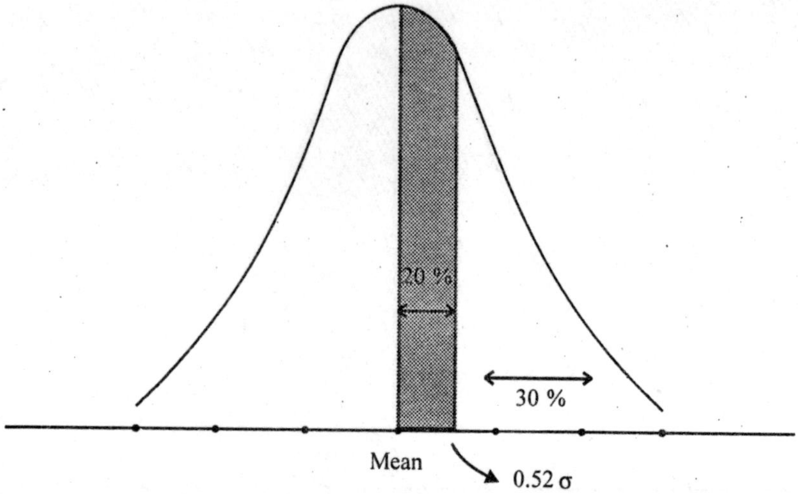

These results can be summarizal as follows :

Question	Passed by	σ value	σ difference
1	10%	1.28	–
2	20%	0.84	0.44
3	30%	0.52	0.32

Comparison of the three questions on the difficulty level based on σ value :

(i) Question 1 has a difficulty value 0.44 σ higher than Question 2.

(ii) Question 2 has a difficulty value 0.32 σ higher than Question 3.

The difference in difficulty value between Question 2 and Question 3 is 0.32 which is roughly 3/4 of the σ difference in difficulty between Question 1 and 2.

(Check : $3/4 \times 0.44 = 0.33 \doteqdot 0.32$)

It is clear that the difference in percentages (which is equal to 10 percent in each case here) is not as good index of differences in difficulty as the σ difference is.

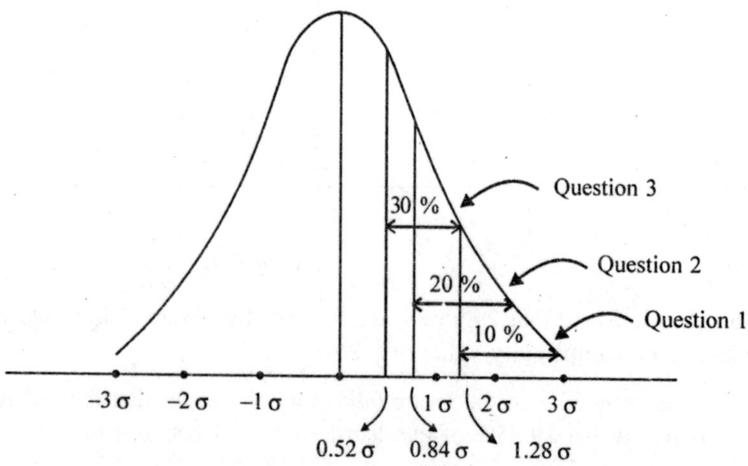

Example : A test item is answered correctly by 20% of a large unselected group; second item solved correctly by 30% of the same group, and a third problem solved by 40%. Assuming normal distribution of capacity to solve test problems, what is the relative difficulty of items 1, 2 and 3?

Solution : First of all, we shall find out the cut off points of the base line of the Normal Probability Curve which shows

(i) top 20% of the cases.

(ii) top 30% of the cases.

(iii) top 40% of the cases.

Since all the distances are to be taken from the mean, the highest 20% of the cases has (50–20)% i.e., 30% cases between its lower limit and the mean. From the Table A we find that 29.40% (i.e., 30%) of the normal distribution falls between the mean and $0.84\,\sigma$. Thus, $0.84\,\sigma$ may be set down as the difficulty value of Question 1.

Question 2 is attempted correctly by 30% falls at point in the distribution (50–30)% i.e., 20% above the mean.

From Table A it is seen that 19.85% (i.e., 20%) of the group falls between mean and $0.52\,\sigma$, hence Question 2 has a difficulty value of $0.52\,\sigma$.

Question 3, passed by 40% of the group falls at a point in the distribution (50–40)% is 10% above the mean. From Table A it is found that 9.87% (i.e., 10%) of the distribution falls between the mean and $0.25\,\sigma$. The results can be summarized as follows :

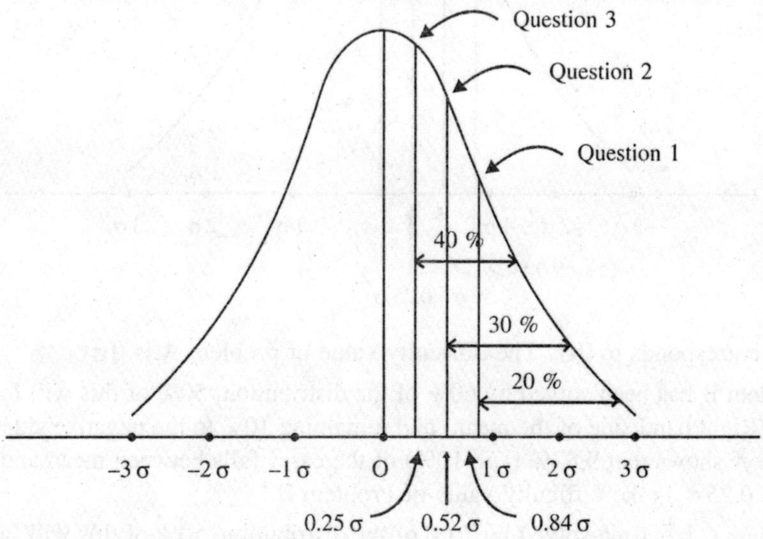

Comparison of relative difficulty value of questions based on σ differences.

Question	Passed by	σ value	σ difference
1	20%	0.84	–
2	30%	0.52	0.32
3	40%	0.25	0.27

(4) Comparison of the three questions on the difficulty level based on σ value :

(i) Question 1 has a difficulty value 0.84 σ higher than Question 2.

(ii) Question 2 has a difficulty value 0.52 σ higher than Question 3.

The difference in difficulty value between Question 2 and 3 is 0.27 which is roughly 3/4 of the difference in difficulty between Question 1 and 2.

(Check : $3/4 \times 0.32/1 = 3 \times 0.8 = 0.24 \doteq 0.27$)

It is thus clear that the difference in percentages (which is equal to 10% in each case here) is not as good index of differences in difficulty as the σ difference is.

Example : Four problems A, B, C and D have been solved by 50%, 60%, 70% and 80% respectively of a large group. Compare the difference in difficulty between A and B with the difference in difficulty between C and D.

Solution :

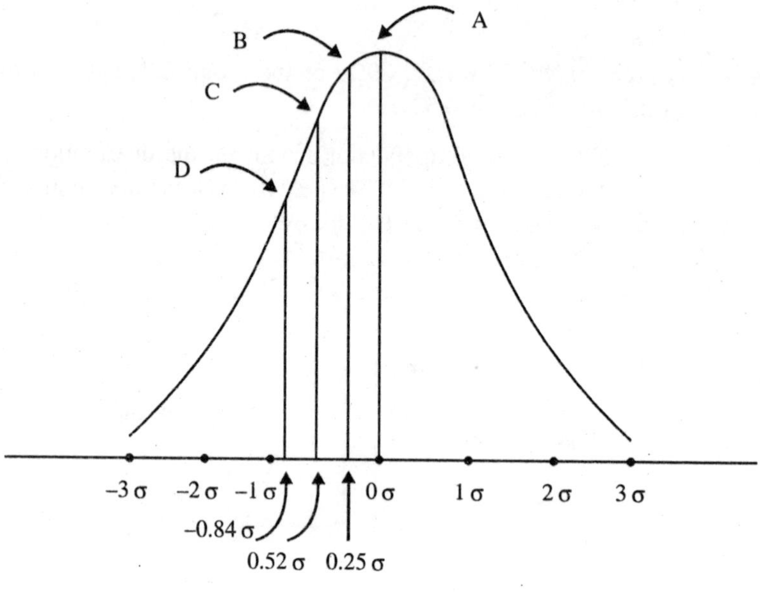

(i) 50% corresponds to 0 σ. The difficulty value of problem A is 0 σ.

(ii) Problem B has been solved by 60% of the distribution. 50% of this will fall to the positive side (Right hand side of the mean) and remaining 10% to the negative side of the base line. Table A shows that 9.87% (i.e., 10%) of the cases falls between mean and – 0.25 σ. Thus, the – 0.25 σ is the difficulty value of Problem B.

(iii) Problem C has been solved by 70% of the distribution. 50% of this will fall to the positive side of the mean and remaining 20% to the negative side. Table A shows that 19.85% (i.e., 20%) of the cases lie between mean and – 0.52 σ. The difficulty value of Problem C is therefore – 0.52 σ.

(iv) Problem D has been solved by 80% of the group. 50% of this will fall to the right side or positive side of the mean. The remaining 30% will fall to negative side of mean. Table A shows that 29.95% (i.e., 30%) of the cases falls between mean and – 0.84 σ. The difficulty value of problem D is thus – 0.84 σ.

The summary is given in the following table.

Problems	Passed by	σ value	σ difference
A	50%	0	0.25
B	60%	– 0.25	
C	70%	– 0.52	0.32
D	80%	– 0.84	

The difference between A and B is 0.25 σ and the difference between C and D is 0.32 σ.

Example : A test consisting of 20 questions was administered to a large unselected group. Question number 13, 14 and 15 were answered correctly by 33%, 20% and 7% resp. of the group. What percentage of the group should answer Question number 16 correctly, so that the difference in difficulty value between Question 13 and 14 may become equal to the difference in difficulty value between Question 15 and 16?

Solution : First of all we shall find out the cut off points of the base line of the Normal Curve which shows

(i) top 33% of the cases

(ii) top 20% of the cases

(iii) top 7% of the cases.

Since all the distances are to be taken from the mean the top 33% of the cases has (50–33)% i.e., 17% cases between its lower limit and the mean. From a Table A it is found that 17.00% of the normal distribution falls between the mean and + 0.44 σ. Thus, 0.44 σ may be set down as the difficulty value for Question 13.

Question 14 is attempted correctly by 20% fall at a point in the distribution (50–20)% i.e., 30% above the mean. Table A shows that 29.95% (i.e., 30%) of the group falls between mean and 0.84 σ, hence Question 14 has a difficulty value of 0.84 σ.

Question 15 passed by 7% of the group falls at a point in the distribution (50–7)% or 43% above the mean. Table A indicates that 42.92% (i.e., 43%) of the distribution falls between the mean and 1.47 σ.

Let Question 16 be solved accurately by x% of the candidates. x% of the normal distribution falls at a point (50–x)% above these mean.

The informations are summarised below.

Questions	Passed by	σ value	σ difference
13	33%	0.44	0.40
14	20%	0.84	
15	7%	1.47	0.40
16	x%	1.87	

As the difference between Questions 13 and 14 should be same as the difference between Questions 15 and 16, therefore σ value for question 16 should be 1.87.

Table A indicates that 1.87 σ corresponds to 46.93% of the area of normal curve.

$\therefore\ 50 - x = 46.93$

$\therefore\ -x = -50.00 + 46.93$

$\therefore\ -x = -3.07$

$\therefore\ +x = 3.07$

$\therefore\ x \doteqdot 3$

$\therefore$ 3% of the group should answer Question 16 correctly.

(5) To separate a given group into sub-groups according to capacity, when the trait is normally distributed :

Example : An entrance examination is administered to 100 college students. This groups of 100 students are to be classified into five sub-groups A, B, C, D and E according to ability, the range of ability to be equal in each sub-group on the assumption that the trait measured by the examination is normally distributed. How many students should be placed in group A, B, C, D and E?

Solution : The base line of the normal curve is considered to extend from -3σ to $+3\sigma$, that is, over a range of 6σ. Dividing this range by 5 (the number of sub-groups) we get 1.2σ. Each group is to be allotted an equal extent of 1.2σ on the base line. These five intervals may be laid of on the base line as shown in the figure, and perpendiculars erected to demarcate the various sub-groups.

(i) Group A covers the upper 1.2σ

(ii) Group B the next 1.2σ

(iii) Group C lies 0.6σ to the right and 0.6σ to the left of the mean.

(iv) Group D occupies the same relative position in the lower half of the curve as B occupies in the upper half.

(v) Group E occupies the same relative position in the lower half of the curve as A occupies in the upper half.

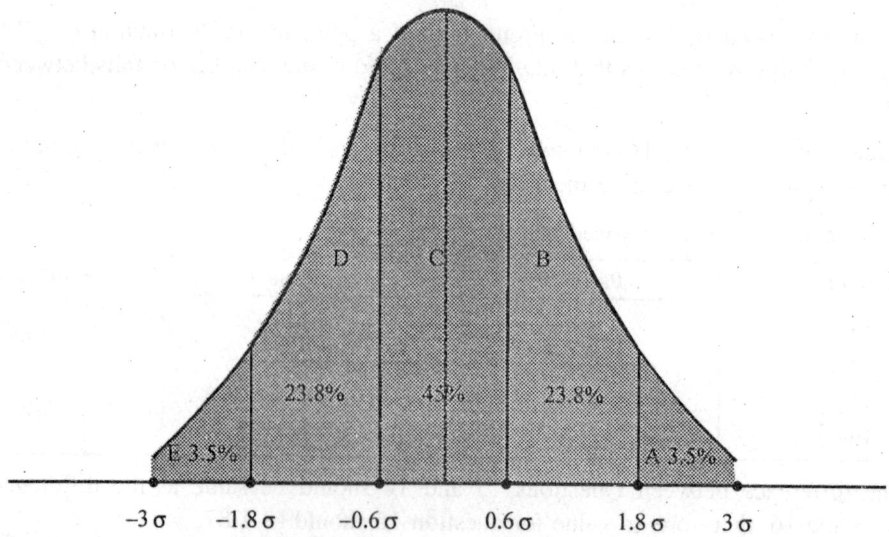

Classification of a Group into sub-groups.

The next step is to find out the percentage of the area that falls in the upper and lower limits of each sub-group.

Grade	Upper Limit		Lower Limit		% in sub-group	Cases out of 100
	σ	%	σ	%		
A	+ 3.0	49.86	+ 1.8	46.41	49.86 – 46.41 = 3.45	4 or 3
B	+ 1.8	46.41	+ 0.6	22.57	46.41 – 22.57 = 23.84	24
C	+ 0.6	22.57	– 0.6	22.57	22.57 + 22.57 = 45.14	45
D	– 0.6	22.57	– 1.8	46.41	46.41 – 22.57 = 23.84	24
E	– 1.8	46.41	– 3.0	49.86	49.86 – 46.41 = 3.45	4 or 3

On the assumption that the capacity measured follows the normal curve, it is clear that 3 to 4 in the group of 100 should be placed in group A, the "marked" ability group, 24 in group B, the "high average" ability group; 45 in group C the "average" ability group; 24 in group D, the "low average" ability group and 3 or 4 in group E, the "very low" or "inferior" group.

The above procedure may be used to determine how many students in a class should be assigned to each of any given number of grade groups. The assumption is always made that performance in the subject upon which the individuals are being marked can be represented by the normal curve. The larger and more unselected the group, and the better the test, the more nearly this assumption justified.

Example : In a certain college, ten grades, A+, A, A–, B+, B, B–, C+, C, C– and D are assigned. If ability in mathematics in distributed normally, how many students in a group of 500 should receive each grade?

Solution : The base line of the normal curve is considered to extend from -3σ to $+3\sigma$, that is, over a range of 6σ. Dividing this range by 10 (the number of grades) we get 0.6σ. Each group is to be allotted an equal extent of 0.6σ on the base line. These ten groups are represented diagramatically on a normal curve as shown in the figure.

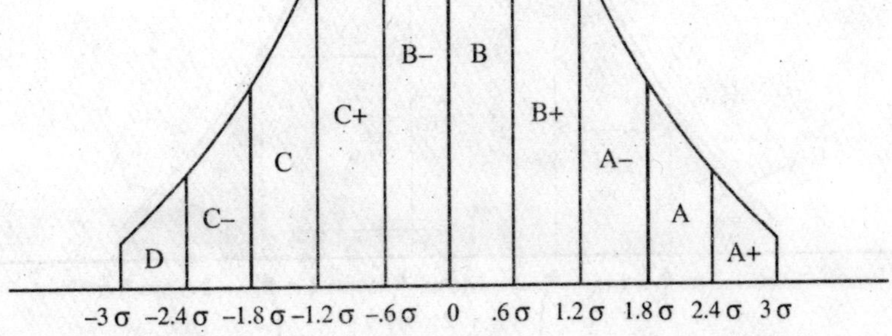

Classification of Group into sub-groups.

The next step is to find out the percentage of the area that falls in the upper and lower limits of each sub-groups.

Calculation of percent area and number of cases in each sub-group :

Grade	Upper Limit		Lower Limit		% in sub-group	Cases out of 500
	σ	%	σ	%		
A+	3.0	49.86	2.4	49.18	49.86 – 49.18 = 0.68	3
A	2.4	49.18	1.8	46.41	49.18 – 46.41 = 2.77	14
A–	1.8	46.41	1.2	38.49	46.41 – 38.49 = 7.92	40
B+	1.2	38.49	0.6	22.57	38.49 – 22.57 = 15.92	80
B	0.6	22.57	0	00.00	22.57 – 00.00 = 22.57	113
B–	0	00.00	– 0.6	22.57	22.57 – 00.00 = 22.57	113
C+	– 0.6	22.57	– 1.2	38.49	38.49 – 22.57 = 15.92	80
C	– 1.2	38.49	– 1.8	46.41	46.41 – 38.49 = 7.92	40
C–	– 1.8	46.41	– 2.4	49.18	49.18 – 46.41 = 2.77	14
D	– 2.4	49.18	– 3.0	49.86	49.86 – 49.18 = 0.68	3

The number of cases in each sub-group as shown in the last column have been obtained by multiplying the percentage of area within a sub-group by $\frac{500}{100}$ or 5.

Example : Assume that the distribution of grades in a class of 500 freshmen is normal with M = 72 and SD = 10. The instructor wants to give letter grades as follows :

10% A's, 30% B's, 40% C's, 15% D's, and 5% E's.

Compute to the closest score the divisions between A's and B's; B's and C's ; C's and D's; D's and F's.

Solution : The positions of the five sub-groups are represented diagramtically on a normal curve as shown in the following figure.

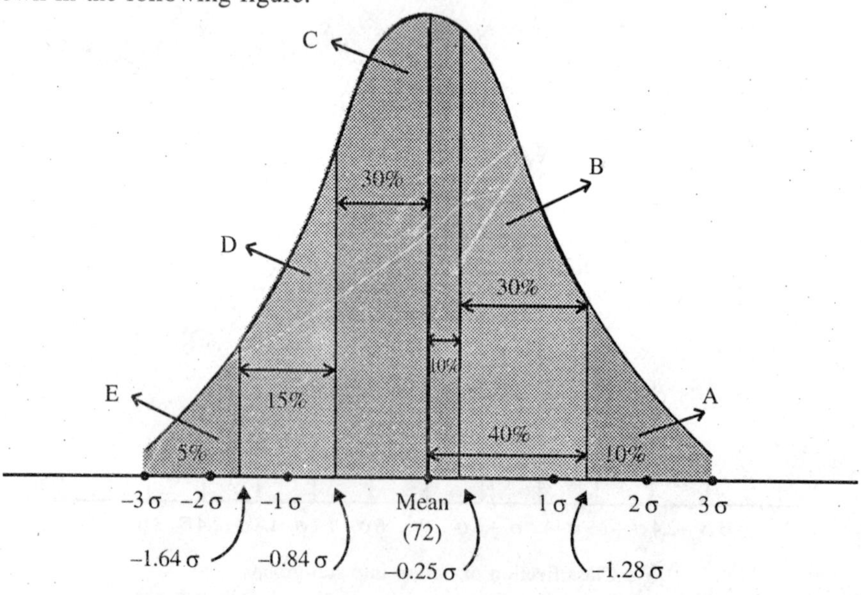

(1) The highest 10% are given A grade. To get the highest 10% of the cases we have to find out the 40% (50 – 10) % above the mean. The normal area tables are to be consulted in the reverse manner. The following steps are followed :

(i) Locate the 40% area in table A.

(ii) Read the z-equivalent to this area.

(iii) Get the raw score using the formula.

Raw Score (X) = M + σz

In this case the following are the readings :

Area Percentage	Equivalent z with sign	$\sigma \times z$	Raw Score = M + σz
40	+ 12.8	10 × 1.28 = 12.8	72 + 12.8 = 84.8 ≑ 85

(2) 30% below A are to be assigned B grade. Hence, the lower score of this group will be 10% above the mean. (As cases getting A and B grades together cover 40% of the upper half of the normal curve).

The following will be the reading

Area Percentage	Equivalent z with sign	$\sigma \times z$	Raw Score = M + σz
10	+ 0.25	10 × 0.25 = 2.5	72 + 2.5 = 74.5 ≑ 75

(3) 40% below B are to be given C grade. The group consists of 10% above and 30% below mean. Thus, the lower score can be obtained by considering 30% of the area below mean.

Area Percentage	Equivalent z with sign	$\sigma \times z$	Raw Score = M + σz
30%	– 0.84	10 × (0.84) = – 8.4	72 – 8.4 = 63.6 ≑ 64

(4) 15% below C are to be assigned D grade. The lower score of this grade can be obtained by 45% of the area below mean.

Area Percentage	Equivalent z with sign	$\sigma \times z$	Raw Score = M + σz
45	– 1.64	10 × 1.64 = – 16.4	72 – 16.4 = 55.6 ≑ 56

From the above calculations it is seen the divisions between A's and B's, B's and C's, C's and D's and D's and E's to the closest scores are 85, 75, 64 and 56.

IMPORTANCE OF NORMAL DISTRIBUTION

The normal distribution is by far the most used distribution in inferential statistics. There are some very important reasons for the same.

(1) A good fit to many phenomena. Phenomena which follow the normal probability curve (at least approximately) many be classified as follow :

(a) **Biological statistics :** e.g., sex ratios in births in a country over a number of years; and the proportion of different types of plants and animals in cross fertilization etc.

(b) **Anthropometrical data :** Height, weight etc., for large groups of the same age and sex.

(c) **Social and Economic data :** e.g., rates of births, marriages or deaths.

(d) **Psychological measurements :** e.g., intelligence, speed of association, perception span, reaction time, educational test scores.

(e) **Errors of observation :** e.g., chance errors which cause observation of heights and weights to deviate above or below their true value.

(2) It may be convenient, on mathematical grounds alone, to assume a normally distributed population.

The normal function has important mathematical properties shared by no other theoretical distribution. Assuming a normal distribution gives the statistician an extremely rich set of mathematical consequences that he can use in developing methods.

(3) The normal distribution can be used as a good approximation to a number of other theoretical distributions like the binomial and can allow the calculation of probabilities that are either tedious or impossible to work out exactly.

(4) There is a very intimate connection between the size of the sample and the extent to which a sampling distribution approaches the normal form.

The central limit theorem states that many sampling distributions based on large N follow the normal curve even though the population distribution is definitely non-normal. This is one of the most remarkable and useful principles used in inferential statistics.

Why frequency Distributions deviate from Normal form :

It is often important for the researcher to know why certain distributions deviate from normal form. The reasons why such deviations occur or the distributions exhibit skewness and kurtosis are numerous.

The following may be the causes of such deviations.

(1) Selection :

(i) Selection is an important cause of skewness. The distribution would be naturally non-normal if the I.Q's of 50 genius students are considered. Similarly, we cannot except normal distribution if a special class of dull normal boys.

(ii) Scores made by small and homogeneous groups are likely to yield narrow and leptokurtic distributions. Similarly scores from large and heterogenous groups are more likely to be broad and platykurtic in form.

(2) Unsuitable or poorly made test :

If a test is too easy, the frequency of the high score will be more resulting into a negatively skewed curve. On the contarary if the examination or test consists of only difficult and complex problems then the frequency of the lower score will be more resulting into a positively skewed curve.

Besides the matter of difficulty in the test, asymmetry may be appear due to ambiguous or poorly made items and by other technical faults.

(3) Errors in the administration of tests :

Error in timing or in giving instructions, errors in the use of scoring stencils, etc., may cause some students to score higher and other to score lower than they normally would yield skewness in the distribution.

(4) The total frequencies involved :

If the total frequencies involved are significantally small then this may unpset the tendency to Normality.

DIVERGENCE FROM NORMALITY

Skewness :

In the normal curve

(i) the mean the median and the mode all coincide and

(ii) there is perfect balance between the right and left halves of the figure.

When a distribution of scores is not symmetrical it is said to be asymmetrical or skewed. By skewness, then we mean the degree of its departure from symmetry.

Types of skewness : There are two types of skewness.

(1) Negative skewness.

(2) Positive skewness.

Negative skewness :

(i) Distributions show negative skewness when scores are massed at the high end of the scale (the right end) and are spread out more gradually toward the low end (or left).

(ii) mean < median in negatively skewed distribution

(iii) mean lies to the left of median.

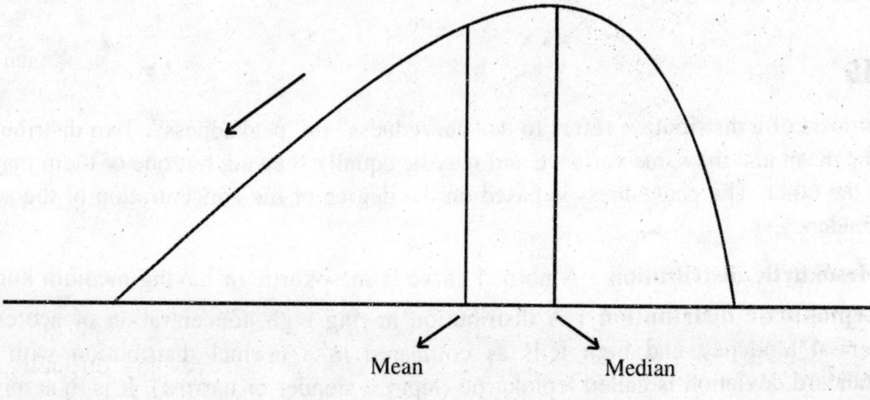

Negative Skewness (to the left)

Positive skewness :

(i) Distributions show negative skewness when the scores are massed at the low (or left) end of the scale and are spread out gradually towards the high or right end.

(ii) mean > median in positively skewed distribution.

(iii) mean lies to the right of median.

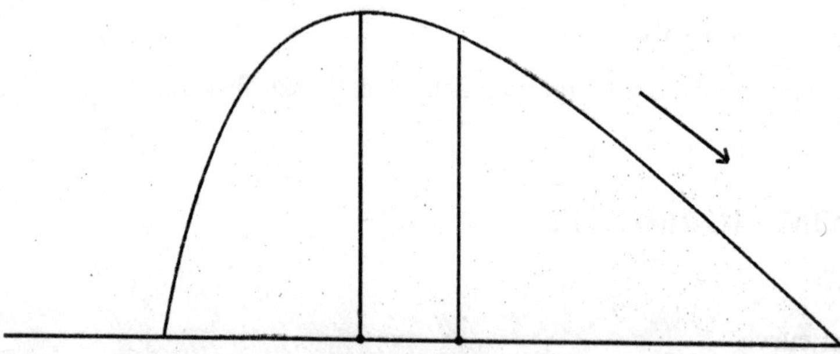

Positive Skewness (to the right)

Measures of skewness :

(i) A measure of skewness based or mean and median is given by the formula

$$Sk = \frac{3\,(\text{mean} - \text{median})}{\sigma}$$

In normal curve mean = mean, hence it has Sk = 0.

(ii) A measure of skewness based on percentiles is given by the formula

$$Sk = \frac{P_{90} + P_{10}}{2} - P_{50}$$

The two measures are not mathematically equivalent. A normal curve has Sk = 0. Deviations from normality can be in negative or positive directions, leading to negatively skewed and positively skewed distributions respectively.

KURTOSIS

The Kurtosis of a distribution refers to its "curvedness" or "peakedness". Two distributions may have the same mean and the same variance and may be equally skewed, but one of them may be more peaked than the other. The peakedness is based on the degree of the concentration of the scores near the central tendency.

(1) Mesokurtic distribution : A normal curve is mesokurtic or having medium kurtosis.

(2) Leptokurtic distribution : A distribution having high concentration of scores near the central tendency and high tails as compared to a normal distribution with the same standard deviation is called leptokurtic (lepto = slender or narrow). It is thus more peaked than normal.

(3) **Platykurtic distribution :** A distribution having low concentration of scores in the neighbourhood of the central tendency and low tails as compared to a normal distribution with the same standard deviation is called platykurtic. (platy = flat, broad or wide)

Thus, it is flatter than the normal.

The following figure shows three curves depicting mesokurtosis, leptokurtosis and platykurtosis.

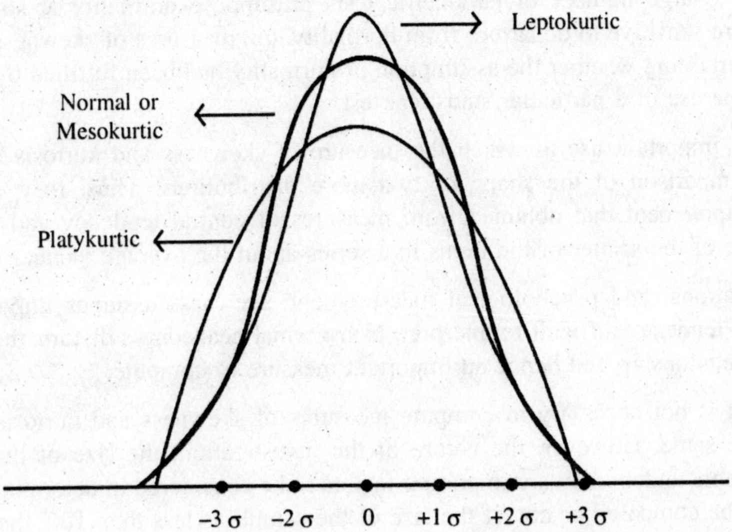

Kurtosis can be measured by the following formula based on percentiles :

$$Ku = \frac{Q}{(P_{90} - P_{10})}$$

From table for normal curve

$PE\ (Q) = 0.6745\ \sigma$

$P_{90} = 1.28\ \sigma$

$P_{10} = -1.28\ \sigma$

$$\therefore \text{Ku (for normal curve)} = \frac{0.6745}{(1.28 - (-1.28)}$$

$$= \frac{0.6745}{2.56} = 0.263$$

If

(i) Ku = 0.263 it is normal distribution.

(ii) Ku is less than 0.263 the distribution is leptokurtic

(iii) Ku is greater than 0.263 the distribution is platykurtic.

IMPORTANCE OF MEASURES OF SKEWNESS AND KURTOSIS

(1) Measures of skewness and kurtosis together with measures of central tendency and variability and the number of cases (N), convey all the information ordinarily needed to understand and interpret any distribution.

(2) Measures of skewness and kurtosis indicate the extent of "non-normal" variation in a series of scores. Since a large number of parametric tests presuppose normality at some point of their application and are sensitive to departure from normality, the measures of skewness and kurtosis can be helpful in ascertaining whether the assumption of normality had been fulfilled by the experimental data to warrant the use of a particular statistical test.

(3) Another important use to which the measure of skewness and kurtosis are generally put, relates to the comparison of the shape of two more distributions. Thus, they furnish additional information to supplement that obtained from measures of central tendency and variability. These indicate the shape of the scatter of the items in a series about the average value.

(4) In educational and psychological measurement, skewness assumes importance because it makes the central tendency difficult to interpret. Non-normal peakedness distorts the normal standard scores and area relationship and hence an important measure to compute.

Ordinarily it is not necessary to compute measures of skewness and kurtosis unless there are indications to the same. However, the nature of the investigation, the size of the sample and the nature of the variable under study are important factors to be considered in determining whether these measures should be compared or not. If the size of the sample is less than 100, these measures may not give very reliable results.

❑❑❑

CHAPTER VI

THE SIGNIFICANCE OF MEAN AND OTHER STATISTICS

In any field we cannot study all the elements in the population. What we do is to select a sample, study the characteristics of this sample and draw conclusions about population based upon the sample studies. Through statistical inference, it is possible to generalise from a sample description to some larger population of which the sample is a part. Inferential statistics is that branch of statistics which primarily deals with inferences from a sample to a larger population from which the sample has been taken. Thus, statistical inferences help us to generalise some characteristic of the population.

A parameter is any measure based upon an entire population. Parameters are perhaps more widely known as "true" measures. For example, a true mean which is a parameter, is the mean of all members of the population.

Thus measures descriptive of a population are known as "parameters". A statistic is any measure derived from a sample and is frequently referred to as an "obtained" measure or an "observed" measure. A parameter always has an exact constant value, although usually unknown; a statistic varies in values from sample to sample. Parameters do exist but are seldom determinable, since usually the entire population is not accessible, in most instances, the best we can do is to estimate the parameter by drawing a sample and calculating the corresponding statistic. For example the best estimate of a true mean that may be derived from a random sample is the mean of that sample. Usually there exists a *sampling error*. A sampling error is the difference between a parameter and an estimate of that parameter which is derived from a sample. As the sample size increases the statistics tend to approximate the parameters and there is decrease in the sampling error.

Under specified conditions, the parameters may be forecast from sample statistics with known degree of accuracy. The degree to which a sample mean represents its parameter is an index of the *significance* or trustworthiness of the computed sample mean. When a statistics has been calculated, the question which is generally asked is : How good an estimate is this statistic of the parameter based upon the entire population from which this sample was drawn? This question applies to all statistics, but only a few more important ones will be discussed in this chapter.

THE STANDARD ERROR OF THE MEAN (SE_M) IN LARGE SAMPLES

The need for a standard error of sample mean can be best understood when we have examined the factors upon which the stability of mean depends. Suppose we wish to estimate the mean weight of boys studying in Std.X in Mumbai. To find the mean weight in general we should find the weight of all the male students studying in Std.X in Mumbai. It will involve a huge expense in terms of money and time and will defeat the very purpose of the experiment itself. We should therefore be satisfied with a sample. But this sample should be as large and as randomly drawn as possible. Thus, the degree to which a sample mean approximates its parameter depends for one thing upon how impartially we have drawn the sample. The sample mean depends on (1) Number of cases in sample and (2) σ, the variability or spread of scores around the mean.

If a large number of samples are taken from the same population, each sample will have its own mean. If all such sample means are arranged graphically we get a normal curve. It has been found that even if the distribution of scores is skewed, the sampling distribution of mean tends to reach a normal shape. The Standard Error (SE) is the standard deviation of the sampling distribution of the mean. The sampling distributions, though, are not calculated, yet they exist. The SE is also not calculated directly from the sampling distribution but it is estimated from the sample standard distributions but it is estimated from the sample standard deviation which is the only value available to us.

COMPUTATION OF THE STANDARD ERROR OF THE MEAN (SE_M)

The formula for the Standard Error of the mean is

$$SE_M \text{ or } \sigma_M = \frac{\sigma}{\sqrt{N}}$$

where σ = the standard deviation of the population

N = the number of cases in the sample.

However, the standard deviation of the population is generally unknown, we go for the best substitute which is the standard deviation of the sample.

Some authors suggest the use of N in the denominator of the formula SE_M for large sample ($N \geq 30$) and ($N - 1$) for small samples ($N < 30$). In the social science, the sample is very large hence subtraction of 1 from N makes no appreciable difference in the computed SD.

APPLICATION AND INTERPRETATION OF SE_M IN LARGE SAMPLE

Standard Error of mean measures the degree to which the mean is affected by the errors of measurement as well as by the errors of sampling or sampling fluctuations from one random sample to the other. The interpretation of the SE of the mean is done to answer - how dependable is the mean? Further it may be asked, as to how good an estimate is the sample mean or the population mean. To answer to these questions is provided by setting up the *confidence limits*. or the fiduciary limits* of the mean. These limits, for a particular level of confidence are supposed to embrace the population mean. Thus, the interpretation of the SE_M is done in terms of the confidence intervals for the population mean.

The following example will illustrate the computation and interpretation of the SE of the mean in large samples.

Example :

The mean achievement of a random sample of 500 students on a test of Algebra is 59 and the SD is 12. How dependable is the mean? How good an estimate is it of the population mean?

Solution :

The example can be solved in the following steps :

Step 1 : Calculate SE_M

$$SE_M = \frac{\sigma}{\sqrt{N}} = \frac{12}{\sqrt{500}}$$

$$= \frac{12}{22.361} = 0.536 \doteqdot 0.54$$

SD of the sample is used as our estimate of the population σ. When the means of such many samples are plotted we get a normal curve. SE_M is the standard deviation of a distribution of sample means around the fixed population mean ($M_{pop.}$).

The position of the SE_M is shown in the following figure.

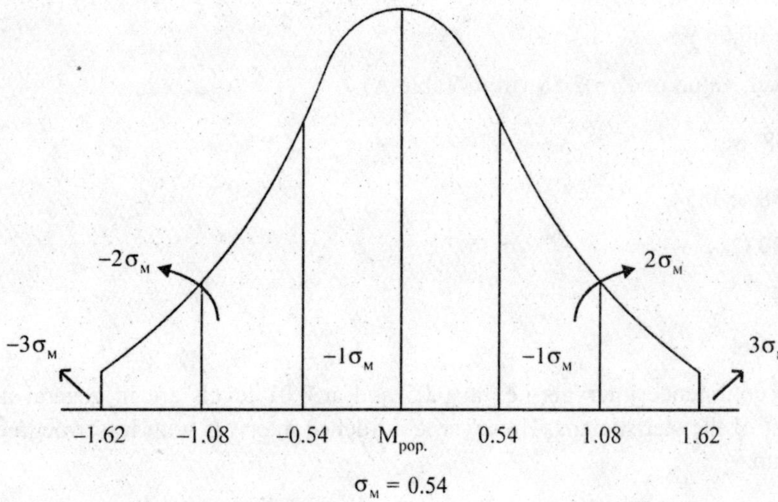

(sampling distribution of means, showing variability of obtained Means around Population mean in terms of σ_M .)

*R.A. Fisher termed the confidence intervals of a parameter as fiduciary limits and the confidence placed in the interval defined by the limits as containing the parameter, as fiduciary probability.

Step 2 : Set up Confidence Intervals.

In the figure $M_{pop.}$ which is unknown, is at the centre of the curve. It is noted

(i) 62.26% of the sample means fall between $\pm 1\sigma_M$ of $M_{pop.}$ i.e., within a range of $\pm$ 0.54 units.

(ii) 95% of the sample means fall between $\pm 2\sigma_M$

More exactly 1.96 $\sigma_{M.}$

Two confidence intervals are generally set up by the statistician to interpret the $M_{pop.}$ In any distribution of sample means 95% cases must theoretically be included $M \pm 1.96\sigma_M$ and 99% of them should fall with $M \pm 2.58\sigma_M$ Thus, M_{pop} will fall within $M \pm 1.96\sigma_M$ is 95% cases and within $M \pm 2.58\sigma_M$ in 99% cases. It is already stated that the limits of confidence intervals are also known as fiduciary limits of the M_{pop} or true mean. We say that the fiduciary probability is 0.95 that $M_{pop.}$ lies within the interval $M \pm 1.96\sigma_M$ and 0.05 that it falls outside this interval.

Let us consider the further solution of the problem in hand. At 0.05 level

value of Z = 1.96 (from Table A)

$M \pm 1.96\ \sigma_M$

$= 59 \pm 1.96 \times 0.54$

$= 59 \pm 1.0584$

$= 59 \pm 1.06$

= 57.94 to 60.06

At 0.01 level, value of Z = 2.58 (from Table A)

$M \pm 2.58\ \sigma_M$

$= 59 \pm 2.58 \times 0.54$

$= 59 \pm 1.3932$

$= 59 \pm 1.4$

= 57.6 to 60.4

The above confidence intervals i.e., at 0.05 and at 0.01 levels are in general use accepted as standard by most of the statisticians. However, confidence intervals with lesser degrees of assurance can also be set up.

Step 3 : Interpret the Results :

The confidence intervals represent a range within which the parameter $M_{pop.}$ is likely to fall. Hence, with respect to our data above, there are 95 chances out of 100, the $M_{pop.}$ would fall between the score value 57.94 to 60.06; and there are 99 chances out of 100, that $M_{pop.}$ would fall between the score values 57.06 to 60.4. Our confidence that these intervals contain $M_{pop.}$ is 95 per cent of P of 0.95 and 99 per cent or P of 0.99 respectively.

Example :

On a test of clerical aptitude, a randomly selected group of 400 candidates obtain a mean = 25.6 and σ = 5.00. Use 0.95 and 0.99 confidence and set up the two confidence intervals.

Solution :

Step 1 : Calculate SE_M.

$$SE_M = \frac{\sigma}{\sqrt{N}} = \frac{5}{\sqrt{400}} = \frac{5}{20} = 0.25$$

Step 2 : Set up Confidence Intervals

At 0.05 level

$$M \pm 1.96\ \sigma_M$$

$$= 25.6 \pm 1.96 \times 0.25$$

$$= 25.6 \pm 0.49$$

$$= 25.11 \text{ to } 26.09$$

At 0.01 level,

$$M \pm 2.58\ \sigma_M$$

$$= 25.6 \pm 2.58 \times 0.25$$

$$= 25.6 \pm 0.645$$

$$= 24.955 \text{ to } 26.245$$

Example :

The mean of a test of Numerical ability for 135 students is 270.16 with a standard deviation of 25.1.

How dependable is the mean? How good an estimate is of the population mean?

Solution :

Step 1 : Calculate SE_M

$$SE_M = \frac{\sigma}{\sqrt{N}} = \frac{25.1}{\sqrt{135}}$$

$$= \frac{25.1}{11.619}$$

$$= 2.16$$

Step 2 : Set up Confidence Intervals

At 0.05 level

$$M \pm 1.96\ \sigma_M$$

$$= 270.16 \pm 1.96 \times 2.16$$

$$= 270.16 \pm 4.2336$$

$$= 265.93 \text{ to } 274.39$$

At 0.01 level,

$$M \pm 2.58\ \sigma_M$$

$$= 270.16 \pm 2.58 \times 2.16$$

$$= 270.16 \pm 5.5728$$

$$= 264.5872 \text{ to } 275.7328$$

Step 3 : Interpret the results

At 0.05 level the means lies between 265.93 to 274.39, i.e., there is 95% chance that the mean of the population will lie between these two limits.

At 0.01 level the mean lies between 264.59 to 275.73 i.e., there is 99% chance that the mean of the population will be between these two limits.

Example :

Given M = 26, σ = 5.20, N = 100

Compute the 0.95 confidence interval for the true mean.

Solution :

Step 1 : Calculate SE_M

$$SE_M = \frac{\sigma}{\sqrt{N}} = \frac{5.20}{\sqrt{100}}$$

$$= \frac{5.20}{10} = 0.52$$

Step 2 : Set up the confidence interval

It is to be computed as the 0.95 interval for true mean

$$M \pm 2.58\ \sigma_M$$

$$= 26.40 \pm 2.58 \times 0.52$$

$$= 26.40 \pm 1.3416$$

$$= 25.0584 \text{ to } 27.7416$$

$$= 25.06 \text{ to } 27.74$$

THE STANDARD ERROR OF THE MEAN IN SMALL SAMPLES

In sample (N < 30) the formula for the standard error for mean (σ_M) becomes

$$S_M = \frac{S}{\sqrt{N}} \quad \text{where}$$

$$S = \sqrt{\frac{\Sigma x^2}{(N-1)}} \quad \text{and}$$

N = size of the sample.

Apart from this modified formula for standard error for small sample, there is one more significant difference between the treatment of large and small samples. The sampling distribution of means computed from small samples is known as 't distribution*' which closely compares with the normal distribution. When N increases in the size the shape of the 't', distribution approximates the shape of the normal distribution.

The t ratio is obtained by the formula

$$t = \frac{M - M_{pop}}{S_M} \quad \text{where}$$

M = Mean of the sample

M_{pop} = Population mean

S_M = An estimate of the σ_M obtained from SD of the sample.

Gossett has shown that for random samples drawn from normal populations, the sampling distribution of t is given by.

$$y = \frac{y_0}{\left(1 + \frac{t^2}{n-1}\right)^{n/2}}$$

(equation for sampling distribution of t) in which

n = number of cases in the sample.

y = length of the ordinate.

The denomination of this equation has its minimum value when y = 0 and hence the curve has its maximum ordinate at this point. It is also noted that the squared value of t is used, therefore the ordinate is same for given value of t (whether t is positive or negative) and the distribution is therefore symmetrical. Finally, as t increases, the ordinate y decreases or the height of the curve

* This theoretical 't distribution' was discovered by an English statistician, W.S. Gossett in 1908 writing under the pen name "Student" in respect of his teacher R.A. Fisher.

decreases. The curve is asymptotic to the base line. The curve is much like the normal curve except that it is more peaked for small values of 'n'. For large values of n, the distribution approaches the form of the normal distribution.

It is to be noted that 't distribution' is not a single distribution but a family of distributions depending upon df. A different distribution of t, off course will be found for each value of n, or for each number of degrees of freedom. Fisher has prepared a table (Table D) showing for each value of df from 1 to 30, what absolute value of 't' would be expected in 1 per cent of all samples, as well as in 2 per cent, 5 per cent .... 90 per cent of all such samples.

DEGREES OF FREEDOM (df)

The concept of degrees of freedom is of key importance in inferential statistics. Almost all tests of significance require the calculation of degrees of freedom. It is a mathematical concept. The geometric interpretation of the concept relates to the movement of a point in relation to the number of dimensions it is attached with. A point on a line is free to move in one dimension only and thus has 1 degree of freedom. A point on a plane has freedom of movement in two dimensions, and thus has two degrees of freedom. A point in space of three dimensions has 3 degrees of freedom.

The expression degrees of freedom is abbreviated from the full expression "degrees of freedom to vary". When a sample statistic is used to estimate a parameter, the number of degrees of freedom depends upon the number of restrictions placed upon the scores, each restriction reducing one df.

The idea of df is illustrated with the help of the following example.

Set I (Given Scores)	Set II (Altered Scores)	
5	21	Can vary in any way.
13	11	
8	5	
9	7	
15	[6] →	its value gets fixed or automatically determined.
$\Sigma X = 50$	$\Sigma X = 50$	

In set I, original scores have been presented. The sum total of all the five scores is 50. We can vary the first four scores in any way we like. But the value of the 5th score gets fixed due to the restriction that Σx in each case must be 50. Here four scores out of five are free to vary, hence the df $= (N - 1) = 5 - 1 = 4$.

(The concept of df has also been explained in the chapter of Chi-square).

LEVELS OF SIGNIFICANCE

Researchers have selected some arbitrary standards called levels of significance to serve as the cut off points or critical points along the probability scale, to separate the significant difference from the non-significant difference between the two statistics like means or standard deviations. The 0.05

and the 0.01 levels of significance are most popular in social science research. The confidence with which a researcher rejects – or retains a null hypothesis depends upon the level of significance adopted. Hence, they are sometimes called as levels of confidence. The following table will make its meaning clear.

MEANING OF LEVELS OF CONFIDENCE

Level	Amount of confidence	Interpretation
0.05	95%	If the experiment is repeated 100 times only on 5 occasions, the obtained mean will fall outside the limits M $\pm$ 1.96 SE
0.01	99%	If the experiment is repeated 100 times only on one occasion, the obtained mean will fall outside the limit M $\pm$ 1.96 SE

It is clear that if an obtained value of t is significant at 0.01 level, it is automatically significant at 0.05 level but the reverse is not always true.

APPLICATION AND INTERPRETATION OF SE_M IN SMALL SAMPLES

The procedure of calculation and interpretation of standard error of Mean in small samples differs from that of large sample in two respects.

(1) In the calculation of SD of the sample, (N – 1) is used instead of N in the formula.

(2) "t distribution" is used instead of normal distribution.

The rest of the line of reasoning in determining and interpreting SE_M in small samples is similar to that for the large samples.

Example :

A randomly selected group of 25, VI grade students have a mean height of 135 cm, and SD = 10 cm. How well does this value estimate the population mean? Use 0.99 and 0.95 confidence intervals.

Solution :

Step 1 : Calculate SE_M

$$SE_M = \frac{\sigma}{\sqrt{N}} = \frac{10}{\sqrt{25}} = \frac{10}{5} = 2$$

Step 2 : From Table D pick up the values of t :

For df = N – 1 = 25 – 1 = 24

t at 0.05 level = 2.06

t at 0.01 level = 2.80

Step 3 : Set up confidence intervals

At 0.95

$M \pm 2.06\ SE_M$

$= 135 \pm 2.06 \times 2$

$= 135 \pm 4.12$

$= 130.88$ to 139.12

At 0.99

$M \pm 2.80\ SE_M$

$= 135 \pm 2.80 \times 2$

$= 135 \pm 5.60$

$= 129.40$ to 140.60.

Step 4 : Interpret the results

There is a probability of 0.95 that the M_{pop} will be within the score 130.88 to 139.12 and 0.99 probability that M_{pop} will be within the score range of 129.40 to 140.60.

Example :

The mean of 16 independent observations of a certain magnitude is 100 and the SD is 24.

(a) At the 0.05 confidence level, what are the fiduciary limits of the true mean?

(b) Taking the 0.99 confidence interval as our standard, we may be assured the true mean is at least as large as what value.

Solution :

Step 1 : Calculate SE_M

$$SE_M = \frac{\sigma}{\sqrt{N}} = \frac{24}{\sqrt{16}} = \frac{24}{4} = 6$$

Step 2 : From Table D pick up the values of t :

For df $= N - 1 = 16 - 1 = 15$

t at 0.05 level $= 2.13$

t at 0.01 level $= 2.95$

Step 3 : Set up confidence intervals

At 0.05 confidence level the fiduciary limits of true mean are :

$M \pm 2.13\ SE_M$

$= 100 \pm 2.13 \times 6$

$= 100 \pm 12.78$

$= 87.22$ to 112.78

At 0.99 confidence interval

$M \pm 2.95\ SE_M$

$= 100 \pm 2.95 \times 6$

$= 100 \pm 17.70$

$= 82.30$ to 117.70

(a) At 0.05 confidence level, the fiduciary limits of true mean are 87.22 to 112.78

(b) At 0.99 confidence interval the true mean is atleast as large as 82.30.

Example :

A test of Numerical ability was given to a group of 10 students which yielded the following estimates M = 35.00 and SD = 6. Determine the fiduciary limits of the Population Mean at 0.99 and 0.95 probabilities.

Solution :

Step 1 : Calculate SE_M

$$SE_M = \frac{\sigma}{\sqrt{N}} = \frac{6}{\sqrt{10}} = \frac{6}{3.162}$$

$= 1.89$

$\doteqdot 1.9$

Step 2 : From Table D pick up the values of t :

For df $= N - 1 = 10 - 1 = 9$

t at 0.05 level $= 2.26$

t at 0.01 level $= 3.25$

Step 3 : Set up confidence intervals

At 0.95 confidence interval.

$M_{pop} = M \pm 2.06\ SE_M$

$= 35 \pm 2.26 \times 1.9$

$= 35 \pm 4.294$

$= 30.706$ to 39.294

At 0.99 confidence interval

$M_{pop} = M \pm 3.25\ SE_M$

$= 35 \pm 3.25 \times 1.9$

$= 35 \pm 6.175$

$= 28.82$ to 41.17

Example :

For a given group of 500 students the mean score is 95 and the SD is 25.

(a) Determine the 0.99 confidence interval for the true mean.

(b) It is unlikely that the true mean is larger than what value?

Solution :

The sample is large (N > 30) hence normal distribution is used.

Step 1 : Calculate SE_M

$$SE_M = \frac{\sigma}{\sqrt{N}} = \frac{25}{\sqrt{500}}$$

$$= \frac{25}{22.361}$$

$$\div 1.12$$

Step 2 : Set up Confidence Intervals

At 0.01 level

$$M \pm 2.58\ \sigma_M$$

$$= 95 \pm 2.58 \times 1.12$$

$$= 95 \pm 2.89$$

$$= 92.11 \text{ to } 97.89$$

Step 3 : Interpretation

(a) The range of scores for the 0.99 confidence interval is 92.11 to 97.89

(b) It is unlikely that the true mean is larger than 97.89.

Example :

The following measures of perception span for unrelated words are obtained from 5 children :

5, 6, 4, 7, 5.

(a) Find the 0.99 confidence interval for the true mean of these scores.

(b) Compare the fiduciary limits (0.99 confidence interval) when calculated by large sample methods with the results in (a)

Solution :

Here mean and SD are not given, hence both are to be worked out.

(i) $M = \frac{\Sigma x}{N} = \frac{27}{5} = 5.4$

(ii) Calculation of SD

Scores (X)	x = X – M	x^2
5	– 0.4	0.16
6	0.6	0.36
4	– 1.4	1.96
7	1.6	2.56
5	– 0.4	0.16

N = 5 $\Sigma x^2 = 5.20$

$$SD = \sqrt{\frac{\Sigma x^2}{N}}$$

As the sample is small, (N – 1) is used instead of N

$$SD = \sqrt{\frac{\Sigma x^2}{(N-1)}}$$

$$SD = \sqrt{\frac{5.20}{4}}$$

$$= \sqrt{1.3}$$

$$= 1.140$$

Now M = 5.4 and SD = 1.14

The steps for small samples are now followed.

Step 1 : Calculate SE_M

$$SE_M = \frac{\sigma}{\sqrt{N}} = \frac{1.14}{\sqrt{5}} = \frac{1.14}{2.236}$$

$$= 0.5098$$

$$\doteqdot 0.51$$

Step 2 : From table D pick up the value of t :

For df = N – 1 = 5 – 1 = 4

t at 0.05 level = 2.78

t at 0.01 level = 4.60

Step 3 : Set up confidence intervals

At 0.99 interval

$M \pm 4.60\ SE_M$

$= 5.4 \pm 4.60 \times 0.51$

$= 5.4 \pm 2.346$

$= 3.05$ to 7.75

(b) In large sample SD is calculated using the formula

$$SD = \sqrt{\frac{\Sigma x^2}{N}}$$

$$= \sqrt{\frac{5.2}{5}} = \sqrt{1.04}$$

$$= 1.02$$

In large sample normal distribution is used instead of t distribution.

Step 1 : Calculate SE_M

$$SE_M = \frac{\sigma}{\sqrt{N}} = \frac{1.02}{\sqrt{5}}$$

$$= \frac{1.02}{2.236}$$

$$= 0.4561$$

$$\doteqdot 0.46$$

Step 2 : Set up the confidence interval

At 0.99 interval

$M \pm 2.58\ SE_M$

$= 5.4 \pm 2.58 \times 0.46$

$= 5.4 \pm 1.19$

$= 4.21$ to 6.59

Example :

Suppose it is known that the SD of the scores in a certain population is 20. How many cases would we need in a sample in order that the SE of the sample M be 2?

Solution :

$$SE_M = \frac{\sigma}{\sqrt{N}}$$

$$2 = \frac{20}{\sqrt{N}}$$

$$2 \times \sqrt{N} = 20$$

$$\sqrt{N} = 10$$

Squaring both the sides we get

$$N = 100$$

The required size of the sample is 100.

THE STANDARD ERROR OF A MEDIAN

It has been established that the variability of the sample medians is about 25% greater than the variability of means in a normally distributed population. The following formulae are used to estimate standard error of a median.

(a) Standard error in terms of standard deviation

$$SE_{Mdn} = (\sigma_{Mdn}) = \frac{1.253\,\sigma}{\sqrt{N}}$$

(b) Standard error in terms of quartile deviation

$$SE_{Mdn} = (\sigma_{Mdn}) = \frac{1.858\,Q}{\sqrt{N}}$$

We know

$$SE_M = \frac{\sigma}{\sqrt{N}}$$

From (a) we know

$$\sigma_{Mdn} = \frac{1.253\,\sigma}{\sqrt{N}}$$

$$= 1.253\left(\frac{\sigma}{\sqrt{N}}\right)$$

$$= 1.253 \times SE_M$$

$$= 1\frac{1}{4} \text{ times } SE_M \qquad \left(1.253 = 1\frac{1}{4}\right)$$

Thus, SE_{Mdn} is roughly $1\frac{1}{4}$ times the $SE_{M.}$ Hence, σ_{Mdn} is less dependable and more subject to sampling fluctuations as compared to σ_M.

Example :

The median score of 225 students randomly selected is 24.5 and Q = 4.2. Set up the fiduciary limits within which the population median is likely to fall. Use 0.99 and 0.95 confidence levels.

Solution :

Step 1 : Calculate σ_{Mdn}

$$\sigma_{Mdn} = \frac{1.858\ Q}{\sqrt{N}}$$

$$= \frac{1.858 \times 4.2}{\sqrt{225}}$$

$$= \frac{7.8036}{15}$$

$$\doteqdot 0.52$$

Step 2 : Set up confidence intervals.

Since N is large, we can use normal curve tables to set up the confidence intervals.

z for 99% = 2.58

z for 95% = 1.96

Hence, the confidence intervals are :

(i) 0.99 confidence

$$\text{Mdn} \pm 2.58\ \sigma_{Mdn}$$

$$= 24.5 \pm 2.58 \times 0.52$$

$$= 24.5 \pm 1.34$$

$$= 23.16 \text{ to } 25.84$$

(ii) 0.95 confidence

$$\text{Mdn} \pm 1.96\ \sigma_{Mdn}$$

$$= 24.5 \pm 1.96 \times 0.52$$

$$= 24.5 \pm 1.0192$$

$$= 23.4808 \text{ to } 25.5192$$

$$= 23.48 \text{ to } 25.52$$

Step 3 : Interpret the Results :

(i) There are 99 chances out of 100 that the Median (pop) would fall between the score values 23.16 to 25.84.

(ii) There are 95 chances out of 100 that the Median (pop) would fall between the score values 23.48 to 25.52.

Example :

Suppose it has been found out that the median weight of 550 students of Std.IX randomly selected is 45 kg. and SD = 8.5. How well does this value estimate the population median? Use 0.99 and 0.95 confidence interval.

Solution :

Step 1 : Calculate σ_{Mdn}

$$\sigma_{Mdn} = \frac{1.253\ \sigma}{\sqrt{N}}$$

$$= \frac{1.253 \times 8.5}{\sqrt{550}}$$

$$= \frac{10.6505}{23.452}$$

$$= 0.454$$

Step 2 : Set up confidence intervals.

(i) at 0.95 confidence interval.

$$\text{Median (pop.)} = \text{Mdn} \pm 1.96\ \sigma_{Mdn}$$
$$= 45 \pm 1.96 \times 0.454$$
$$= 45 \pm 0.89$$
$$= 44.11 \text{ to } 45.89$$

(ii) at 0.99 confidence interval.

$$\text{Median (pop.)} = \text{Mdn} \pm 2.58\ \sigma_{Mdn}$$
$$= 45 \pm 2.58 \times 0.454$$
$$= 45 \pm 1.17$$
$$= 43.83 \text{ to } 46.17$$

Step 3 : Interpret the Result :

(i) There are 95 chances out of 100 that the Median (pop.) would fall between 44.11 to 45.89.

(ii) There are 99 chances that the Median (pop.) would fall between 43.83 to 46.17.

THE STANDARD ERROR OF A STANDARD DEVIATION (SE_σ) :

The standard deviation records fluctuate from sample to sample. The standard error of a standard deviation is found by computing the probable divergence of the sample SD from its parameter (population SD). the formula for SE_σ or σ_σ is

$$SE_\sigma = \frac{0.71\,\sigma}{\sqrt{N}} \quad \text{or}$$

$$SE_\sigma = \frac{\sigma}{\sqrt{2N}}$$

For small samples ($N < 100$) the sampling distribution of SD is somewhat skewed but approaches normality as N increases. Hence, inferences based on normal distribution can be drawn.

We have

$$SE_M = \frac{\sigma}{\sqrt{N}} \qquad \text{(i)}$$

$$SE_\sigma = \frac{0.71\,\sigma}{\sqrt{N}} \qquad \text{(ii)}$$

Dividing (i) by (ii) we get

$$\frac{SE_M}{SE_\sigma} = \frac{\frac{\sigma}{\sqrt{N}}}{\frac{0.71\,\sigma}{\sqrt{N}}}$$

$$\frac{SE_M}{SE_\sigma} = \frac{\sigma}{\sqrt{N}} \times \frac{\sqrt{N}}{0.71\sigma} = \frac{1}{0.71} = 1.41$$

$$\frac{SE_M}{SE_\sigma} = 1.41$$

$$SE_M = 1.41\, SE_\sigma$$

It is therefore clear that SE_σ is always smaller than SE_M and SE_M is about 41% greater than SE_σ. Hence, SE_M is less stable than the SE_σ.

Example :

The standard deviation of the intelligence score of a group of 200 randomly selected students is 10.2. How dependable is the SD?

Step 1 : Calculation SE_σ

$$SE_\sigma = \frac{\sigma}{\sqrt{2N}} = \frac{10.2}{\sqrt{400}} = \frac{10.2}{20}$$

$$SE_\sigma = \frac{5.1}{10} = 0.51$$

Step 2 : Set up confidence intervals.

Since N is large, we can use normal curve tables to set up the confidence intervals.

(i) at 0.95 confidence interval

$$\begin{aligned} SD_{pop} &= SD \pm 1.96\ \sigma_\sigma \\ &= 10.2 \pm 1.96 \times 0.51 \\ &= 10.2 \pm 0.99 \\ &= 9.21 \text{ to } 11.19 \end{aligned}$$

(ii) at 0.99 confidence interval

$$\begin{aligned} SD_{pop} &= SD \pm 2.58\ \sigma_\sigma \\ &= 10.2 \pm 2.58 \times 0.51 \\ &= 10.2 \pm 1.32 \\ &= 8.88 \text{ to } 11.52 \end{aligned}$$

Step 3 : Interpret the Results.

(i) There are 95 chances out of 100 that the SD_{pop} would fall between 9.21 to 11.19.

(ii) There are 99 chances out of 100 that SD_{pop} would fall between 8.88 to 11.52.

Example :

The standard deviation of the test scores of a group of 484 randomly selected students is 33. How dependable is the SD?

Solution :

Step 1 : Calculate SE_σ

$$SE_\sigma = \frac{0.71\sigma}{\sqrt{N}} = \frac{0.71 \times 33}{\sqrt{484}} = \frac{23.43}{22} = 1.065$$

Step 2 : Set up the confidence intervals.

(i) at 0.95 confidence interval

$$\begin{aligned} SD_{pop} &= SD \pm 1.96\ \sigma_\sigma \\ &= 33 \pm 1.96 \times 1.065 \\ &= 33 \pm 2.087 \\ &= 30.91 \text{ to } 35.09 \end{aligned}$$

(ii) at 0.99 confidence interval

$$SD_{pop} = SD \pm 2.58\ \sigma_\sigma$$
$$= 33 \pm 2.58 \times 1.065$$
$$= 33 \pm 2.747$$
$$= 30.25 \text{ to } 35.75$$

Step 3 : Interpret the Results.

(i) There are 95 chances out of 100 that SD_{pop} would fall between 30.91 to 35.09.

(ii) There are 99 chances out 100 that SD_{pop} would fall between 30.25 to 35.75.

Example :

Suppose it is known that the SD of the scores in a certain population is 20. How many cases would we need that the SE of the sample SD be 1?

Solution :

$$SE_\sigma = \frac{\sigma}{\sqrt{2N}}$$

$$1 = \frac{20}{\sqrt{2N}}$$

$$\sqrt{2N} = 20$$

Squaring both the sides.

$$2N = 400$$
$$N = 200$$

The required size of the sample is 200.

THE STANDARD ERROR OF PERCENTAGES AND PROPORTIONS

Sometimes it is difficult or impossible to measure certain traits. The only information available is the percentage of the group that possesses the trait. It is necessary to compute the SE of a percentage to know how reliable is the percentage as the index of the incidence of the behaviour in which we are interested. The formula for the SE of the percentage is :

$$SE_{\%} = \sqrt{\frac{PQ}{N}}$$

in which

P = percentage of the group possessing the trait.

Q = (1 – P)

N = number of cases.

The following examples will make clear the computation of $SE_{\%}$

Example :

In a sample of 625 voters, 55 percent favour a particular political party. How dependable is this percentage?

Solution :

Step 1 : Calculate $SE_{\%}$

$$SE_{\%} = \sqrt{\frac{PQ}{N}}$$

$$P = 55\%$$

$$Q = 1 - P = 1 - \frac{55}{100} = \frac{100-55}{100} = \frac{45}{100} = 45\%$$

$$N = 625$$

Substituting the values in the formula we get

$$SE_{\%} = \sqrt{\frac{55\% \times 45\%}{625}}$$

$$= \sqrt{\frac{55 \times 45}{100 \times 100 \times 625}}$$

$$SE_{\%} = \sqrt{\frac{99}{100 \times 100 \times 25}} = \frac{\sqrt{99}}{100 \times 5}$$

$$= \frac{9.950}{100 \times 5} = \frac{1.99}{100} = 1.99\%$$

$\therefore$ SE of the percentage of voters favouring a particular political party = 1.99%

Step 2 : Set up the confidence interval :

The sampling distribution of percentages can be taken as normal when N is large (N > 50) and when P is less than 95% and greater than 5%. The $SE_{\%}$ is interpreted like the σ_M.

In the present problem

(i) The 0.95 confidence interval will be :

$$P \pm 1.96\ \sigma_{\%}$$

$$= 55\% \pm 1.96 \times 1.99\%$$

$$= 55\% \pm 3.90\%$$

$$= 51.1\% \text{ to } 58.90\%$$

(ii) The 0.99 confidence interval will be

$$P \pm 2.58\ \sigma_{\%}$$
$$= 55\% \pm 2.58 \times 1.99\%$$
$$= 55\% \pm 5.13\%$$
$$= 48.87\% \text{ to } 60.13\%$$

Step 3 : Interpretation of the result :

(i) There are 95 chances out of 100 that the percentage of the voters favouring the political party is 51.1% to 58.90%.

(ii) There are 99 chances out of 100 that the percentage of the voters favouring the political party is 48.87% to 60.13%.

Example :

In a newspaper article of 1600 words in Marathi, 64% of the words are found to be of Sanskrit origin. Assuming the simple sampling conditions hold good, estimate the proportion of Sanskrit words in the writer's vocabulary and assign limits to that proportion.

Solution :

Step 1 : Calculate the $SE_{\%}$

Standard error of the proportion of words of

$$\text{Sanskrit origin} = \sqrt{\frac{PQ}{N}}$$

$$SE_{\%} = \sqrt{\frac{64\% \times 36\%}{1600}}$$

$$= \sqrt{\frac{64 \times 36}{100 \times 100 \times 1600}}$$

$$= \frac{8 \times 6}{10 \times 10 \times 40} = \frac{48}{100 \times 40}$$

$$= \frac{12}{1000} = 1.2\%$$

Step 2 : Set up the confidence interval.

(i) at 0.95 confidence level

$$P \pm 1.96\ \sigma_{\%}$$
$$= 64\% \pm 1.96 \times 1.2\%$$
$$= 64\% \pm 2.35\%$$
$$= 61.65\% \text{ to } 66.35\%$$

(ii) at 0.99 confidence level

$$P \pm 2.58 \times 1.2\%$$
$$= 64 \pm 3.1\%$$
$$= 60.9\% \text{ to } 67.1\%$$

Step 3 : Interpretation of the result :

Taking 64% to be the estimate of words of Sanskrit origin in the writer's vocabulary

(i) at 0.95 confidence interval the limits are 61.65% to 66.35% and

(ii) at 0.99 confidence interval the limits are 60.9% to 67.1%.

Example :

In a sample of 200 students, 80 students were found to have shown signs of tiredness after a strenuous physical exercise. Assuming that the sample was randomly drawn from a specified population, how well do our results represent the population percentage?

Solution :

Step 1 : Calculate $\sigma_{\%}$

$$P = \frac{80}{200} = \frac{40}{100} = 40\%$$

$$\therefore Q = 60\%$$

$$= \sqrt{\frac{P \times Q}{N}} = \sqrt{\frac{40\% \times 60\%}{200}}$$

$$= \sqrt{\frac{40}{100} \times \frac{60}{100} \times \frac{1}{200}}$$

$$= \sqrt{\frac{12}{100 \times 100}} = \frac{\sqrt{12}}{100}$$

$$= \frac{3.464}{100} = 3.464\%$$

$$\doteqdot 3.46\%$$

Step 2 : Set up the confidence intervals.

(i) The 0.99 confidence interval will be :

$$P \pm 2.58\ \sigma_{\%}$$
$$= 40\% \pm 2.58 \times 3.46\%$$
$$= 40\% \pm 8.93\%$$
$$= 31.07\% \text{ to } 48.93\%.$$

(ii) at 0.95 confidence interval will be

$$P \pm 1.96 \times \sigma_{\%}$$

$$= 40\% \pm 1.96 \times 3.46\%$$

$$= 40\% \pm 6.78\%$$

$$= 33.22\% \text{ to } 46.78\%$$

Step 3 : Interpret the Results :

We may feel sure with 99 percent confidence that the percentage of children in the population who are likely to be tired after the physical exercise will not be less than 31% and more than 48.93%.

THE STANDARD ERROR OF A CORRELATION COEFFICIENT (SE_r)

If a large number of samples are drawn randomly from a population, coefficient of correlation is computed for each sample and a frequency distribution of correlation coefficients is prepared, then the shape of this distribution depends upon r_{pop}. To test the dependability of r, in terms of its SE, we assume the sampling distribution of r to be normal place, the "true or population r" at the centre of the distribution. As population r (r_{pop}) departs from zero, the sampling distribution of r's become increasingly skewed. A high positive value of r_{pop} produces an extremely negative skewness, while a high negative value of r_{pop} gives rise to an extremely positive skewness. The SE of r is given by the formula.

$$\sigma_r = \frac{1-r^2}{\sqrt{N}}$$

Example :

In a group of 200 students selected at random, the coefficient of correlation between two variables is 0.65. How dependable is this value?

Solution :

Step 1 : Calculate σ_r

$$SE_r = \frac{1-r^2}{\sqrt{N}} = \frac{1-(0.65)^2}{\sqrt{200}}$$

$$= \frac{1-0.4225}{14.142}$$

$$= \frac{0.5775}{14.142}$$

$$\div \ 0.041$$

Step 2 : Set up the confidence intervals.

(i) At 0.95 confidence interval

$$r_{pop} = r \pm 1.96\ \sigma_r$$
$$= 0.65 \pm 1.96 \times 0.041$$
$$= 0.65 \pm 0.08$$
$$= 0.57 \text{ to } 0.73$$

(ii) At 0.99 confidence interval

$$r_{pop} = r \pm 2.58\ \sigma_r$$
$$= 0.65 \pm 2.58 \times 0.041$$
$$= 0.65 \pm 0.11$$
$$= 0.54 \text{ to } 0.76$$

Step 3 : Interpret the Results :

(i) There are 5 chances out of 100 (or one chance in 20) that an error of $\pm$ 1.96 σ_r is present in our r. Thus, there are 95 chances out of 100 that r_{pop} would fall between 0.57 to 0.73

(ii) There is one chance out of 100 that an error of $\pm$ 2.58 σ_r is present in our r. Thus, there are 99 chances out of 100 that r_{pop} would fall between 0.54 to 0.76.

Example :

In a sample of 60 students selected randomly, the coefficient of correlation between two variables is 0.40. How dependable is the mean? Use 0.05 and 0.01 confidence intervals.

Solution :

Step 1 : Calculate σ_r

$$SE_r = \frac{1-r^2}{\sqrt{N}} = \frac{1-(0.40)^2}{\sqrt{60}}$$

$$= \frac{1-0.16}{7.746} = \frac{0.84}{7.746} = 0.108$$

Step 2 : Set up the confidence intervals.

(i) At 0.95 confidence interval

$$r_{pop} = r \pm 1.96\ \sigma_r$$
$$= 0.40 \pm 1.96 \times 0.108$$
$$= 0.40 \pm 0.21$$
$$= 0.19 \text{ to } 0.61$$

(ii) At 0.99 confidence interval

$$r_{pop} = r \pm 2.58\ \sigma_r$$
$$= 0.40 \pm 2.58 \times 0.108$$
$$= 0.40 \pm 0.28$$
$$= 0.12 \text{ to } 0.68$$

Step 3 : Interpret the results

(i) There are 95 chances out of 100 that r_{pop} would fall between 0.19 to 0.61.

(ii) There are 99 chances out of 100 that r_{pop} would fall between 0.12 to 0.68.

DEFECTS IN THE FORMULA FOR SE_r

(1) The r, in the formula is really the true or population r. Since r_{pop} is not available we must substitute the calculated r in the formula to get an estimate of the SE_r. If the obtained r is in error, our estimate also will be in error.

(2) The sampling distribution of r is not normal except when population r = 0. and N is large. Thus, the theoretical model of normal distribution is not a good fit to the sampling distribution of r's. Hence, we cannot use the normal probability integral table to interpret SE_r exactly.

CONVERSION OF r's INTO FISHER'S z FUNCTION :

Difficulties resulting from the non-normality of the sampling distribution of r were resolved by R.A. Fisher. Fisher suggested the conversion of r's into z function.

Table C is used for this purpose. The test of significance is applied to z and not to r's.

The function z has two advantages over r

(1) Its sampling distribution is approximately normal

(2) Its SE depends only upon the size of the sample N and is independent of the size of r.

The formula for the SE for Fisher's z function (σ_z) is as follows :

$$\sigma_z = \frac{1}{\sqrt{N-3}}$$

The following example will make the application of Fisher's z function and σ_z.

Example :

An r of 0.74 is obtained from sample of 39 cases. Use z conversion and set up the fiduciary limits of the 0.99 and 0.95 confidence intervals.

Solution :

Step 1 : Convert r into z.

r = 0.74

consulting Table C, r = 0.74 is converted to z which is equal to 0.95

Step 2 : Calculate SE_z

$$\sigma_z = \frac{1}{\sqrt{N-3}} = \frac{1}{\sqrt{39-3}} = \frac{1}{\sqrt{36}}$$

$$= \frac{1}{6}$$

$$= 0.17$$

Step 3 : Set up the confidence intervals

(i) at 0.95 confidence interval

$$\begin{aligned} & z \pm 1.96\ \sigma_z \\ &= 0.95 \pm 1.96 \times 0.17 \\ &= 0.95 \pm 0.33 \\ &= 0.62 \text{ to } 1.28 \end{aligned}$$

Convert back into r's = 0.55 to 0.85

(ii) at 0.99 confidence interval

$$\begin{aligned} & z \pm 2.58\ \sigma_z \\ &= 0.95 \pm 2.58 \times 0.17 \\ &= 0.95 \pm 0.44 \\ &= 0.51 \text{ to } 1.39 \end{aligned}$$

Convert back into r's = 0.47 to 0.88

Step 4 : Interpret the results.

(i) There are 95 chances out of 100 that the r_{pop} would fall between 0.55 to 0.85.

(ii) There are 99 chances out of 100 that the r_{pop} would fall between 0.47 to 0.88.

Example :

An 'r' of 0.81 is obtained from a random sample of 37 cases. Establish the fiduciary limits of the true r at the 0.01 level using the z - conversion.

Solution :

Step 1 : Convert r into z

r = 0.81

consulting Table C, it is noted that for r = 0.81

z = 1.13

Step 2 : Calculate SE_z

$$\sigma_z = \frac{1}{\sqrt{N-3}} = \frac{1}{\sqrt{37-3}} = \frac{1}{\sqrt{34}}$$

$$= \frac{1}{5.831} = 0.17$$

Step 3 : Set up the confidence interval.

at 0.99 confidence interval.

$$\begin{aligned} & z \pm 2.58\ \sigma_z \\ &= 1.13 \pm 2.58 \times 0.17 \\ &= 1.13 \pm 0.44 \\ &= 0.69 \text{ to } 1.57 \end{aligned}$$

convert back into r's = 0.60 to 0.915

÷ 0.60 to 0.92

Step 4 : Interpret the result.

There 99 chances out of 100 that the r_{pop} would fall between 0.60 to 0.92.

TESTING r AGAINST THE NULL-HYPOTHESIS

The significance of an obtained r may be tested also against the hypothesis, the population r is in fact zero.

To make the test against the null-hypothesis enter in the following table with (N – 2) degree of freedom; and compare the obtained r with the tabulated value of r. Two significance levels 0.05 and 0.01 are given in the table. When the obtained value of r is greater than the tabulated value of r then the null hypothesis is rejected, otherwise it is accepted.

Correlation coefficients of the 5% and 1% levels of significance.

Example :

When N is 52 and df is 50, an r must be .273 to be significant at .05 level and .354 to be significant at .01 level.

Degrees of freedom (N – 2)	.05	.01	Degrees of freedom (N – 2)	.05	.01
1	.997	1.000	24	.388	.496
2	.950	.990	25	.381	.487
3	.878	.959	26	.374	.478
4	.811	.917	27	.367	.470
5	.754	.874	28	.361	.463
6	.707	.834	29	.355	.456
7	.666	.798	30	.349	.449
8	.632	.765	35	.325	.418
9	.602	.735	40	.304	.393
10	.576	.708	45	.288	.372
11	.553	.684	50	.273	.354
12	.532	.661	60	.250	.325
13	.514	.641	70	.232	.302
14	.497	.623	80	.217	.283
15	.482	.606	90	.205	.267
16	.468	.590	100	.195	.254
17	.456	.575	125	.174	.228
18	.444	.561	150	.159	.208
19	.433	.549	200	.138	.181
20	.423	.537	300	.113	.148
21	.413	.526	400	.098	.128
22	.404	.515	500	.088	.115
23	.396	.505	1000	.062	.081

The following example will illustrate the point.

Example :

In a sample of 30 students selected randomly the coefficient of correlation is 0.22 between two variables. Test the significance of obtained r against Null Hypothesis.

Solution :

Step 1 : Find degrees of freedom using df = (N – 2)

N = 30

∴ df = (N – 2) = (30 – 2) = 28

Step 2 : Refer the table with 28 degrees of freedom and compare the obtained r with tabulated entries.

(i) at 0.05 the entry against 28 df is 0.361.

(ii) at 0.01 the entry against 28 df is 0.463.

Step 3 : Interpret the results

(i) Only 5 times in 100 trials an 'r' as large as ± 0.361 arise from.

Example :

In a random sample of 82 students the coefficient of correlation between two variables is 0.40. Test the significance of obtained r against Null Hypothesis.

Solution :

Step 1 : Find degrees of freedom

df = (N – 2) = (80 – 2) = 80

Step 2 : Consult the tablet with 80 df.

(i) at 0.05 the entry against 80 df is 0.217.

(ii) at 0.01 the entry against 80 df is 0.283.

❑❑❑

CHAPTER VII

ANALYSIS OF VARIANCE (ANOVA)

ANALYSIS OF VARIANCE (ANOVA)

Analysis of Variance (abbreviated as ANVOA) is an extremely useful technique concerning research in the fields of economics, biology, education, psychology, sociology, business, industry and in researches of serveral other disciplines. This technique is used when multiple sample cases are involved.

The significance of the difference between the means of two samples can be judged through either Z-test or t-test, but the difficulty arises when we happen to examine the significance of the difference amongst more than two sample means at the same time. If there are three samples say A, B, and C. The use of t-test would still be possible and would involve taking two group means at a time and testing the significance of difference. The number of mean comparisons in this case would be three *viz.*

(i) A and B

(ii) A and C

(iii) B and C

However, the problem arises when the number of group is larger say five or more. If we have ten groups, the number of comparisons which would be required under the t-test would be given by the formula :

$$^{n}C_2 = {}^{10}C_2 = \frac{10!}{2!(10-2)!}$$

$$= \frac{10 \times 9 \times 8!}{2 \times 8!}$$

$$= \frac{10 \times 9}{2}$$

$$= 45$$

ANOVA is thus very useful as it helps testing differences among all of the means at the same time. The analysis of variance and the corresponding test of significance based upon F distribution permits us to do this. Another important consideration which rules out the use of t-test and warrants the use of more sophisticated F test of significance, is the case of situations in which two or more experimental variables or one experimental and one or more control variables are simultaneously operating and not only comparison of means within each variable is required but also the joint operation or interaction of two or more variables is of interest.

The ANOVA technique is important in the context of all those situations where we want to compare more than two populations such as in comparing the smoking habits of five groups of university students, comparing the effectiveness of three different methods of teaching map reading etc.

The ANOVA technique enables the researcher to perform the simultaneous test. Using this technique one can draw inferences about whether the samples have been drawn from populations having the same mean.

WHAT IS ANOVA?

Prof. Sir R. A. Fisher, an English statistician was the first man to use the term 'Variance'* He is considered to be the father of modern statistics as applied to social and behavioural sciences. It was first reported in 1923, and its early applications were in the field of agriculture. Later on Prof. Snedecor and many others contributed to the development of this technique.

ANVOA is essentically a procedure for testing the difference among the different groups of data for homogeneity. "The essence of ANOVA is that the total amount of variation in a set of data is broken down into two types;

(i) that amount which can be attributed to chance, and

(ii) that amount which can be attributed to specific causes."

---

* Variance is an important statistical measure as it is described as the mean of the squares of deviations taken from the mean of the given series of data. It is a frequently used measure of variation. Its square root is known as standard deviation i.e.

$$SD = \sqrt{\text{Variance}}$$

There may be variation between samples and also within sample items. ANOVA consists in splitting the Variance for analytical purposes. Hence, it is a method of analysing the variance to which a response is subject into its various components corresponding to various sources of variation. The analysis of variance, as the name indicates, deals with variances rather than with standard deviations and standard errors.

Thus, through ANOVA technique one can, in general, investigate any number of factors which are hypothesised or said to influence the dependent variable. One may as well investigate the differences amongst various categories within each of these factors which may have a large number of possible values.

If we take only one factor and investigate the differences amongst its various categories having numerous possible values, we are said to use one way ANOVA.

In case we investigate two factors at the same time, then we use two way ANOVA.

In a two or more way ANOVA, the interaction (i.e., inter-relation between two independent variables/factors), if any, between two independent variable affecting a dependent variable can as well be studied for better decisions.

THE BASIC PRINCIPLE OF ANOVA

The basic principle of ANOVA is to test for differences among the means of the populations by examining the amount of variation within each of these samples, relative to the amount of variation between the samples. In terms of variation within the given population, it is assumed that the values of (Xij) differ from the mean of this population only because of random effect i.e., there are influences on (Xij) which are unexplainable, whereas in examining differences between populations we assume that the difference between the mean of the jth population and the grand means is attributable to what is called a 'specific factor' or what is technically described as treatment effect. Thus, while using ANOVA, we assume that each of the samples is drawn from a normal population and that each of these populations has the same variance. We also assume that all factors other than the one or more being tested are effectively controlled. This, in other words, means that we assume the absence of many factors that might affect our conclusions concerning the factor (s) to be studied.

In short, we have to make two estimates of population variance *viz.* one based on between samples variance and the other based on within samples variance. Then the said two estimates of Population variance are compared with F-test, wherein we work out.

$$F = \frac{\text{Estimate of population variance based on between samples variance}}{\text{Estimate of pupulation variance based on within samples variance}}$$

This value of F is to be compared to the F-limit for given degrees of freedom. If the F value we work out exceeds the F limit values (to be seen from F tables given in appendix), we may say that there are significant differences between the sample means.

ONE WAY OR SINGLE CLASSIFICATION ANOVA

It is also known as single factor ANOVA. Under the one-way ANOVA, we consider only one factor and then observe that the reason for said factor to be important is that several possible types of samples can occur within that factor. We then determine if there are differences within that factor. The technique involves the following steps:

Steps :

(i) Obtain the mean of each sample i.e., obtain

$$\overline{X}_1, \overline{X}_2, \overline{X}_3 \text{ .... } \overline{X}_k$$

when there are k samples.

(ii) Work out the mean of the sample means as follows :

$$\overline{\overline{X}} = \frac{\overline{X}_1 + \overline{X}_2 + \overline{X}_3 + \text{........} \overline{X}_K}{\text{No. of samples (k)}}$$

(iii) Take the deviations of the sample means from the mean of the sample means and calculate the square of such deviations which may be multiplied by the number of items in the corresponding sample, and then obtain their total. This is known as the sum of squares for variance between the samples (or SS between). Symbolically, this can be written :

$$SS_{between} = n_1 (\overline{X}_1 - \overline{\overline{X}})^2 + n_2 (\overline{X}_2 - \overline{\overline{X}})^2 + \text{..........}$$

$$+ n_k (\overline{X}_k - \overline{\overline{X}})^2$$

(iv) Divide the result of the (iii) step by the degrees of freedom between the sample to obtain variance or mean square (MS) between samples. Symbolically, this can be written :

$$MS_{between} = \frac{SS_{between}}{(k-1)}$$

where (k-1) represents degrees of freedom (d. f.) between samples.

(v) Obtain the deviations of the value of the sample items for all the samples from corresponding means of the samples and calculate the squares of such deviations and then obtain their total. This total is known as the sum of squares for variance within samples (or SS within). Symbolically, this can be written as :

$$SS_{within} = \Sigma (X_{1i} - \overline{X}_1)^2 + \Sigma (X_{2i} - \overline{X}_2)^2$$

$$+ \Sigma (K_{ki} - \overline{X}_k)^2$$

$$i = 1, 2, 3, \ldots$$

(vi) Divide the result of (v) step by the degrees of freedom within samples to obtain the variance or mean square (MS) within samples. Symbolically, this can be written as :

$$MS_{within} = \frac{SS_{within}}{(n-k)}$$

where (n-k) represents degrees of freedom within samples.

n = total number of items in all the samples i.e.,

$n_1 + n_2 + ... + n_k$.

k = number of samples.

(vii) For a check, the sum of squares of deviations for total variance can also be worked out by adding the squares of deviations when the deviation for the individual items in all the samples have been taken from the mean of the sample means. Symbolically, this can be written as :

$$\text{SS for total variance} = \Sigma (X_{ij} - \overline{\overline{X}})^2 \quad i = 1, 2, 3....$$
$$j = 1, 2, 3....$$

This total should be equal to the total of the result of the (iii) and (v) steps explained above i.e.,

$$\text{SS for total variance} = \text{SS between} + \text{SS within.}$$

The degrees of freedom for total variance will be equal to the number of items in all samples minus one i.e., (n – 1). The degrees of freedom for between and within must add up to the degrees of freedom for total variance i.e.,

$$(n - 1) = (k - 1) + (n - k)$$

This fact explains the additive property of the ANOVA technique.

(viii) Finally, F ratio may be worked out as under :

$$F - \text{ratio} = \frac{\text{MS between}}{\text{MS within}}$$

This ratio is used to judge whether the difference among several sample means is significant or is just a matter of sampling fluctuations. For this purpose we look into the table, giving the values of F for given degrees of freedom at different levels of significance. If the worked out value of F, as stated above, is either equal to or less than the table value of F, the difference is taken as insignificant i.e., due to chance and the null-hypothesis of no difference between sample means stands. In case the calculated value of F happens to be more than its table value, the difference is considered as significant (which means the samples could not have come from the same universe) and accordingly the conclusion may be drawn. The higher the calculated value of F is above the table value, the more definite and sure one can be about his conclusions.

Example:

The following data represent the scores of 4 students in each of the three schools of a city on science practical examination. By analysis of variance, test the difference between the means.

Schools		
A	**B**	**C**
6	5	5
7	5	4
3	3	3
8	7	4

Solution:

(i) Calculate the mean of each of these samples.

$$\overline{X}_1 = \frac{6+7+3+8}{4} = 6$$

$$\overline{X}_2 = \frac{5+5+3+7}{4} = 5$$

$$\overline{X}_3 = \frac{5+4+3+4}{4} = 4$$

Mean of the Samples means :

$$\overline{\overline{X}} = \frac{6+5+4}{3} = 5$$

Now we work out SS between and SS within samples

$$SS_{between} = n_1 (\overline{X}_1 - \overline{\overline{X}})^2 + n_2 (\overline{X}_2 - \overline{\overline{X}})^2 + n_3 (\overline{X}_3 - \overline{\overline{X}})^2$$

$$= 4\,(6-5)^2 + 4\,(5-5)^2 + 4\,(4-5)^2$$

$$= 4(1)^2 + 4\,(0)^2 + 4\,(-1)^2$$

$$= 4 + 0 + 4$$

$$= 8$$

$$SS_{within} = \Sigma\,(X_{1i} - \overline{X}_1)^2 + \Sigma\,(X_{2i} - \overline{X}_2)^2 + \Sigma\,(X_{3i} + \overline{X}_3)^2$$

$$i = 1, 2, 3, 4$$

$$= \{(6\text{-}6)^2 + (7\text{-}6)^2 + (3\text{-}6)^2 + (8\text{-}6)^2\} + \{(5\text{-}5)^2 + (5\text{-}5)^2 + (3\text{-}5)^2 + (7\text{-}5)^2\} + \{(5\text{-}4)^2 + (4\text{-}4)^2 + (3\text{-}4)^2 + (4\text{-}4)^2\}$$

$$= (0 + 1 + 9 + 4) + (0 + 0 + 4 + 4) + (1 + 0 + 1 + 0)$$

$$= 14 + 8 + 2$$

$$= 24$$

$$\text{SS for total variance} = \Sigma\,(X_{ij} - \overline{\overline{X}})^2 \quad i = 1, 2, 3, \ldots \quad j = 1, 2, 3, \ldots$$

$$= (6\text{-}5)^2 + (7\text{-}5)^2 + (3\text{-}5)^2 + (8\text{-}5)^2 + (5\text{-}5)^2 + (5\text{-}5)^2 + (3\text{-}5)^2 + (7\text{-}5)^2 + (5\text{-}5)^2 + (4\text{-}5)^2 + (3\text{-}5)^2 + (4\text{-}5)^2$$

$$= 1 + 4 + 4 + 9 + 0 + 0 + 4 + 4 + 0 + 1 + 4 + 1$$

$$= 32$$

SS for total variance can also be worked out as follows :

$$\begin{aligned} \text{SS for total} &= SS_{between} + SS_{within} \\ &= 8 + 24 \\ &= 32 \end{aligned}$$

We can now set up the ANOVA table for this problem.

SUMMARY OF ANOVA

Soures of Variation	SS	df	MS	F-ratio	5% F-limit (from the F-table)
Between Sample	8	(3-1) = 2	8/2 = 4	$\frac{4}{2.67} = 1.5$	F(2,9) = 4.26
Within Sample	24	(12-3) = 9	24/9 = 2.67		
Total	32	(12-1) = 11.			

INTERPRETATION

The above table shows that the calcultated value of F is 1.5 which is less than the table value of 4.26 at 5% level with d.f. being $V_1 = 2$ and $V_2 = 9$ and hence could have arisen due to chance. This analysis supports the null hypothesis, of no difference in sample means. We may therefore conclude that the difference in achievement at science practical due to different schools, is insignificant and is just a matter of chance.

SHORT CUT METHOD FOR ONE WAY ANOVA

ANOVA can be performed by following the short cut method which is usually used in practice since the same happens to be a very convenient method particularly when means of the samples and/ or means of the sample means happen to be non-integer values. The various steps involved in the short cut method are as under :

(i) Set up the values of individual items in all samples under $X_1, X_2, X_3, \ldots\ldots\ldots X_n$.

(ii) Square the scores of all the individual items in all samples under $X^2_1, X^2_2, X^2_3, \ldots\ldots\ldots X^2_n$.

(iii) Obtain the total of the values of individual items in all the samples i.e., work out ΣX and call it as T.

(iv) After these intermediate calculations, we are now ready for calculation of various sums of squares.

(v) Calculate correction term, C as it is required for the adjustment of origin when raw scores are used for the calculation of variance. In fact, the assumed mean here is zero and all scores from deviation is zero.

$$\text{Correction factor} = C = \frac{(\Sigma X)^2}{N} = \frac{T^2}{N}$$

(vi) Calculate SS for total variance (SS_T) which is sum of squared scores minus C.

(vii) Square each set sum and divide by respective n, and over all the set of the example. Deduct correction factor C, to obtain SS between. In case of equal n's a common denominator n can be used.

If number of scores in the sample are n_1, n_2, n_3 .... nn etc., then –

$$SS_{between} = \frac{(\Sigma X_1)^2}{n_1} + \frac{(\Sigma X_2)^2}{n_2} + \frac{(\Sigma X_3)^2}{n_3} + ... \frac{(\Sigma X_k)^2}{n_k} - C$$

If number of scores in all the sample is same say n then

$$SS_{between} = \frac{(\Sigma X_1)^2 + (\Sigma X_2)^2 + (\Sigma X_3)^2 + ... (\Sigma X_k)^2}{n} - C$$

(viii) Subtract $SS_{between}$ from SS_T to obtain SS_{within}. SS_{within} can also be calculated directly without computing SS_T.

$$SS_{within} = \Sigma X^2 - \frac{(\Sigma X_1)^2 + (\Sigma X_2)^2 + ... (\Sigma X_k)^2}{n}$$

(ix) Table of summary of ANOVA can be set up Degrees of freedom, MS, and F can be calculated.

(x) F-table is then consulted to interpret the result.

The example solved previously can be worked out by short method which is as follows:

Solution:

	Set I		Set II		Set III	
	X_1	X_1^2	X_2	X_2^2	X_3	X_3^2
	6	36	5	25	5	25
	7	49	5	25	4	16
	3	9	3	9	3	9
	8	64	7	49	4	16
	24	158	20	108	16	66
	(ΣX_1)	(ΣX_1^2)	(ΣX_2)	(ΣX_2^2)	(ΣX_3)	(ΣX_3^2)
Mean of sample	6		5		4	

$n_1 = n_2 = n_3 = 4$

$N = n_1 + n_2 + n_3 = 4 + 4 + 4 = 12$

ΣX or $T = 24 + 20 + 16 = 60$

(a) Correction term $C = \frac{(\Sigma X)^2}{N} = \frac{T^2}{N} = \frac{60^2}{12} = \frac{3600}{12} = 300$

(b) Total sum of squares i.e.,

$$\therefore SS_{total} = \Sigma X^2 - C$$

$$= 6^2 + 7^2 + 3^2 + 8^2 + 5^2 + 5^2 + 3^2 + 7^2 + 5^2 + 4^2 + 3^2 + 4^2 - 300$$

$$= 36 + 49 + 9 + 64 + 25 + 25 + 9 + 49 + 25 + 16 + 9 + 16 - 300$$

$$= 332 - 300$$

$$= 32.$$

(c) Sum of squares among set means

$$SS_{between} = \frac{(\Sigma X_1)^2}{n_1} + \frac{(\Sigma X_2)^2}{n_2} + \frac{(\Sigma X_3)^2}{n_3} - C$$

$$= \frac{(24)^2}{4} + \frac{(20)^2}{4} + \frac{(16)^2}{4} - 300$$

$$= 144 + 100 + 64 - 300$$

$$= 308 - 300$$

$$= 8.$$

(d) Sum of squares within sets,

$$SS_{within} = SS_{total} - SS_{between}$$

$$= 32 - 8$$

$$= 24$$

(e) Summary of Analysis of Variance.

Soures of Variation	SS	df	MS	F-ratio	5% F-limit (from the F table)
Between Sample	8	(3-1) = 2	8/2 = 4	4/2.67 = 1.5	F(2,9) = 4.26
Within Sample	24	(12-3) = 9	24/9 = 2.67		

It may be noted that we get exactly the same result as we had by the first method.

Example : Set up the table for ANOVA and work out the F-ratio in respect of the following. Is the F ratio significant?

Set I	Set II	Set III
X_1	X_2	X_3
10	3	10
7	3	11
6	3	10
10	3	5
4	3	6
3	3	8
2	3	9
1	3	12
8	3	9
9	3	10

Solution : We can solve the problem by the direct method or by short cut method, but in each case we shall get the same result. We try below both the methods:

Direct Method:

Set I	Set II	Set III
10	3	10
7	3	11
6	3	10
10	3	5
4	3	6
3	3	8
2	3	9
1	3	12
8	3	9
9	3	10
$\Sigma X = 60$	$\Sigma X = 30$	$\Sigma X = 90$

(i) First we calculate the mean of each of these samples:

which comes out to be $\frac{60}{10}, \frac{30}{10}$ and $\frac{90}{10}$ resp.

i.e., $\bar{X}_1 = 6, \bar{X}_2 = 3, \bar{X}_3 = 9$

(ii) Mean of the sample means $= \frac{6+3+9}{3} = \frac{18}{3} = 6$

$\therefore \bar{\bar{X}} = 6$

Now we work out $SS_{between}$ and SS_{within} Samples:

(iii) $SS_{between} = n_1 (\bar{X}_1 - \bar{\bar{X}})^2 + n_2 (\bar{X}_2 - \bar{\bar{X}})^2 + n_3 (\bar{X}_3 - \bar{\bar{X}})^2$

$= 10 (6-6)^2 + 10 (3-6)^2 + 10 (9-6)^2$

$= 10 \times 0 + 10 \times 9 + 10 \times 9$

$$= 0 + 90 + 90$$

$$= 180.$$

(iv) $MS_{between} = \frac{SS_{between}}{k-1} = \frac{180}{3-1} = \frac{180}{2} = 90$

(v) $SS_{within} = \Sigma (X_{1i} - \bar{X}_1)^2 + \Sigma (X_2^i - \bar{X}_2)^2 + \Sigma (X_{3i} - \bar{X}_3) + \ldots\ldots\ldots$

where i = 1, 2, 3, 4, 5, 6, 7, 8, 9, 10

$$\therefore SS_{within} = \{(10-6)^2 + (7-6)^2 + (6-6)^2 + (10-6)^2 + (4-6)^2 + (3-6)^2 + (2-6)^2 + (1-6)^2 + (8-6)^2 + (9-6)^2\}$$
$$+ \{(3-3)^2 + (3-3)^2 + (3-3)^2 + (3-3)^2 + (3-3)^2 + (3-3)^2 + (3-3)^2 + (3-3)^2 + (3-3)^2 + (3-3)^2\}$$
$$+ \{(10-9)^2 + (11-9)^2 + (10-9)^2 + (5-9)^2 + (6-9)^2 + (8-9)^2 + (9-9)^2 + (12-9)^2 + (9-9)^2 + (10-9)^2\}$$

$$= \{(4)^2 + (1)^2 + (0)^2 + (4)^2 + (-2)^2 + (-3)^2 + (-4)^2 + (-5)^2 + (2)^2 + (3)^2\}$$
$$+ \{(0)^2 + (0)^2 + (0)^2 + (0)^2 + (0)^2 + (0)^2 + (0)^2 + (0)^2 + (0)^2 + (0)^2\}$$
$$+ \{(1)^2 + (2)^2 + (1)^2 + (-4)^2 + (-3)^2 + (-1)^2 + (0)^2 + (3)^2 + (0)^2 + (1)^2\}$$

$$= 16 + 1 + 0 + 16 + 4 + 9 + 16 + 25 + 4 + 9 + 0 + 0 + 0 + 0 + 0 + 0 + 0 + 0 + 0 + 0 + 1 + 4 + 1 + 16 + 9 + 1 + 0 + 9 + 0 + 1$$

$$= 142.$$

(vi) $MS_{within} = \frac{SS_{within}}{(n-k)} = \frac{142}{30-3} = \frac{142}{27} = 5.26$

where $n = n_1 + n_2 + n_3 = 10 + 10 + 10 = 30$

$k = 3$

(vii) SS for total variance should be equal to the total of $SS_{between}$ and SS_{within}.

SS for total Variance = $SS_{between} + SS_{within}$

SS for total Variance = $\Sigma (X_{ijk} - \bar{\bar{X}})^2$

Here,

$$SS_{total} = \{(10-6)^2 + (7-6)^2 + (6-6)^2 + (10-6)^2 + (4-6)^2 + (3-6)^2 + (2-6)^2 + (1-6)^2 + (8-6)^2 + (9-6)^2\}$$

$$+\left\{(3-6)^2+(3-6)^2+(3-6)^2+(3-6)^2+(3-6)^2\right.$$

$$\left.+(3-6)^2+(3-6)^2+(3-6)^2+(3-6)^2+(3-6)^2\right\}$$

$$+\left\{(10-6)^2+(11-6)^2+(10-6)^2+(5-6)^2+(6-6)^2\ (8-6)^2\right.$$

$$\left.+(9-6)^2+(12-6)^2+(9-6)^2+(10-6)^2\right\}$$

$$=\left\{(4)^2+(1)^2+(0)^2+(4)^2+(-2)^2+(-3)^2+(-4)^2+(-5)^2+(2)^2+(3)^2\right\}$$

$$+\left\{(-3)^2+(-3)^2+(-3)^2+(-3)^2+(-3)^2+(-3)^2+(-3)^2+(-3)^2\right.$$

$$\left.+(-3)^2+(-3)^2\right\}$$

$$+\left\{(4)^2+(5)^2+(4)^2+(-1)^2+(0)^2+(2)^2+(3)^2+(6)^2+(3)^2+(4)^2\right\}$$

$$= 16+1+0+16+4+9+16+25+4+9+9+9+9+9+9+9$$
$$+9+9+9+9+16+25+16+1+0+4+9+36+9+16$$

$$= 322.$$

$SS_{between} + SS_{within} = 180 + 142 = 322.$

Thus, SS for total Variance = $SS_{between} + SS_{within}$.

CALCULATION OF DEGREES OF FREEDOM (df)

Degrees of freedom can be calculated as follows :

df (total) = (Total number of scores - 1)
= (N-1)
= (30-1) = 29

df (between) = (No. of sets - 1) = (S-1)
= (3-1)
= 2

df (within) = (Number of scores in each set minus 1) multiplied by number of sets.
= (n-1) x s
= (10-1) x 3
= 27

Note : df (total) = df (between) + df (within).

We can set up the ANOVA table for this problem

Source of variations	Sum of Squares	df	Mean square variance	F-ratio	5% F-limit (from the F-table)
Between sample	180	2	$\frac{180}{2} = 90$	$\frac{90}{5.26} = 17.11$	
Within sample	142	27	$\frac{142}{27} = 5.26$		F (2, 27) = 3.35

F (2,27) = 5.49 at 0.01 or 1% level.

INTERPRETATION

The calculated value of F is higher than both the values of F at 0.05 and 0.01 levels. Since 0.01 level or 1% level is higher we can interpret that the calculated value of F is significant at 0.01 level. Hence, the null hypothesis (HO) cannot be accepted. It can be said that the over all differences among the three set means are significant and not due to chance. The three sets do not belong to the same population with regards to their means.

Solution through short cut method

Set I		Set II		Set III	
X_1	X_1^2	X_2	X_2^2	X_3	X_3^2
10	100	3	9	10	100
7	49	3	9	11	121
6	36	3	9	10	100
10	100	3	9	5	25
4	16	3	9	6	36
3	9	3	9	8	64
2	4	3	9	9	81
1	1	3	9	12	144
8	64	3	9	9	81
9	81	3	9	10	100
$\Sigma X_1 = 60$	$\Sigma X_1^2 = 460$	$\Sigma X_2 = 30$	$\Sigma X_2^2 = 90$	$\Sigma X_3 = 90$	$\Sigma X_3^2 = 852$

$$\text{Mean of sample } X_1 = \frac{60}{10} = 6$$

$$\text{Mean of sample } X_2 = \frac{30}{10} = 3$$

$$\text{Mean of sample } X_3 = \frac{90}{10} = 9$$

$n_1 = n_2 = n_3 = 10$

$N = n_1 + n_2 + n_3 = 30$

$\Sigma X = \Sigma X_1 + \Sigma X_2 + \Sigma X_3$

$= 60 + 30 + 90$

$= 180$

$\Sigma X = T = 180$

$$\text{(i) Correction term} = \frac{(\Sigma X)^2}{N} = \frac{T^2}{N} = \frac{(180)^2}{30} = 1080$$

(ii) Total sum of squares $= SS_{total} = \Sigma X^2 - C$

$$SS_{total} = \Sigma X_1^2 + \Sigma X_2^2 + \Sigma X_3^2 - C$$

$$= 460 + 90 + 852 - 1080$$

$$= 1402 - 1080$$

$$= 322$$

$$\text{(iii) } SS_{between} = \frac{(\Sigma X_1)^2}{n^1} + \frac{(\Sigma X_2)^2}{n^2} + \frac{(\Sigma X_3)^2}{n^3} - C$$

$$= \frac{60^2}{10} + \frac{30^2}{10} + \frac{90^2}{10} - 1080$$

$$= 360 + 90 + 810 - 1080$$

$$= 1260 - 1080$$

$$= 180$$

$$\text{(iv) } SS_{within} = SS_{total} - SS_{between}$$

$$= 322 - 180$$

$$= 142$$

With the help of the above information and calculation we can set up the ANOVA table for this problem as done in the solution by direct method. After setting up ANOVA table the result can be interpreted as done in the previous solution.

❑❑❑

CHAPTER VIII
COEFFICIENT OF CORRELATION

A good teacher is always interested in finding out the relationship between the marks obtained in two subjects; *viz.* Science and English, or Mathematics and Science, or the teacher may also be interested in finding out the relationship between height and weight of the pupils or between marks obtained in the subject of Mathematics and the Intelligent Quotient, and so on. So also, we very often hear people saying 'If supply increases, price will fall down, 'If there are adequate rains, there will be adequate production.' Now, such statements also show nothing but a sort of established relationship between supply and price, between rains and production. Further, we also find a large number of abilities and traits of the individuals mutually related with one another. When such relationship is quantitative, then, we try to find it by means of measures of correlation in Statistics; and after determining its quantity and nature, this method, we put them in the shape of a formula. Thus, it means then, that, when we are to study and measure the relationship of two or more than two variables, then, we take the help of Statistical Correlation.

So far, we have come to the understanding that correlation is the relationship or interdependence between two qualities. If any measurable factor is responsible for any rise or decline in the value of two variables, it is easy to establish the relationship between them. In a particular case, if the rise in the variable A is always accompanied by the rise in B or *vice versa*, it shows some mutual dependence which is known as correlation. Yet, one may still want to know or ask a question 'what is the exact meaning of the term Correlation? and, as an answer to this question, it is better to quote definitions given by some eminent people.

According to Bayliss, "Correlation is the comparison between two or more different groups of data in order to ascertain whether any relationship exists between them and to obtain a numerical expression of the degree of such relationship".

According to D.N. Shrivastava, "whenever two variables are so related that the increase in one variable corresponds to the increase or decrease in the other variable or decrease in one variable corresponds to increase or decrease in other variable or *vice versa*, variables are said to be correlated."

Hence, to find out the relation between two variables, it is necessary to calculate the coefficient of correlation, which is a single number that tells us to what extent the variations in one variable go with the variation in the second variable. Thus, correlation is nothing but the most common method of reporting the answer to such questions as 'Are certain abilities closely related and other relatively independent?', 'Does a given aptitude test predict success on the job?' 'Are football players good in academic achievement?', etc. In order to answer such questions, it is necessary to have a pair of measures for each individual. One can never compute a coefficient of correlation on one person alone nor can anybody compute it without having made two sets of measurements on the same individual or two matched groups; the method of defining this relationship is called correlation.

KINDS OF CORRELATION

We have already seen that Correlation is nothing but the relationship or interdependence between two quantities and it is not difficult to show the relationship between two different performances. In fact, if any measurable factor is responsible for any rise or decline in the value of two variables, then, it is easy to establish the relationship between them. However, all this will soon become more clear if we try to understand or know about the kinds or types of correlation.

Correlations are of the following kinds as discussed below:

Correlation broadly falls under two categories or classifications *viz*, Quantitative Correlation and Qualitative Correlation. Under the classification of quantitative correlation, three kinds of correlation are discussed. They are positive correlation, negative correlation and zero correlation whereas, under the classification of qualitative correlation, there are two kinds of correlation and they are linear correlation and curvelinear correlation.

Let us now have a detailed discussion of all the kinds of correlation that have been stated above.

POSITIVE CORRELATION

A correlation is said to be positive when an increase (or decrease) in one corresponds to an increase (or decrease) in the other. That means, when two variables change in the same direction, it is said to be positive correlation.

For Example : If increase in physical development shows increase in mental development and decrease in physical development shows decrease in mental development, then, it is said that there is positive correlation between physical and mental development.

NEGATIVE CORRELATION

When two variables change in the opposite direction, then there is said to be a negative correlation., i.e., if one variable increases, the other decreases or if one variable decreases, the other increases.

For Example : If a group of individuals have high I.Q. and the suggestibility of exhibited by the same group of individuals is low, then there exists negative correlation between I.Q. and suggestibility.

ZERO CORRELATION

When the change in one variable shows no systematic change in another variable, then, the correlation is termed as zero correlation.

For Example : The physical size of the skill of an adult has no relationship with his/her intelligence. Similarly, taller people may be bright or dull, and bright people may be tall or short. So too, if there is no relationship between marks secured at one examination and marks secured at another examination, it means there exists zero correlation.

LINEAR CORRELATION

This is the simplest kind of correlation to be found between the two sets of scores or variables. Actually, when the relationship between two sets of scores or variables can be represented graphically by a straight line, it is known as Liner Correlation. Such type of correlation clearly reveals how the change in one variable is accompanied by a change in the other or to what extent increase or decrease in one is accompanied by an increase or decrease in another. This type of correlation is calculated by Pearson's Moment Method.

CURVELINEAR CORRELATION

When the correlation between two variables are positive to some extent and after that it becomes negative; and the graph of this relation is seen like (inverse) on x-axis, then, this type of correlation is calculated by Spearman's Rank Difference Method.

DEGREE OF CORRELATION

So far it is clear, that the coefficient of correlation represents the extent to which two variables are related. It is, therefore, a numerical measure of the correlation between two variables. But it is also important to note that there exists what is called as a degree of relationship between the two sets of measures or variables, and for expressing the degree of relationship quantitatively between two sets of measures or variables, usually help of an index is taken. This index is a sort of ratio that indicates the extent to which changes in one variable are accompanied by changes in the other variable. It involves no unit and varies from + 1.00 (indicating perfect positive correlation) through zero to - 1.00 (indicating perfect negative correlation). It means, that, the coefficient of correlation is measured in degrees, and as per the degree of correlation, there are two extremities, *viz*, Perfect Positive Correlation and Perfect Negative Correlation. Now, let us see in detail about these two degrees of correlation.

PERFECT POSITIVE CORRELATION

When one variable is perfectly correlated with another variable, and the increase (or decrease) in one variable corresponds to the increase (or decrease) in the other variable, then it is said to be Perfect Positive Correlation.

For Example : Pupil scoring the highest marks in one test, say Geography and also obtains highest marks in the test of Science, then, there exists perfect positive correlation which is represented as + 1.00.

As the temperature increases, the height of the mercury column in the thermometer also increases by the same extent. This too is an example of perfect positive correlation.

PERFECT NEGATIVE CORRELATION

When one variable is perfectly correlated with another variable, and increase in one corresponds to the decrease in other variable, then it is said to be a case of Perfect Negative Correlation. It is represented as - 1.00.

Example : More intelligent persons are less suggestible. If I.Q. of a group of persons and their corresponding suggestibility are enlisted then perfect negative correlation will be observed.

Thus, the coefficients of correlation are computed in order to determine whether there is any correlation between the two variables; and, if so, to determine the significance of the degree or closeness of relationship. Sometimes 0.20 or - 0.30 may also turn out to be very significant and even 0.70 or - 0.75 may turn out to be insignificant. But for this, it is required to know about interpreting coefficient of correlation - Let us see it.

INTERPRETING THE COEFFICIENT OF CORRELATION

While interpreting coefficient of correlation, two things are to be considered. First is the sign of correlation and second thing is the magnitude or the size of the correlation.

Sign of Correlation indicates the direction of relationship. Positive (+) coefficients indicate direct relationship, i.e., there is a tendency for the two variables to vary in the same direction. Negative (–) coefficients indicate inverse relationship i.e., the two variables have a tendancy to vary in opposite direction.

A coefficient of correlation of + 0.82 denotes just as strong direct relationship as a coefficient of correlation of – 0.82 indicates inverse covariation. Both have equal predictive value.

The magnitude or the size of coefficient of correlation indicates the degree or closeness of relationship.

The following classification may turn out to be useful while interpreting a coefficient of correlation :

(i)	r	from	0.00	to	$\pm$ 0.20	denotes an indifferent, negligible relationship.
(ii)	r	from	$\pm$ 0.20	to	$\pm$ 0.40	denotes a definite but low slight relationship.
(iii)	r	from	$\pm$ 0.40	to	$\pm$ 0.70	denotes a substantial, marked relationship.
(iv)	r	from	$\pm$ 0.70	to	$\pm$ 0.90	denotes to very high relationship.
(v)	r	from	$\pm$ 0.90	to	$\pm$ 1.00	denotes a perfect relationship.

Our interpretation of the size of coefficient of correlation depends very much upon what we propose to do with it or the reasons why we computed it. What would be regarded as large coefficient of correlation for one purpose would be a small one for another. Hence, interpretation is largely a relative matter e.g., a coefficient of correlation of 0.65 between Intelligence test and Achievement in school may be considered fairly high, whereas, a coefficient of correlation of 0.65 between scores on two parallel forms of the same test may be considered as low.

The above classification is broad and tentative and can only be accepted as general guide with certain reservations; and once again it may be stated that a correlation coefficient is always to be judged with reference to the conditions under which it is obtained and the objectives of the experiment. Therefore, while interpreting the coefficient of correlation, one must consider the purpose for which it is being used.

While interpreting the correlation coefficient, the following two points should be borne in mind.

(i) They are not an indication of cause effect. One may come across all sorts of variables that are related but have no causal relationship. For example, among children, the size of the big toe is slightly correlated with mental age, yet, one does not cause the other. They are correlated simply because they are both related to a third variable - chronological age.

(ii) The coefficient is a very complex function of the degree of relationship, and two coefficients cannot be directly compared. A given r should not be interpreted directly as a percentage.

r of .45 does not mean 45% relationship. r of .60 does not indicate twice the relationship that is indicated by r of .30. An increase in correlation from r = .50 to .70 is not equivalent to an increase in r = .20 to .40.

COMPUTATION OF COEFFICIENT OF CORRELATION

There are different methods of computing coefficient of correlation. These are :

(i) Spearman's Rank-difference Method.

(ii) Scatter Diagram Method.

(iii) Pearson's Product Moment Method.

Lets us discuss each one by one.

SPEARMAN'S RANK-DIFFERENCE METHOD

If the data are in the form of ranks rather than raw scores, Spearman's Rank-difference Method is applied. The coefficient is indicated by the Greek letter rho (ρ). Formula employed to find out the correlation by Rank difference method is as follows :

$$\rho \text{ (rho)} + 1 - \frac{6\,\Sigma D^2}{N\,(N^2 - 1)}$$

where,

D represents the difference of ranks of two variables.

N represents the number of variables or cases.

ρ (rho) represents coefficient of correlation.

Difference among individuals in many traits can often be expressed by ranking the subjects in 1-2-3 order when such differences cannot be measured directly. For example, persons may be ranked in order of merit for honesty, athletic ability, salesmanship or social adjustment, when it is impossible to measure these complex behaviours. In like manner, various products or specimens, such as advertisements, colour combinations, compositions, jokes and pictures, which are admittedly hard to evaluate numerically may be put in order of merit for aesthetic quality, beauty, humour, or some other characteristic. In computing the correlation between two sets of ranks, special methods which take account of relative position have been devised. These techniques may also be applied to measurements (i.e., to scores) when these have been arranged in order of merit. If we have very few scores, it is often advisable to rank these scores and to compute the correlation coefficient ρ by the rank-difference method.

In case where we do not have scores and have to work with data in which differences between the individuals in the possession of certain characteristics can be expressed only by ranks, and Rank Correlation Coefficient is the only correlation coefficient that can be computed. But this does not mean that it cannot be computed from the usual data given in scores. In case the data contains scores of individuals, we can compte ρ by converting the individuals. For examples if the marks of a group of 5 students are given as 17, 25, 9, 35, 18, we will rank them as 4,2,5,1 and 3. We determine the ranks or position of the individuals in both the given sets of scores. These ranks are then subjected to further calculation for the determination of the coefficient of correlation.

CALCULATION OF ρ FROM RANKED DATA

Following table shows how to compute the correlation from rank-difference.

TABLE - To illustrate the calculation of (ρ)

	(1)	(2)	(3)	(4)
Traits	**Judge X**	**Judge Y**	**D**	**D^2**
A	2	1	1	1
B	1	2	-1	1
C	4	5	-1	1
D	3	6	-3	9
E	6	4	2	4
F	5	3	2	4
			0	$\Sigma D^2 = 20$

$$\rho = 1 - \frac{6\,\Sigma D^2}{N(N^2-1)}$$

$$\rho = 1 - \frac{6 \times 20}{6 \times 35} = .43$$

Six traits (A,B,C,D,E,F,) believed to be important in the work of an executive have to be ranked in order of merit by Judges X and Y. In column (3), the differences (D) between each pair of ranks is entered, Judge Y's ranks being subtracted from those of Judge X. The sum of the D's is zero. This calculation is of no value *per se*, but is a check on the computation to this point. Each D is now squared in column (4), and the column is summed to give D^2. The coefficient of correlation, is given by the formula –

$$= 1 - \frac{6 \times \Sigma D^2}{N\,(N^2 - 1)}$$

(rank difference correlation coefficient)

Let us solve one more example given below.

Example : Compute the coefficient of correlation by the rank difference method between two sets of scores obtained by ten students in Mathematics and Hindi :

Student	A	B	C	D	E	F	G	H	I	J
Marks in Mathematics	45	92	67	21	56	70	58	37	53	41
Marks in Hindi	52	69	62	31	39	57	60	28	44	50

Solution :

Procedure :

(1) First of all assign ranks against the scores obtained by the students in two subjects. These ranks are put in columns R_1 and R_2 of the table.

(2) Find the difference between the ranks $(R_1 - R_2)$ in column D.

(3) Check that the sum total of all D should be zero.

(4) Square D and put it in the column D^2.

(5) Add all D^2 to get ΣD^2.

(6) Use the following formula to get coefficient of correlation.

$$\rho = 1 - \frac{6\, \Sigma D^2}{N(N^2 - 1)}$$

Students	**Marks in Mathematics**	**Marks in Hindi**	**Rank in Maths (R_1)**	**Rank in Maths (R_2)**	**$D = R_1 - R_2$**	**D^2**
A	45	52	7	5	2	4
B	92	69	1	1	0	0
C	67	62	3	2	1	1
D	21	31	10	9	1	1
E	56	39	5	8	– 3	9
F	70	57	2	4	– 2	4
G	58	60	4	3	1	1
H	37	28	9	10	– 1	1
I	53	44	6	7	– 1	1
J	41	50	8	6	2	4
N = 10						$\Sigma D^2 = 26$

$$\rho = 1 - \frac{6\,\Sigma D^2}{N(N^2-1)}$$

$$= 1 - \frac{6 \times 26}{10\,(10^2-1)}$$

$$= 1 - \frac{156}{10\,(100-1)}$$

$$= 1 - \frac{156}{10 \times 99}$$

$$= 1 - \frac{156}{990}$$

$$= 1 - 0.158$$

$$= 0.842$$

$$= 0.84$$

Interpretation : There is very high correlation.

Example : Calculate rank difference correlation coefficient (ρ) from the following scores of a groups of ten students in two subjects.

Student	A	B	C	D	E	F	G	H	I	J
Score in History	13	16	11	17	16	12	19	20	20	16
Score in Geography	14	19	10	16	15	18	26	29	23	10

Solution :

In the example,

(i) Two students get 20 marks in History. Their ranks have therefore been calculated as: $\frac{1+2}{2} = \frac{3}{2} = 1.5$ each.

(ii) Three students get 16 marks in History

$\therefore$ Each of the three students has rank $\frac{5+6+7}{3} = \frac{18}{3} = 6$

(ii) Similarly two students get 10 marks in Geography

$\therefore$ Each of the two students is assigned rank $= \frac{9+10}{2} = \frac{19}{2} = 9.5$

Students	Score in History	Score in Geography	Rank in History	Rank in Geography	Rank Difference D	D^2
A	13	14	8	8	0	0
B	16	19	6	4	2	4
C	11	10	10	9.5	0.5	0.25
D	17	16	4	6	– 2	4
E	16	15	6	7	– 1	1
F	12	18	9	5	4	16
G	19	26	3	2	1	1
H	20	29	1.5	1	0.5	0.25
I	20	23	1.5	3	– 1.5	2.25
J	16	10	6	9.5	– 3.5	12.25
N = 10						$\Sigma D^2 = 41$

$$\rho = 1 - \frac{6\,\Sigma D^2}{N(N^2 - 1)}$$

$$= 1 - \frac{6 \times 41}{10\,(10^2 - 1)}$$

$$= 1 - \frac{246}{10 \times 99}$$

$$= 1 - \frac{246}{990}$$

$$= 1 - 0.248$$

$$= 0.752$$

$$= 0.75$$

There is very high correlation.

Let us have one more illustration which is solved as shown below :

Students	Marks in Mathematics	Marks in Science	R_1	R_2	$D = R_1 - R_2$	D^2
A	30	55	4	3	1	1
B	40	75	3	1	2	4
C	50	60	1	2	–1	1
D	20	12	6	7	–1	1
E	10	11	8	8	0	0
F	45	38	2	4	–2	4
G	22	25	5	5	0	0
H	18	15	7	6	1	1
						$\Sigma D^2 = 12$

$$\rho = 1 - \frac{6\,\Sigma D^2}{N(N^2-1)}$$

$$= 1 - \frac{6 \times 12}{8\,(8^2-1)}$$

$$= 1 - \frac{72}{8\,(64-1)}$$

$$= 1 - \frac{72}{8 \times 63}$$

$$= 1 - \frac{9}{63}$$

$$= 1 - \frac{1}{7}$$

$$= \frac{6}{7}$$

$$\therefore \rho = 0.86$$

Interpretation : There is very high correlation.

ILLUSTRATION

Calculate the coefficient of correlation for the given data.

Family Member	1	2	3	4	5	6	7	8	9	10	11
Brothers (X)	71	68	66	67	70	71	70	73	72	68	66
Sisters (Y)	69	64	65	63	65	62	65	64	66	69	62

Solution :

Family Members	X	Y	R_1	R_2	R_1-R_2	D^2
1	71	69	3.5	1.5	2	4.00
2	68	64	7	7.5	–.5	0.25
3	66	65	9.5	5	4.5	20.25
4	67	63	8	9	–1	1.00
5	70	65	5.5	5	.5	0.25
6	71	62	3.5	10.5	–7	49.00
7	70	65	5.5	5	.5	0.25
8	73	64	1	7.5	–6.5	42.25
9	72	66	2	3	-1	1.00
10	65	69	11	1.5	9.5	90.25
11	66	62	9.5	10.5	–1	1.00
N = 11					D = 0	D^2 = 209.50

In column X, 71 occurs twice and rank for that will be $\frac{3+4}{2} = 3.5$

Similarly for 70,70 rank will be X $\frac{5+6}{2} = 5.5$, and, as dissussed earlier, ranks are given.

$$\rho = 1 - \frac{6 \times 209.50}{11\,(121-1)}$$

$$\rho = 1 - \frac{1257.00}{11 \times 120}$$

$$\rho = 1 - \frac{1257}{1320}$$

$$\rho = 1 - 0.95$$

$$\rho = 0.05$$

Interpretation – very negligible correlation.

ONE MORE ILLUSTRATION

Persons	Height in Inches	Weight in Pounds	R_1	R_2	R_1-R_2	D^2
A	73	150	1	4	–3	9
B	72	145	2	5	–3	9
C	71	160	3	2	1	1
D	70	165	4	1	3	9
E	69	140	5	6	–1	1
F	68	135	6	7	–1	1
G	67	155	7	3	4	16
H	66	125	8	9	–1	1
I	65	130	9	8	1	1
N = 9						$\Sigma D^2 = 48$

$$\rho = 1 - \frac{6\,\Sigma D^2}{N(N^2-1)}$$

$$\rho = 1 - \frac{6 \times 48}{9\,(81-1)}$$

$$\rho = 1 - \frac{288}{9\,(80)}$$

$$\rho = 1 - \frac{288}{720}$$

$$\rho = 1 - \frac{2}{5}$$

$$\rho = 1 - 0.40$$

$$\rho = 0.60$$

Interpretation – Correlation is quite good.

CHARACTERISTICS OF Rho (ρ)

The size of the coefficient is directly affected by the size of the rank differences. If the ranks are the same for both tests, each rank difference will be zero and ultimately D^2 will be zero. This means that correlation is perfect; i.e., 1.00. If the rank differences are very large and the fraction is greater than one, then the correlation will be negative.

ADVANTAGES OF RANK DIFFERENCE METHOD

So far we have understood the method of computing the correlation through Rank-Difference Method of Spearman. But along with this it is also essential to know the advantages of this method. These are as follows :

(i) It is much easier to compute than the coefficient of correlation (r) computed by Pearson's Product Moment Method.

(ii) "It is quite easy to interpret."

LIMITATIONS OF RANK DIFFERENCE METHOD

No doubt there are advantages of Rank Differences Method while computing coefficient of correlation. But there are certain limitations too which are as follows :

(i) When the interval data are converted into rank-ordered data, the information about the size of that score difference is lost, e.g., if pupil gets scores in History from 78 upto 90, his/her rank may not change. Whereas, if next pupil scores in Geography from 45 upto 61, his/her rank may go higher than the first pupil.

(ii) If the number of cases are more, giving rank to them becomes a tedious job.

PRODUCT MOMENT METHOD OF COMPUTING COEFFICIENT OF CORRELATION

This method is also known as Pearson's Product Moment Method in the honour of the English Statesman Karl Pearson who is said to be the inventor of this method. The coefficient of correlation computed by this method is known as product Moment Coefficient of Correlation and is symobolically represented as ' '

(a) The Calculation of ' ' from ungrouped Data :

The basic formula for the computation of ' ' for the ungrouped data by this method is as given below :

Where X and Y represent the deviations of scores in the tests X and Y from the means of each distributions.

Procedure can be understood from the following illustration.

Individuals	Scores in Test X	Scores in Test Y	X	Y	XY	X^2	Y^2
A	15	60	–10	10	–100	100	100
B	25	70	0	20	0	0	400
C	20	40	–5	–10	50	25	100
D	30	50	5	0	0	25	0
E	35	30	10	–20	–200	100	400
					$\Sigma XY = -250$	$\Sigma X^2 = 250$	$\Sigma Y^2 = 1000$

Means of series X (MX) = 25

Means of series Y (MY) = 50

$$\text{Formula : r} = \frac{\Sigma XY}{\Sigma X^2 \cdot \Sigma Y^2}$$

$$= \frac{-250}{250 \times 1000}$$

$$= \frac{-250}{250000}$$

$$= \frac{-250}{500}$$

$$= -\frac{1}{2}$$

$$= -0.5$$

Computation of r directly from raw scores when deviations are taken from zero (without calculating deviations from the means)

The formula applied here is as follows :

$$r = \frac{N\Sigma XY - \Sigma X \cdot \Sigma Y}{\left(N\Sigma X^2 - (EX)^2\right) \cdot \left(N\Sigma Y^2 - (\Sigma Y)^2\right)}$$

This can be understood by solving the following example :

Subject	Score in First Test X	Score in Second Test Y	XY	X^2	Y^2
A	5	12	60	25	144
B	3	15	45	9	225
C	2	11	22	4	121
D	8	10	80	64	100
E	6	18	108	36	324
N = 5	$\Sigma X = 24$	$\Sigma Y = 66$	$\Sigma XY = 315$	$\Sigma X^2 = 138$	$\Sigma Y^2 = 914$

$$r = \frac{N\Sigma XY - \Sigma X \cdot \Sigma Y}{\left(N\Sigma X^2 - (EX)^2\right)\cdot\left(N\Sigma Y^2 - (\Sigma Y)^2\right)}$$

$$r = \frac{5 \times 315 - 24 \times 66}{(5 \times 138 - 576)\ (5 \times 914 - 66 \times 66)}$$

$$= \frac{1575 - 1650}{(690 - 576)\ (4570 - 4356)}$$

$$= \frac{-75}{114 \times 214}$$

$$= \frac{-75}{34396}$$

$$= \frac{-75}{156.2}$$

$$= -0.48$$

Answer r = – 0.48

The Calculation of the coefficient of correlation by the Product Moment Method

There are four methods of finding out whether two given variables are related or not.

(i) Scatter Diagram or Scattergram or Scatter plot.

(ii) Correlation table

(iii) Correlation graph

(iv) Coefficient of correlation

SCATTER DIAGRAM

A principal of a training college gets number of applications for the admission to B. Ed. course, he conducts content knowledge test. But after admitting them, he wants to know whether there is any relation between the marks obtained in practice teaching lessons and the marks gained in content knowledge test. The data for eight trainees are as follows :

Trainees	A	B	C	D	E	F	G	H
Marks in Content Test	45	48	63	51	60	62	77	83
Marks in Practice Lesson	51	52	68	60	66	75	85	90

The marks in Content Test are plotted on the X axis and marks in Practice Lesson on the Y axis. For the trainee A ($X_1 = 45$, $Y_1 = 51$) point (45,51) is plotted. Similarly, the remaining 7 points are plotted. The resulting diagram is called scatter diagram. For the above example the scatter diagram is shown in the following figure.

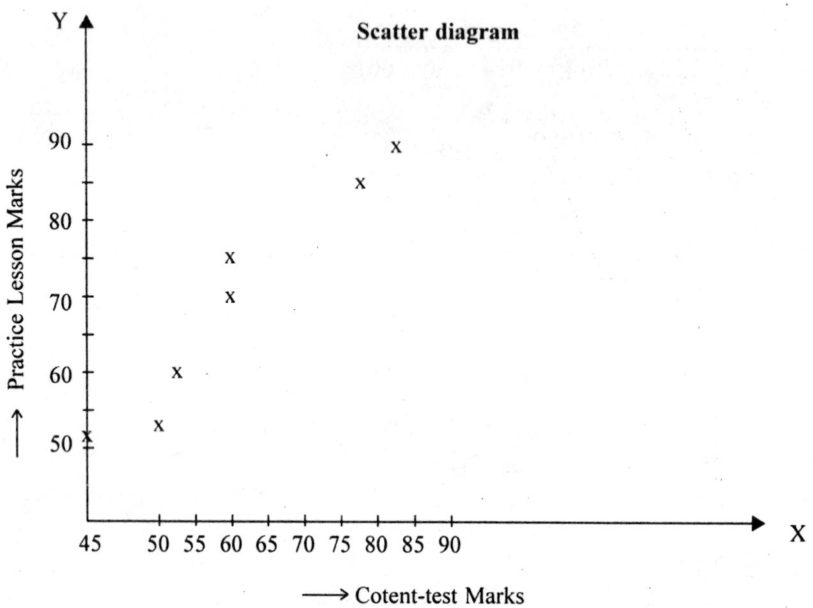

Here it can be noted that as X increases, Y increases, therefore the two variables are positively related. It is also seen that the points tend to fall along a line running from the lower left hand corner to the upper right hand corner. The Principal knows by this, that it is useful to select students on the basis of the content knowledge test as conducted in this case.

If the points tend to fall along a line running from upper left had corner to the lower right hand corner, then the two variables are said to be negatively correlated as shown in the following figure.

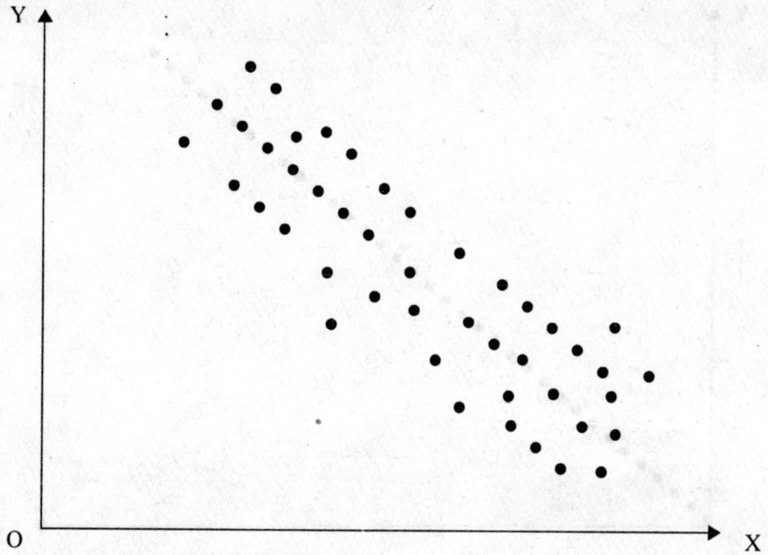

Scatter diagram showing negative correlation

Sometimes, the items are randomly distributed. It means both small and large values of Y can be found corresponding to small as well as large values of X. In such case, the two variables are said to be uncorrelated. The following scatter diagram shows zero correlation.

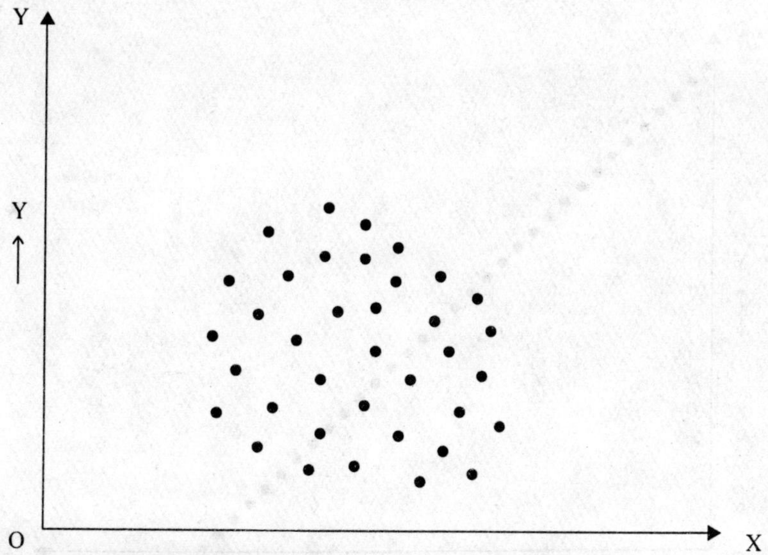

Scatter diagram showing absence of correlation

⟶ X

If the correlation is perfect positive, all the points will lie in a straight line as shown in the following figure.

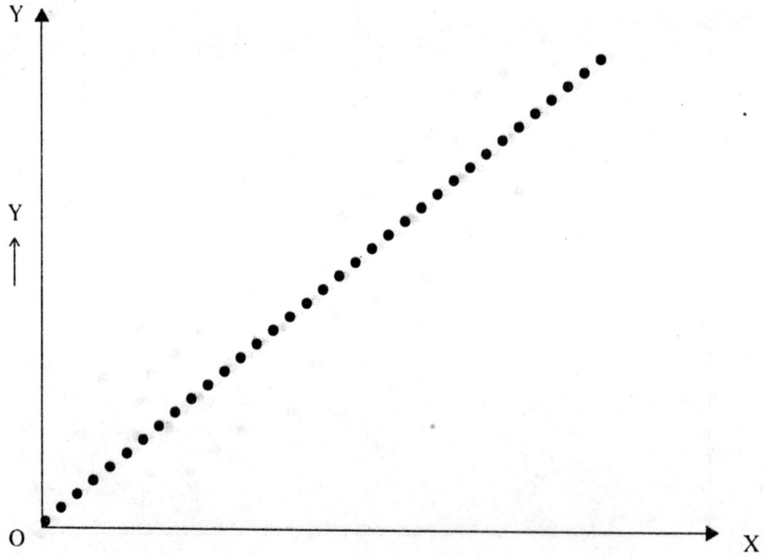

Scatter diagram showing perfect positive correlation

⟶ X

When the correlation is perfect negative, all the points will lie on a line as shown in the following figure. (compare the direction with that of the line showing perfect positive correlation.)

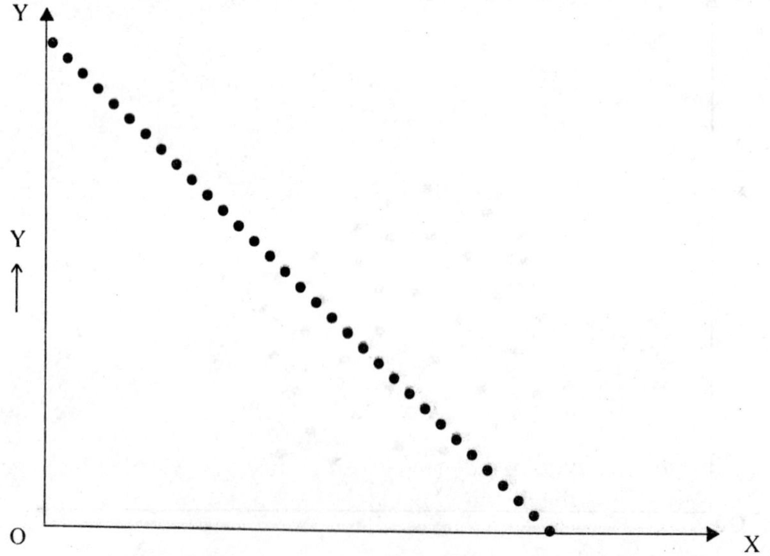

Scatter diagram showing perfect negative correlation

⟶ X

COEFFICIENT OF CORRELATION

The three methods discussed above give us the direction of correlation if it exists. It is more useful to have a numerical measure of correlation which is independent of the units of original data so that the two variables can be compared. For this, coefficient of correlation is calculated. The following are the characteristics of this measure :

(i) It is independent of the units of the variables.

(ii) Its value always lies between – 1 and + 1

(iii) The sign of the coefficient of correlation indicates whether the variables are positively or negatively related.

(iv) Its value indicates the degree of relationship between two variables.

THE CALCULATION OF THE COEFFICIENT OF CORRELATION BY THE PRODUCT MOMENT METHOD

When the relationship between two sets of measures is 'Linear' i.e., can be described by straight line, the correlation between scores may be expressed by the 'product moment' coefficient of correlation, designated by the letter 'r'. The coefficient of correlation 'r' is often called the "Pearson r"after Prof. Karl Pearson who developed the product moment method after the earlier work of Galton and Bravais.

Definition : The coefficient of correlation denoted by 'r' or "Pearson r" can be defined as

$$r = \frac{\Sigma\, Zx\, Zy}{N} \text{ where}$$

(i) Z score $Zx = \dfrac{X - Mx}{\sigma_x}$

(ii) $Zy = \dfrac{Y - Mx}{\sigma_y}$

(iii) there are N pairs (x,y)

Using standard scores for the calculation of coefficient of correlation involves a tedious process. However, several formula exist which have been derived from the basic definitional formula and involves less labour in the computation of 'r'.

(i) Scatter diagram :

Scatter diagram is an important step in analyzing correlation. When the amount of data is limited, a scatter diagram is easy to make manually. It graphically portrays the joint behaviour of the two variables. But it gives only the direction of correlation. It does not give the numerical measure of the degree of correlation.

(ii) Correlation Table :

Here the data are expressed in a bivariate table as shown below.

Marks in Geography	Marks in History				
	30–40	40–50	50–60	60–70	70–80
70 – 80					4
60 – 70			8	3	
50 – 60		2	7	4	
40 – 50		4			
30 – 40	3				

The interpretation is same as that of scatter diagram. If the frequencies are along a diagonal from lower left hand corner to the upper right hand corner, the two variables are positively correlated. In the given table, marks in two subjects shows a positive correlation. The students getting good marks in History get good marks in Geography and *vice-versa*. Similarly, students getting low marks in one subject score low marks in the other subject also.

If the frequencies lie along a diagonal from upper left hand corner to lower right hand corner the two variables are said to be negatively correlated.

(iii) Correlation Graph :

Here two curves are drawn to represent the movements of the two variables.

(a) If the two curves move in the same direction, the variables are positively correlated.

(b) If the two curves move in the opposite directions they are negatively correlated.

(c) If there is no consistency in their joint movements, the two variables are uncorrelated.

CALCULATION OF PRODUCT MOMENT r BY TWO DIFFERENT FORMULAE

(a) Raw Score Method :

The calculation of 'r' may often be carried out most readily especially when the calculating machine is available by means of the following formula which is based upon "raw" scores

$$r = \frac{N\Sigma XY - \Sigma X \cdot \Sigma Y}{\sqrt{(N\Sigma X^2 - (\Sigma X)^2)(N\Sigma Y^2 - (\Sigma Y)^2)}}$$

Example :

Calculate the product Moment r from the following ungrouped data.

Student	A	B	C	D	E
Marks in X	10	8	6	4	2
Marks in Y	11	7	2	6	4

Solution :

Student	X	Y	X^2	Y^2	XY
A	10	11	100	121	110
B	8	7	64	49	56
C	6	2	36	4	12
D	4	6	16	36	24
E	2	4	4	16	8
N = 5	$\Sigma X = 30$	$\Sigma Y = 30$	$\Sigma X^2 = 220$	$\Sigma Y^2 = 226$	$\Sigma XY = 210$

$$r = \frac{N\Sigma XY - \Sigma X \cdot \Sigma Y}{\sqrt{(N\Sigma X^2 - (\Sigma X)^2)(N\Sigma Y^2 - (\Sigma Y)^2)}}$$

$$= \frac{5(210) - 30 \times 30}{\sqrt{(5 \times (220) - (30)^2\ )(5 \times (226) - (30)^2}}$$

$$= \frac{1050 - 900}{\sqrt{(1100 - 900)(1130 - 900)}}$$

$$= \frac{150}{\sqrt{200 \times 230}} = \frac{150}{\sqrt{46000}} = \frac{150}{214.47}$$

$$= 0.7$$

$$r = +0.7$$

Steps :

(1) Calculate squares of each X and Y score as shown in the columns 3 and 4.

(2) Calculate products of X and Y for each pair.

(3) Sum up all columns.

(4) Substitute the values in the formula.

(5) Simplify to get the value of 'r'.

Example :

Calculate Pearson's Product Moment r from the following set of scores.

X	23	21	19	18	17	15	15	13	11	8
Y	15	19	13	17	15	13	12	11	10	5

Solution :

X	Y	X^2	Y^2	XY
23	15	529	225	345
21	19	441	361	399
19	13	361	169	247
18	17	324	289	306
17	15	289	225	255
15	13	225	169	195
15	12	225	144	180
13	11	169	121	143
11	10	121	100	110
8	5	64	25	40
$\Sigma X = 160$	$\Sigma Y = 130$	$\Sigma X^2 = 2748$	$\Sigma Y^2 = 1828$	$\Sigma XY = 2220$

$$r = \frac{N\Sigma XY - \Sigma X \cdot \Sigma Y}{\sqrt{(N\Sigma X^2 - (\Sigma X)^2\ (N\Sigma Y^2 - (\Sigma Y)^2)}}$$

$$= \frac{10 \times 2220 - 160 \times 130}{\sqrt{(10 \times 2748 - (160)^2\ (10 \times 1828 - (130)^2\ )}}$$

$$= \frac{22200 - 20800}{\sqrt{(27480 - 25600)\ (18280 - 16900)}}$$

$$= \frac{1400}{\sqrt{(1880)\ (1380)}}$$

$$= \frac{1400}{\sqrt{2594400}}$$

$$= \frac{1400}{1610.7141}$$

$$= 0.8691$$

$$= 0.87$$

Example : Calculate the Person's Product Moment r from the following set of scores.

Student	A	B	C	D	E	F	G	H	I
Marks in Marathi.	40	50	30	50	45	35	30	55	25
Marks in Sanskrit	79	88	76	82	94	82	73	85	79

Solution :

Student	Marks in Marathi X	Marks in Sanskrit Y	X^2	Y^2	XY
A	40	79	1600	6241	3160
B	50	88	2500	7744	4400
C	30	76	900	5776	2280
D	50	82	2500	6724	4100
E	45	94	2025	8836	4230
F	35	82	1225	6724	2870
G	30	73	900	5329	2190
H	55	85	3025	7225	4675
I	25	79	625	6241	1975
N = 9	ΣX = 360	ΣY = 738	$\Sigma X^2 = 15300$	$\Sigma Y^2 = 60840$	ΣXY = 29880

$$r = \frac{N\Sigma XY - \Sigma X \cdot \Sigma Y}{\sqrt{N\Sigma X^2 - (\Sigma X)^2 \, (N\Sigma Y^2 - (\Sigma Y)^2}}$$

$$= \frac{9 \times 29880 - 360 \times 738}{\sqrt{9 \times 15300 - (360)^2 \; (9 \times 60840 - (738)^2}}$$

$$= \frac{268920 - 265680}{\sqrt{137700 - 129600\,)\,(547560 - 544644)}}$$

$$= \frac{3240}{\sqrt{8100 \times 2916}}$$

$$= \frac{3240}{90 \times 54}$$

$$= \frac{3240}{4860}$$

$$= 0.666$$

$$= +0.67$$

(b) Deviation Score Method :

Product Moment 'r' can also be calculated by deviation score method. In this method the following formula is used.

$$r = \frac{\Sigma XY}{\sqrt{\Sigma X^2 \cdot \Sigma Y^2}}$$

The following steps are involved in this method :

(1) Calculate Means of X and Y scores.

(2) Obtain deviation scores x and y as follows :

$x = X - Mx$ and $y = Y - My$

where Mx = Mean of all X scores.

and My = Mean of all Y scores.

(3) Obtain squares of deviation scores.

(4) Multiply the corresponding values of x and y to get xy for each pair.

(5) Sum up all columns to get the values of Σxy, Σx^2 and Σy^2

(6) Substitute the values in the formula.

(7) Simplify to get the values of r.

Example : Calculate Pearson's Product Moment r from the following set of score using deviation score method.

Student	A	B	C	D	E
Marks in X	10	8	6	4	2
Marks in Y	11	7	2	6	4

Solution : Mean of X scores (Mx) $= \frac{\Sigma X}{N} = \frac{10 + 8 + 6 + 4 + 2}{5}$

$$= \frac{30}{5} = 6$$

$$\therefore Mx = 6$$

Mean of Y scores (My) $= \frac{\Sigma Y}{N}$

$$= \frac{11 + 7 + 2 + 6 + 4}{5}$$

$$= \frac{30}{5} = 6$$

$$\therefore My = 6.$$

Student	X	Y	x = X – Mx	y = Y – My	X²	Y²	xy
A	10	11	4	5	16	25	20
B	8	7	2	1	4	1	2
C	6	2	0	– 4	0	16	0
D	4	6	– 2	0	4	0	0
E	2	4	– 4	– 2	16	4	8
					$\Sigma x^2 = 40$	$\Sigma y^2 = 46$	$\Sigma xy = 30$

$$r = \frac{\Sigma xy}{\sqrt{\Sigma x^2 \cdot \Sigma y^2}}$$

$$= \frac{30}{\sqrt{40 \times 46}}$$

$$= \frac{30}{\sqrt{1840}}$$

$$= \frac{30}{42.89}$$

$$= 0.699$$

$$= +0.7$$

$$\therefore r = +0.7$$

Example : Calculate Product Moment coefficient of correlation from the following data using deviation score method.

Height in cms (X)	120	125	127	130	134	144
Weight in Kgs (Y)	42	47	48	46	50	49

Solution :

$$\text{Mean of height (Mx)} = \frac{\Sigma x}{N}$$

$$= \frac{120 + 125 + 127 + 130 + 134 + 144}{6}$$

$$= \frac{780}{6}$$

$$= 130$$

$$\therefore Mx = 130 \text{ cms.}$$

$$\text{Mean Weight (My)} = \frac{\Sigma Y}{N}$$

$$= \frac{42 + 47 + 48 + 46 + 50 + 49}{6}$$

$$= \frac{282}{6}$$

$$\therefore (My) = 47 \text{ Kg.}$$

X	Y	x = X – Mx	y = Y – My	x^2	y^2	xy
120	42	– 10	– 5	100	25	50
125	47	– 05	0	25	0	0
127	48	– 03	1	9	1	– 03
130	46	0	– 1	0	1	0
134	50	4	3	16	9	12
144	49	14	2	196	4	28
				$\Sigma x^2 = 346$	$\Sigma y^2 = 40$	$\Sigma xy = 87$

$$r = \frac{\Sigma xy}{\sqrt{\Sigma x^2 \cdot \Sigma y^2}}$$

$$= \frac{87}{\sqrt{346 \times 40}}$$

$$= \frac{87}{\sqrt{13840}}$$

$$= \frac{87}{177.64352}$$

$$= 0.739$$

$$= 0.74$$

$$\therefore r = +0.74$$

Example : Calculate the Product Moment coefficient of correlation from the following data using deviation score method.

Pupil	A	B	C	D	E	F	G	H	I	J
Marks in Physics (X)	51	42	48	41	47	40	47	39	47	38
Marks in Chemistry (Y)	69	68	70	64	70	59	68	59	64	59

Solution :

$$\text{Mean of Physics Marks (Mx)} = \frac{\Sigma X}{N} = \frac{440}{10}$$

$$\therefore Mx = 44$$

$$\text{Mean of Chemistry Marks (My)} = \frac{\Sigma Y}{N} = \frac{650}{10}$$

$$\therefore My = 65$$

Pupil	X	Y	x = X – Mx	y = Y – My	x^2	y^2	xy
A	51	69	7	4	49	16	28
B	42	68	– 2	3	4	9	– 6
C	48	70	4	5	16	25	20
D	41	64	– 3	– 1	9	1	3
E	47	70	3	5	9	25	15
F	40	59	– 4	– 6	16	36	24
G	47	68	3	3	9	9	9
H	39	59	– 5	– 6	25	36	30
I	47	64	3	– 1	9	1	– 3
J	38	59	– 6	– 6	36	36	36
N = 10					$\Sigma x^2 = 182$	$\Sigma y^2 = 199$	$\Sigma xy = 156$

$$r = \frac{\Sigma xy}{\sqrt{\Sigma x^2 \cdot \Sigma y^2}} = \frac{156}{\sqrt{182 \times 194}}$$

$$= \frac{156}{\sqrt{35308}}$$

$$= \frac{156}{187.90}$$

$$= +0.83$$

COEFFICIENT OF CORRELATION FROM CORRELATION TABLE

Example : In the following correlation table compute the coefficient of correlation.

Boys : Ages 4.5 to 5.5 years.

Weight in Pounds

Height in Inches	24 – 28	29 – 33	34 – 38	39 – 43	44 – 48	49 – 53	Total
45 – 47			1		2		3
42 – 44			4	35	21	5	65
39 – 41		5	87	90	7	1	190
36 – 38	1	18	72	8			99
33 – 35	5	15	5				25
30 – 32	2						2
Total	8	38	169	133	30	6	384

Solution : The following steps are followed to calculate the coefficient of correlation (r) by the product moment method when the data is in the form of correlation table.

Step I : Construct a scattergram for the two variables to be correlated and from it draw up correlation table. In this example the data is already in the form of correlation table.

Step 2 : The correlation table is rearranged.

Assume a mean for the height distribution and draw double lines to mark the row in which the assumed mean for height/falls.

Similarly, assume a mean for weight distribution and draw double lines to mark the column in which the assumed for weight falls.

The mean for height distribution is 37 (mid-point of interval 36–38) and for weight distribution is 36 (mid-point of interval 34–38).

Step 3 : Assign deviations from the assumed mean of the weight distribution as well as height distribution.

Weight in Pounds (columns); **Height in Inches** (rows)

Deviation	–2	–1	0	1	2	3		F	Y	Y^2
3			1 (0)		2 (12)			3	9	27
2			4 (0)	35 (70)	21 (84)	5 (30)		65	130	260
1		5 (–5)	87 (0)	90 (90)	7 (14)	1 (3)		190	190	190
0	1 (0)	18 (0)	72 (0)	8 (0)				99	0	0
–1	5 (10)	15 (15)	5 (0)					+25	–25	25
–2	2 (8)							2 ↓	–4 ↓	8 ↓
F	8	38	169	133	30	6	→	384	300	510
X	–16	–38	0	133	60	18	→	157		
X^2	32	38	0	133	120	54	→	377		
XY	18	10	0	160	110	33	→	331		

Step 4 : Multiply the frequency of the box or cell with the corresponding deviations and put the product in the bracket in the respective box, e.g., in the first row of the second last column the frequency of the box is 2 and the corresponding deviations are 3 and 2 respectively. The product $2 \times 3 \times 2 = 12$ is written in the bracket and put in the box.

Similarly, the frequency of the box of the first column and second last row is 5; and the corresponding deviations are –1 and –2 respectively. The product $5 \times -1 \times -2 = 10$ is written in the bracket and put in the said box.

Step 5 : Add the frequencies of the rows and put the total in the first column of the right hand side of the table under the heading "F". Similarly, add the frequencies of the column and put the total under the table in the first row against 'F'.

Step 6 : To get Y the 'f' of the row (X axis) is multiplied with the corresponding deviation of Y axis.

E.g., first row frequency total 'f' is 3 and deviation is 3

$\therefore\ Y = 3 \times 3 = 9$

for second row f is 65 and deviation is 2

$\therefore\ Y = 65 \times 2 = 130$

Similarly, X is calculated by multiplying the 'f' of the column (Y axis) with the corresponding deviation of X axis.

Step 7 : To get Y^2 we are required to multiply Y with the corresponding deviation of Y axis (column).

E.g., to get Y^2 for the first row 9 is multiplied with 3 thus $Y^2 = 9 \times 3 = 27$

similarly to get Y^2 for the last row –4 is multiplied with –2

$\therefore\ Y^2 = (-4) \times (-2) = 8$

The same method is followed to work out X^2.

E.g., to get X^2 for the first column X is multiplied with the corresponding deviation of X axis.

$X^2 = -16 \times -2 = 32$

Step 8 : To get XY, the numbers put in all the brackets in each column is added

E.g., for first column XY = 0 + 10 + 8 = 18

for second column XY = –5 + 0 + 15 = 10

Step 9 :

(i) Find N, ΣY, ΣY^2, ΣX, ΣX^2, and ΣXY

Step 10 :

Substitute the values in the following formula to get the value of 'r'.

$$r = \frac{\Sigma XY - \dfrac{\Sigma X \cdot \Sigma Y}{N}}{\sqrt{(\Sigma X^2 - \dfrac{(\Sigma X)^2}{N})(\Sigma Y^2 - \dfrac{(\Sigma Y)^2}{N})}}$$

$$= \frac{331 - \dfrac{157 \times 300}{384}}{\sqrt{(377 - \dfrac{(157)^2}{384})\,(510 - \dfrac{(300)^2}{384})}}$$

$$= \frac{208.664}{\sqrt{(312.81)\ (275.625)}}$$

$$= \frac{208.664}{\sqrt{86218.256}}$$

$$= \frac{208.664}{293.6}$$

$$= 0.71$$

Example : Compute the coefficient of correlation in the table below.

Arithmetic (X)

Science (Y)	12–13	14–15	16–17	18–19	20–21	22–23	24–25	Total
35–37					1		1	2
32–34					6	3		9
29–31		1	2	6	8	1		18
26–28		4	4	6	11	4	1	30
23–25	2	1	6	5	4	1		19
20–22	3	2	1	1				7
Total	5	8	13	18	30	9	2	85

Solution :

Deviation	–3	–2	–1	0	1	2	3		F	Y	Y^2
3					1 (3)		1 (9)		2	6	18
2					6 (12)	3 (12)			9	18	36
1		1 (–2)	2 (–2)	6 (0)	8 (8)	1 (2)			18	18	18
0		4 (0)	4 (0)	6 (0)	11 (0)	4 (0)	1 (0)		30	0	0
–1	2 (6)	1 (2)	6 (6)	5 (0)	4 (–4)	1 (–2)			19	–19	19
–2	3 (18)	2 (8)	1 (2)	1 (0)					7	–14	28
									↓	↓	↓
F	5	8	13	18	30	9	2	→	N = 85	ΣY = 9	ΣY^2 = 119
X	–15	–16	–13	0	30	18	6	→	ΣX = 10		
X^2	45	32	13	0	30	36	18	→	ΣX^2 = 174		
XY	24	8	6	0	19	12	9	→	ΣXY = 78		

$$r = \frac{\Sigma XY - \frac{\Sigma X \cdot \Sigma Y}{N}}{\sqrt{(\Sigma X^2 - \frac{(\Sigma X)^2}{N})\ (\Sigma Y^2 - \frac{(\Sigma Y)^2}{N})}}$$

$$= \frac{78 - \frac{10 \times 9}{85}}{\sqrt{(174 - \frac{(10)^2}{85})\ (119 - \frac{(9)^2}{85})}}$$

$$= \frac{78 - 1.0588235}{\sqrt{(174 - 1.1764)\ (119 - 0.952)}}$$

$$= \frac{76.9412}{\sqrt{(172.8236)\ (118.048)}}$$

$$= \frac{76.9412}{\sqrt{20401.48}}$$

$$= \frac{76.9412}{142.83}$$

$$= 0.538$$

$$= 0.54$$

Example : Compute the coefficient of correlation between the Algebra test and I.Q.'s shown in the table below.

Algebra Test Scores

I.Q.	30–34	35–39	40–44	45–49	50–54	55–59	60–64	65–69	Total
130–139				1		1		1	3
120–129			1		1	2	1		5
110–119	1	2	5	6	11	6	3	2	36
100–109	3	7	9	17	13	5	1	1	56
90–99	4	10	16	12	5	1			48
80–89	4	9	8	2	2				25
Total	12	28	39	38	32	15	5	4	173

Solution :

Algebra Test Scores

I.Q. Deviation	–3	–2	–1	0	1	2	3	4	F	Y	Y^2
2				1 (0)		1 (4)		1 (8)	3	6	12
1			1 (–1)		1 (1)	2 (4)	1 (3)		5	5	5
0	1 (0)	2 (0)	5 (0)	6 (0)	11 (0)	6 (0)	3 (0)	2 (0)	36	0	0
–1	3 (9)	7 (14)	9 (9)	17 (0)	13 (–13)	5 (–10)	1 (–3)	1 (–4)	56	–56	56
–2	4 (24)	10 (40)	16 (32)	12 (0)	5 (–10)	1 (–4)			48	–96	192
–3	4 (36)	9 (54)	8 (24)	2 (0)	2 (-6)				25 ↓	–75 ↓	225 ↓
F	12	28	39	38	32	15	5	4 →	N = 173	ΣY = 216	ΣY² = 490
X	–36	–56	–39	0	32	30	15	16 →	ΣX = –38		
X²	108	112	39	0	32	60	45	64 →	ΣX² = 460		
XY	69	108	64	0	–28	–6	0	4 →	ΣXY = 211		

$$r = \frac{\Sigma XY - \frac{\Sigma X \cdot \Sigma Y}{N}}{\sqrt{(\Sigma X^2 - \frac{(\Sigma X)^2}{N})(\Sigma Y^2 - \frac{(\Sigma Y)^2}{N})}}$$

$$= \frac{211 - \frac{(-38) \times (-216)}{173}}{\sqrt{(460 - \frac{(-38)^2}{173})(490 - \frac{(-216)^2}{173})}}$$

$$= \frac{211 - 47.445}{\sqrt{(460 - 8.346)(490 - 269.687)}}$$

$$= \frac{163.555}{\sqrt{(451.654)(220.313)}}$$

$$= \frac{163.555}{\sqrt{99504.366}}$$

$$= \frac{163.555}{315.443}$$

$$= 0.5184$$

$$= 0.52 \qquad \therefore r = 0.52$$

Example:

Calculate coefficient of correlation between X and Y.

X

Y	20–29	30–39	40–49	50–59	60–69	70–79	80–89
35–39				1			3
30–34		4			6		
25–29			3		3		
20–24			2	5		1	
15–19	1		4		3		
10–14		3		1	2		
5–9		1	2				2
0–4	2	1					

Solution:

Deviation	–3	–2	–1	0	1	2	3	F	Y	Y^2
4				1 (0)			3 (36)	4	16	64
3		4 (–24)			6 (18)			10	30	90
2		3 (–6)	3 (–6)		3 (–6)			6	12	24
1			2 (–2)	5 (0)		1 (2)		8	8	8
0	1 (0)		4 (0)		3 (0)			8	0	0
–1		3 (6)		1 (0)	2 (–2)			6	–6	6
–2		1 (4)	2 (4)				2 (–12)	5	–10	20
–3	2 (18)	1 (6)						3	–9	27
								↓ N = 50	↓ ΣY = 41	↓ ΣY^2 = 239

F	3	9	11	7	14	1	5	→	N = 50
X	–9	–18	–11	0	14	2	15	→	ΣX = –7
X^2	27	36	11	0	14	4	45	→	ΣX^2 = 137
XY	18	–8	–4	0	22	2	24	→	ΣXY = 54

$$r = \frac{\Sigma XY - \frac{\Sigma X \cdot \Sigma Y}{N}}{\sqrt{(\Sigma X^2 - \frac{(\Sigma X)^2}{N})(\Sigma Y^2 - \frac{(\Sigma Y)^2}{N})}}$$

$$= \frac{54 - \frac{-7 \times 41}{50}}{\sqrt{(137 - \frac{(-7)^2}{50})(239 - \frac{(41)^2}{50})}}$$

$$= \frac{54 + 5.74}{\sqrt{(137 - \frac{49}{50})(239 - \frac{1681}{50})}}$$

$$= \frac{59.74}{\sqrt{(137 - 0.98)(239 - 33.62)}}$$

$$= \frac{59.74}{\sqrt{136.02 \times 205.38}}$$

$$= \frac{59.74}{\sqrt{27935.787}}$$

$$= \frac{59.74}{167.14002}$$

$$= 0.3574248$$

$$= 0.36$$

$\therefore r = 0.36.$

Example : In the following correlation table compute the coefficient of correlation.

Group Test I.Q.

School Marks	84 and Low	85–89	90–94	95–99	100–104	105–109	110–114	115–119	120–124	125 Over	Total
90 and over				3	3	15	12	9	9	5	56
85-89				8	17	15	24	13	6	6	89
80-84			4	6	22	21	20	10	5	1	89
75-79			7	25	33	23	10	7	4		109
70-74		4	10	18	14	22	12	1	1		82
65-69	1	3	3	12	7	8	8	1			43
60-64			3	5	3	1	1				12
Total	1	7	26	77	99	105	87	41	25	12	480

Solution :

Deviation	–5	–4	–3	–2	–1	0	1	2	3	4	F	Y	Y^2
3				3 (–18)	3 (-9)	15 (0)	12 (36)	9 (54)	9 (81)	5 (60)	56	168	504
2				8 (–32)	17 (–34)	15 (0)	24 (48)	13 (52)	6 (36)	6 (48)	89	178	356
1			4 (–12)	6 (–12)	22 (–22)	21 (0)	20 (20)	10 (20)	5 (15)	1 (4)	89	89	89
0			7 (0)	25 (0)	33 (0)	23 (0)	10 (0)	7 (0)	4 (0)		109	0	0
–1		4 (16)	10 (30)	18 (36)	14 (14)	22 (0)	12 (–12)	1 (–2)	1 (–3)		82	–82	82
–2	1 (10)	3 (24)	3 (18)	12 (48)	7 (14)	8 (0)	8 (–16)	1 (–4)			43	–86	172
–3			2 (18)	5 (30)	3 (9)	1 (0)	1 (–3)				12 ↓	–36 ↓	108 ↓
F	1	7	26	77	99	105	87	41	25	12 →	N = 480	ΣY = 231	ΣY^2 = 1311
X	–5	–28	–78	–154	–99	0	87	82	75	48 →	ΣX = –72		
X^2	25	112	234	308	99	0	87	164	225	192 →	ΣX^2 = 1446		
XY	10	40	54	52	–28	0	73	120	129	112 →	ΣXY = 562		

$$r = \frac{\Sigma XY - \dfrac{\Sigma X \cdot \Sigma Y}{N}}{\sqrt{(\Sigma X^2 - \dfrac{(\Sigma X)^2}{N})\ (\Sigma Y^2 - \dfrac{(\Sigma Y)^2}{N})}}$$

$$= \frac{562 - \dfrac{(-72)\ (231)}{480}}{\sqrt{(1446 - \dfrac{(-72)^2}{480})\ (1311 - \dfrac{(231)^2}{480})}}$$

$$= \frac{562 + 34.65}{\sqrt{(1446 - \dfrac{5184}{480})\ (1311 - \dfrac{53361}{480})}}$$

$$= \frac{596.65}{\sqrt{(1446 - 10.8)\ (1311 - 111.16875)}}$$

$$= \frac{596.65}{\sqrt{(1435.2 \times 1199.8313}}$$

$$= \frac{596.65}{\sqrt{(1721997.8}}$$

$$= \frac{596.65}{1312.2491}$$

$= 0.4546$

$= 0.46$

Example : In the following correlation table compute the coefficient of correlation between X and Y.

→ X

Scores	0–3	4–7	8–11	12–15	16–19	20–23	24–27
70–79	1	3					1
60–69				2			
50–59					5	2	
40–49		4		7			
30–39	3				3	1	
20–29			2		2		
10–19		1				1	2

→ Y

Solution :

Deviation	–3	–2	–1	0	1	2	3		F	Y	Y^2
3	1 (–9)	3 (–18)					1 (9)		5	15	45
2				2 (0)					2	4	8
1					5 (5)	2 (4)			7	7	7
0		4 (0)		7 (0)					11	0	0
–1	3 (9)				3 (–3)	1 (-2)			7	–7	7
–2			2 (4)		2 (–4)				4	–8	16
–3		1 (6)				1 (–6)	2 (–18)		4	–12	36
									↓	↓	↓
F	4	8	2	9	10	4	3	→	N = 40	ΣY = –1	ΣY^2 = 119
X	–12	–16	–2	0	10	8	9	→	ΣX = –3		
X^2	36	32	2	0	10	16	27	→	ΣX^2 = 123		
XY	0	–12	4	0	–2	–4	–9	→	ΣXY = –23		

$$r = \frac{\Sigma XY - \frac{\Sigma X \cdot \Sigma Y}{N}}{\sqrt{(\Sigma X^2 - \frac{(\Sigma X)^2}{N})(\Sigma Y^2 - \frac{(\Sigma Y)^2}{N})}}$$

$$= \frac{-23 - \frac{(-3)\times(-1)}{40}}{\sqrt{(123 - \frac{(-3)^2}{40})(119 - \frac{(-1)^2}{40})}}$$

$$= \frac{-23 - \frac{3}{40}}{\sqrt{(123 - \frac{9}{40})(119 - \frac{1}{40})}}$$

$$= \frac{-23 - 0.075}{\sqrt{(123 - 0.225)(119 - 0.025)}}$$

$$= \frac{-23.075}{\sqrt{122.775 \times 118.975}}$$

$$= \frac{-23.075}{\sqrt{14607.155}}$$

$$= \frac{-23.075}{120.86006}$$

$$= -0.1909$$

$$\therefore r = -0.1909$$

USE OF THE COEFFICIENT OF CORRELATION

The use of coefficient of correlation is very wide. In almost all social sciences this is now being increasingly used. It is useful whenever each member of a group of individuals has been measured on two or more traits. It expresses at one figure the average degree of resemblance, etc., between the two traits. Its' specific uses may be given as follows :

(i) One of the most important uses of coefficient of correlation is to predict the preformance on the second variable by knowing the score on the first variable *viz.* the test. In a number of studies, the coefficient of correlation is used to predict the success one will achieve in his/her further educational career. For example, the marks obtained by the students in 6th class were correlated with marks obtained in the college examination. The correlation was found to be nearly 60. This showed a marked degree of resemblance. Hence, in the result of this study it can be safely predicted that the student who does well in lower classes will likely to do well in the higher classes. But it is to be remembered that one should not jump to conclusion only on the basis of some results on a limited sample. There are quite a large number of factors that influence the achievement and a correlation between marks at different stages may not be a true indicator. However, it can show a trend.

(ii) Second use of coefficient of correlation is to determine the reliability of the test. Very often the coefficient of correlation has been used to test the reliability. The test is given to the students on two occassions and correlation between the scores of each individual on the two occassions is found out. This helps us to know how precise and consistent the test is. Such a correlation between the results of applying the test to the same group of pupils on two occassions is known as reliability coefficient, which tells us how far the test is consistent.

Through the calculation of this statistics it has been sought to be asserted whether or not a test measures on two successive occassions the same type of thing. The same test if given to the same individuals a second time, there is likelihood of the variation in the scores obtained the second time.

(iii) A third use of coefficient of correlation is to determine the validity of a test e.g., suppose we want to determine the validity of an intelligence test as a predictor of success in the college. In that case, we have to find the coefficient of correlation between the scores on intelligence test and the college examination marks. The coefficient of correlation thus obtained is called validity coefficient and is interpreted like any other coefficient of correlation.

In validating a group intelligence test, the correlation between scores on the group test and scores on an individual test of intelligence is to be found out. A high correlation would indicate that the two tests go together.

(iv) The fourth use of coefficient of correlation is to determine the objectivity of the test e.g., if the answer books have been assessed by the two examiners, the objectivity of their scoring can be determined by finding the coefficient of correlation between the marks given by these two examiners. When papers have been independently assessed twice, either by the same person or by different persons, the coefficient of correlation between the sets of two scores is the objectivity coefficient.

For a highly objective test, the coefficient of correlation should closely approach to + 1.00.

(v) The coefficient of correlation is also being used in the Test-Construction. Wherever a new test is constructed, there is always the question of whether each element of the test is related to other elements or to the test as a whole, and as to whether each element is related to criteria choosen. These relationships are all examined through the technique of correlation.

(vi) Coefficient of correlation is useful in vocational as well as Educational Guidance.

(vii) Coefficient of correlation is useful in comparison of two or more characteristics of a student.

(viii) Coefficient of correlation is useful in factor analysis.

❑❑❑

CHAPTER IX

REGRESSION AND PREDICTION

When we know that two given variables are correlated, we try to establish some relation between the two so that we can estimate the value of one variable, given the value of the other. For example, if there exists positive correlation between the heights and weights of a group of children we can find an equation establishing the relation between the height and weight. Using this equation we can estimate the weight of a child belonging to the same population of his height.

Correlation coefficient only determines whether the variables are related and if so, how strong is the relationship. The equations used for prediction or estimation are known as **regression equations,** i.e., with the help of regression analysis we establish a model which expresses the functional relationship between the two variables. These are also known as estimating equation.

In a simple regression problem there are two regression lines–one for regression of Y on X (predicting X from Y), and the other for the regression of X on Y (predicting Y from X). True, that if two variables are measured on each person in a group, the relationship should be the same regardless of whether one predicts Y from X or X from Y. However, the regression constants will be different depending upon which variable is the predictor and which is the predicted.

EQUATION OF A STRAIGHT LINE

Equation of a straight line can be written in the following forms :

(1) Slope point form.

(2) Double or Two intercept form.

(3) Slope-intercept form.

The equation of a straight line in slope-intercept form is written as follows :

$y = ax + b$

where a is the slope of the line and b is called the y - intercept of the line.

As stated earlier, in a simple problem there are two regression lines. However, if the correlation between the two variables is perfect and linear, the two regression lines will coincide. However, since perfect relationships are rare in social sciences, there are usually two regression lines.

SIMPLE REGRESSION

For predicting a variable from another, it is essential to set up a regression equation or equation of the regression line. It is also to be noted that the equation of a straight line is based on two constants 'a' and 'b', hence it is necessary to calculate the values of these constants before prediction can be made. In the following pages the procedure for setting up regression equations are demonstrated on raw as well as on the information about coefficient of correlation, standard deviations and means.

REGRESSION EQUATIONS FROM RAW SCORES

Example : The following marks have been obtained by five students in two tests X and Y.

X	10	11	12	9	8
Y	12	18	20	10	10

Set up regression equations for predicting Y from X and also X from Y.

Solution :

X	Y	X^2	Y^2	XY
10	12	100	144	120
11	18	121	324	198
12	20	144	400	240
9	10	81	100	90
8	10	64	100	80
$\Sigma X = 50$	$\Sigma Y = 70$	$\Sigma X^2 = 510$	$\Sigma Y^2 = 1068$	$\Sigma XY = 728$

Mean for X = $M_x = 10$

Mean for Y = $M_y = 14$

$N = 5$

Predicting Y from X scores :

Step 1 : Find the value of **b** coefficient for predicting Y from X

$$b_{yx} = \frac{\Sigma XY - \frac{(\Sigma X)(\Sigma Y)}{N}}{\Sigma x^2 - \frac{(\Sigma X)^2}{N}}$$

$$= \frac{N\Sigma XY - (\Sigma X)(\Sigma Y)}{N\Sigma X^2 - (\Sigma X)^2}$$

$$= \frac{5 \times 728 - 50 \times 70}{5 \times 510 - 50 \times 50}$$

$$= \frac{3640 - 3500}{2550 - 2500}$$

$$= \frac{140}{50}$$

$$= 2.8$$

Step 2 : Find the value of **a** coefficient for predicting Y from X.

The formula for calculating the value of a is as follows :

$$a_{yx} = M_y - b_{yx} M_x$$

$$a_{yx} = 14 - 2.8 \times 10$$

$$= 14 - 28$$

$$a_{yx} = -14$$

Step 3 : Set up the full regression equation.

The full regression equation for predicting Y scores from X scores would be

$Y' = bX + a$

where Y' is the predicted score and b and a are regression constants.

Substituting the values of a and b we get

$Y' = 2.8\ X + (-14)$

$Y' = 2.8\ X - 14$

It means that Y score can be viewed as 2.8 times the X score with a constant of 14 subtracted.

Predicting X from Y scores :

Step 1 : Find the value of b coefficient for predicting X from Y

$$b_{xy} = \frac{\Sigma XY - \dfrac{(\Sigma X)(\Sigma Y)}{N}}{\Sigma Y^2 - \dfrac{(\Sigma Y)^2}{N}}$$

$$= \frac{N\,\Sigma XY - (\Sigma X)(\Sigma Y)}{N\Sigma Y^2 - (\Sigma Y)^2}$$

(Note the change in the denominator as compared to the formula used in predicting Y from X)

$$b_{xy} = \frac{5 \times 728 - 50 \times 70}{5 \times 1068 - 70 \times 70}$$

$$= \frac{3640 - 3500}{5340 - 4900}$$

$$= \frac{140}{440}$$

$$= 0.318$$

$$a_{xy} = M_x - b_{xy} M_y.$$

$$a_{xy} = 10 - 0.318 \times 14$$

$$= 10 - 4.452$$

$$= 5.548$$

The regression equation for predicting X from Y will be

$$X' = bY + a$$

$$= 0.318\ Y + 5.548$$

It means that an X score can be viewed as 0.318 times Y score plus a constant of 5.548.

Note : Value of regression coefficient **a** and **b** in both the situations can also be obtained by using and solving the simultaneous normal equations given below :

Predicting Y from X

$\Sigma Y = Na + b\,\Sigma X$ and

$\Sigma XY = a\,\Sigma X + b\,\Sigma X^2$

Predicting X from Y

$$\Sigma X = Na + b\,\Sigma Y \quad \text{and}$$

$$\Sigma XY = a\,\Sigma Y + b\,\Sigma Y^2$$

Example :

Raw scores of five students on an intelligence test (X) and an academic achievement measure (Y) are given below. Set up regression equations for predicting Y from X; and X from Y.

Persons	**1**	**2**	**3**	**4**	**5**
X	5	3	2	8	2
Y	7	5	2	10	6

Solution :

Persons	**X**	**Y**	X^2	Y^2	**XY**
1	5	7	25	49	35
2	3	5	9	25	15
3	2	2	4	4	4
4	8	10	64	100	80
5	2	6	4	36	12
N = 5	$\Sigma X = 20$	$\Sigma Y = 30$	$\Sigma X^2 = 106$	$\Sigma Y^2 = 214$	$\Sigma XY = 146$

Mean for X = $M_x = 4$

Mean for Y = $M_y = 6$.

Predicting Y from X scores :

Step 1 : Find the value of b coefficient for predicting Y from X.

$$b_{yx} = \frac{N\,\Sigma XY - (\Sigma X)(\Sigma Y)}{N\,\Sigma X^2 - (\Sigma X)^2}$$

$$b_{yx} = \frac{5 \times 146 - 20 \times 30}{5 \times 106 - 20 \times 20}$$

$$= \frac{730 - 600}{530 - 400}$$

$$= \frac{130}{130}$$

$$= 1.$$

Step 2 : Find the value of a coefficient for predicting Y from X.

$a_{yx} = M_y - b_{yx} M_x$

$a_{yx} = 6 - 1 \times 4$

$= 6 - 4$

$= 2$

Step 3 : Set up the full regression equation.

The full regression equation for predicting Y scores from X scores would be

$Y' = bX + a$

$Y' = 1 \times X + 2$

$Y' = X + 2$

Predicting X from Y scores :

Step 1 :

$$b_{xy} = \frac{N\,\Sigma XY - (\Sigma X)(\Sigma Y)}{N\,\Sigma Y^2 - (\Sigma Y)^2}$$

$$= \frac{5 \times 146 - 20 \times 30}{5 \times 214 - (30)^2}$$

$$= \frac{730 - 600}{1070 - 900}$$

$$= \frac{130}{170}$$

$= 0.76$

Step 2 :

$a_{xy} = M_x - b_{xy} M_y$

$= 4 - 0.76 \times 6$

$= 4 - 4.56$

$= -0.56$

Step 3 : Set up the full regression equation.

The full regression equation for predicting X scores from Y scores would be

$X = bY + a$

$= 0.76Y + (-0.56)$

$= 0.76Y - 0.56$

Example : Compute the regression equations for the prediction of Y from the following set of data.

X	0	1	2	3	4
Y	1	3	2	4	5

Solution :

X	Y	X^2	Y^2	XY
0	1	0	1	0
1	3	1	9	3
2	2	4	4	4
3	4	9	16	12
4	5	16	25	20
$\Sigma X = 10$	$\Sigma Y = 15$	$\Sigma X^2 = 30$	$\Sigma Y^2 = 55$	$\Sigma XY = 39$

N = 5

Mx = 2

My = 3

Prediction of Y from X

Step 1 : Find the value of **b** coefficient for predicting Y from X.

$$b_{yx} = \frac{N\,\Sigma XY - (\Sigma X)(\Sigma Y)}{N\,\Sigma X^2 - (\Sigma X)^2}$$

$$= \frac{5 \times 39 - 10 \times 15}{5 \times 30 - 10 \times 10}$$

$$= \frac{195 - 150}{150 - 100}$$

$$= \frac{45}{50}$$

$$= 0.9$$

Step 2 : Find the value of **a** coefficient for predicting Y from X.

$$a_{yx} = M_y - b_{yx} \cdot M_x$$

$$= 3 - 0.9 \times 2$$

$$= 3 - 1.8$$

$$= 1.2$$

Step 3 :

$$Y' = bX + a$$

$$Y' = 0.9\,X + 1.2$$

Example : The following marks have been obtained by a group of students in Algebra and Geometry.

Algebra	80	45	55	56	58	60	65	68	70	75	85
Geometry	82	56	50	48	60	62	64	65	70	74	90

Find the two regression equations.

Estimate the marks of a student in Geometry who gets 78 marks in Algebra. Also estimate the marks of a student in Algebra who gets 87 marks in Geometry.

Solution :

Algebra X	**Geometry Y**	X^2	Y^2	**XY**
80	82	6400	6724	6560
45	56	2025	3136	2520
55	50	3025	2500	2750
56	48	3136	2304	2688
58	60	3364	3600	3480
60	62	3600	3844	3720
65	64	4225	4096	4160
68	65	4624	4225	4420
70	70	4900	4900	4900
75	74	5625	5476	5550
85	90	7225	8100	7650
$\Sigma X = 717$	$\Sigma Y = 721$	$\Sigma X^2 = 48149$	$\Sigma Y^2 = 48905$	$\Sigma XY = 48398$

$N = 11$

$M_x = 65.18$, $M_y = 65.54$

Predicting Y from X scores :

Step 1 :

$$b_{yx} = \frac{N\,\Sigma XY - (\Sigma X)\,(\Sigma Y)}{N\,\Sigma X^2 - (\Sigma X)^2}$$

$$= \frac{11 \times 48398 - 717 \times 721}{11 \times 48149 - 717 \times 717}$$

$$= \frac{532378 - 516957}{529639 - 514089}$$

$$= \frac{15421}{15550}$$

$$= 0.99$$

Step 2 :

$$a_{yx} = M_y - b_{yx} M_x$$

$$= 65.54 - 0.99 \times 65.18$$

$$= 65.54 - 64.52$$

$$= 1.02$$

Step 3 :

$$Y' = bX + a$$

$$= 0.99 X + 1.02$$

Now Y' = marks gained in Geometry

X = marks gained in Algebra = 78.

$$Y' = 0.99 \times 78 + 1.02$$

$$= 78.24$$

The student who gets 78 marks in Algebra is expected to get 78 marks in Geometry.

Predicting X from Y scores :

Step 1 :

$$b_{xy} = \frac{N\,\Sigma XY - (\Sigma X)\,(\Sigma Y)}{N\,\Sigma Y^2 - (\Sigma Y)^2}$$

$$= \frac{11 \times 48398 - 717 \times 721}{11 \times 48905 - 721 \times 721}$$

$$= \frac{532378 - 516957}{537955 - 519841}$$

$$= \frac{15421}{18114}$$

$$= 0.85$$

Step 2 :

$a_{xy} = M_x - b_{xy} . M_y$

$= 65.18 - 0.85 \times 65.54$

$= 65.18 - 55.709$

$= 9.471$

Step 3 :

$X' = bY + a$

$X' = 0.85Y + 9.471$

Now X' = marks gained in Algebra.

Y = marks gained in Geometry = 87

$X' = 0.85 \times 87 + 9.471$

$X' = 73.95 + 9.471$

$= 83.421$

The student getting 87 marks in Geometry is expected to get 83 marks in Algebra.

Example : Following data give the age of students and marks obtained in a test. Find the regression marks on age.

Age in year (X)	10	10	11	11	12	13
Marks (Y)	50	60	60	58	70	65

What would be the expected marks if the age of the student is 10.5 years?

Solution : Here Y is to be predicted from X

X	Y	X^2	Y^2	XY
10	50	100	2500	500
10	60	100	3600	600
11	60	121	3600	660
11	58	121	3364	638
12	70	144	4900	840
13	65	169	4225	845
$\Sigma X = 67$	$\Sigma Y = 363$	$\Sigma X^2 = 755$	$\Sigma Y^2 = 22189$	$\Sigma XY = 4083$

$N = 6$

$M_x = 11.16,$

$M_y = 60.5$

Predicting Y from X scores :

Step 1 :

$$b_{yx} = \frac{N\,\Sigma XY - (\Sigma X)\,(\Sigma Y)}{N\,\Sigma X^2 - (\Sigma X)^2}$$

$$b_{yx} = \frac{6 \times 4083 - 67 \times 363}{6 \times 755 - 67 \times 67}$$

$$= \frac{24498 - 24321}{4530 - 4489}$$

$$= \frac{177}{41}$$

$$= 4.317$$

$$\doteqdot 4.32$$

Step 2 :

$$a_{yx} = M_y - b_{yx} \cdot M_x$$

$$= 60.5 - 4.32 \times 11.16$$

$$= 60.5 - 48.21$$

$$= 12.29$$

Step 3 :

$$Y' = bX + a$$

$$= 4.32 \times X + 12.29$$

Now age of the student is 10.5 years.

$$\therefore Y' = 4.32 \times 10.5 + 12.29$$

$$= 45.36 + 12.29$$

$$= 57.65$$

$$\doteqdot 58$$

The expected marks is 58.

Example : Find the regression equations from the following data.

X	4	6	8	9	10
Y	10	11	13	17	20

Solution :

X	Y	X^2	Y^2	XY
4	10	16	100	40
6	11	36	121	66
8	13	64	169	104
9	17	81	289	153
10	20	100	400	200
$\Sigma X = 37$	$\Sigma Y = 71$	$\Sigma X^2 = 297$	$\Sigma Y^2 = 1079$	$\Sigma XY = 563$

$M_x = 7.4$

$M_y = 14.2$

$N = 5$

Regression equation of Y on X :

Step 1 :

$$b_{yx} = \frac{N\ \Sigma XY - (\Sigma X)(\Sigma Y)}{N\ \Sigma X^2 - (\Sigma X)^2}$$

$$= \frac{5 \times 563 - 37 \times 71}{5 \times 297 - 37 \times 37}$$

$$= \frac{2815 - 2627}{1485 - 1369}$$

$$= \frac{188}{116}$$

$$= 1.62$$

Step 2 :

$$a_{yx} = M_y - b_{yx}\ M_x$$

$$= 14.2 - 1.62 \times 7.4$$

$$= 14.2 - 11.98$$

$$= 2.22$$

Step 3 :

$$Y' = bX + a$$

$$Y' = 1.62\ X + 2.22$$

Regression equation of X on Y :

Step 1 :

$$b_{xy} = \frac{N\,\Sigma XY - (\Sigma X)(\Sigma Y)}{N\,\Sigma Y^2 - (\Sigma Y)^2}$$

$$= \frac{5 \times 563 - 37 \times 71}{5 \times 1079 - 71 \times 71}$$

$$= \frac{2815 - 2627}{5395 - 5041}$$

$$= \frac{188}{354}$$

$$= 0.53$$

Step 2 :

$$a_{xy} = M_x - b_{xy} \cdot M_y$$

$$= 7.4 - 0.53 \times 14.2$$

$$= 7.4 - 7.526$$

$$= -0.126$$

Step 3 :

$$X' = bY + a$$

$$X' = 0.53Y - 0.126$$

The required equations are

$Y' = 1.62\,X + 2.22$ and

$X' = 0.53\,Y - 0.126$

II Method

We can obtain the required regression equations by solving the simultaneous equations for

Predicting Y from X

$$Na + b\,\Sigma X = \Sigma Y$$

$$a\,\Sigma X + b\,\Sigma X^2 = \Sigma\,XY$$

Predicting X from Y

$$Na + b\,\Sigma Y = \Sigma X$$

$$a\,\Sigma Y + b\,\Sigma Y^2 = \Sigma XY$$

(i) The regression equation of Y on X :

$N = 5, \ \Sigma X = 37, \Sigma Y = 71$

$\Sigma X^2 = 297, \Sigma XY = 563.$

$5a + 376b = 71$ (I)

$37a + 297b = 563$ (II)

Multiplying (I) by 37 and (II) by 5 we get

$185a + 1369b = 2627$ (III)

$185a + 1485b = 2815$ (IV)

Subtracting (III) from (IV) we get

$116\ b = 188$

$b = 188/116$

$b = 1.62$

Substituting the value of b = 1.62 in (I)

$5a + 37 \times 1.62 = 71$

$5a + 59.94 = 71$

$\therefore 5a = 11.06$

$\therefore a = 2.212$

$Y' = bX + a$

$Y' = 1.62\ X + 2.212$

(ii) Regression equation of X on Y

$Na + b\ \Sigma Y = \Sigma X$

$a\ \Sigma Y + b\ \Sigma Y^2 = \Sigma\ XY$

Substituting the values.

$5a + 71b = 37$ (I)

$71a + 1079b = 563$ (II)

multiplying (I) by 71 and (II) by 5 we get

$355a + 5041\ b = 2627$ (III)

$355a + 5395\ b = 2815$ (IV)

Subtracting (III) from (IV) we get

$354\ b = 188$

$\therefore \ b = 0.53$

Substituting the value of b = 0.53 in (I) we get

$5a + 71 \times 0.53 = 37$

$5a + 37.63 = 37$

$5a = -0.63$

$a = -0.126$

$X' = bY + a$

$X' = 0.53Y - 0.126$

REGRESSION EQUATIONS FROM STANDARD DEVIATIONS, COEFFICIENT OF CORRELATION AND MEANS

The regression equations can be set up by making use of standard deviations, coefficient of correlation and Mean. The following example would make clear the method of setting of the regression equations.

Example :

(a) From the following information, set up regression equations for predicting Y from X and X from Y.

	M	σ	r
X	130	10	0.70
Y	110	18	

(b) Predict values of X for Y = 120, 90, 125 and 130.

(c) Predict values of Y for X = 122, 115, 140, 135, 132 and 128.

Solution :

(a) Predicting Y from X :

The values of the two regression coefficient **a** and **b** can be calculated as follows :

(i) $b_{yx} = r_{yx}\left(\frac{\sigma_y}{\sigma_x}\right)$

substituting the values

$$b_{yx} = 0.70 \times \frac{18}{10}$$

$$= 0.70 \times 1.8$$

$$= 1.26$$

(ii) $a_{yx} = M_y - (M_x)(b_{yx})$

$$= 110 - 130 \times 1.26$$

$= 110 - 163.8$

$= -53.8$

(iii) The complete equation for prediction is

$$Y' = b_{yx} X + a_{yx}$$

$$= 1.26\ X + (-53.8)$$

$$= 1.26\ X - 53.8$$

The entire regression equation can also be obtained by using the following composite formula.

$$Y' = r\left(\frac{\sigma_y}{\sigma_x}\right)(X - M_x) + M_y$$

$$= 0.70 \times \frac{18}{10}(X - 130) + 110$$

$$= 0.70 \times 1.8\ (X - 130) + 110$$

$$= 1.26\ (X - 130) + 110$$

$$= 1.26\ X - 1.26 \times 130 + 110$$

$$= 1.26\ X - 163.8 \times 110$$

$$= 1.26\ X - 53.8$$

$$Y' = 1.26\ X - 53.8 \qquad \text{.......... (I)}$$

Predicting X from Y :

(i) $$b_{xy} = r_{xy}\left(\frac{\sigma_x}{\sigma_y}\right)$$

$$= 0.70 \times \frac{10}{18}$$

$$= 0.70 \times 0.55$$

$$= 0.385$$

(ii) $$a_{xy} = M_x - (M_y)\ (b_{xy})$$

$$= 130 - 110 \times 0.385$$

$$= 130 - 42.35$$

$$= 87.65$$

(iii) The regression equation is

$$X' = b_{xy} Y + a_{xy}$$

$$X' = 0.385\ Y + 87.65$$

The same equation can also be obtained by using composite formula.

$$X' = r\left(\frac{\sigma_x}{\sigma_y}\right)(Y - M_y) + M_x$$

$$= 0.70 \times \frac{10}{18}(Y - 110) + 130$$

$$= 0.70 \times 0.55\ (Y - 110) + 130$$

$$= 0.385\ (Y - 110) + 130$$

$$= 0.385Y - 42.35 + 130$$

$$= 0.385\ Y + 87.65$$

(b) Predicting X values from Y = 120, 90, 125 and 130.

$\because$ X' = 0.385Y + 87.65 (Set up earlier)

$\therefore$ for Y = 120 X' = 0.385 × 120 + 87.65 = 133.85

for Y = 90 X' = 0.385 × 90 + 87.65 = 122.30

for Y = 125 X' = 0.385 × 125 + 87.65 = 135.77

for Y = 130 X' = 0.385 × 130 + 87.65 = 137.70

(c) Predicting Y values from X = 122, 115, 140, 135, 132 and 128.

Y' = 1.26 X –53.8

for X = 122 Y' = 1.26 × 122 – 53.8 = 99.92

for X = 115 Y' = 1.26 × 115 – 53.8 = 91.1

for X = 140 Y' = 1.26 × 140 – 53.8 = 122.6

for X = 135 Y' = 1.26 × 135 – 53.8 = 116.3

for X = 132 Y' = 1.26 × 132 – 53.8 = 112.52

for X = 128 Y' = 1.26 × 128 – 53.8 = 107.48

Example :

A survey was conducted to study the relationship between expenditure on accommodation (X) and expenditure on food and entertainment (Y). The following results were obtained.

	Mean	**SD.**	**r**
Expenditure on accommodation (x)	173	63.15	0.5
Food and entertainment (y)	47.8	22.98	

Find the regression of Y on X and estimate the expenditure on food and entertainment if the expenditure on accommodation is Rs. 200.

Predicting Y from X :

(i) $b_{yx} = r_{yx}\left(\frac{\sigma_y}{\sigma_x}\right)$

$= 0.5 \times \frac{22.98}{63.15} = 0.5 \times 0.36 = 0.18$

(ii) $a_{yx} = M_y - (M_x)\ (b_{yx})$

$= 47.8 - 173 \times 0.18$

$= 47.8 - 31.14$

$= 16.66$

(iii) $Y' = b_{yx}\ X + a_{yx}$

$= 0.18\ X + 16.66$

Now X = Rs. 200

$Y' = 0.18 \times 200 + 16.66$

$= 36 + 16.66$

$= 52.66$

Expenditure on food and entertainment is Rs. 52.66.

Example :

The following data are given for marks of 100 students in Paper I and Paper II in a certain subject.

Mean of Marks (out of 100) in Paper I = 39.5
Mean of Marks (out of 100) in Paper II = 47.5
Standard deviation of marks in Paper I = 10
Standard deviation of marks in Paper II = 16.8
Coefficient of correlation between the marks in Paper I and Paper II = 0.42
Find the expected marks in Paper II of a candidate who secured 50 marks in Paper I.

Solution :

The data can be tabulated as follows :

Papers	Mean	SD	r
I (x)	39.5	10	0.42
II (y)	47.5	16.8	

Predicting Y from X :

(i) $b_{yx} = r_{yx}\left(\frac{\sigma_y}{\sigma_x}\right)$

$= 0.42 \times \frac{16.8}{10}$

$= 0.42 \times 1.68$

$= 0.7$

(ii) $a_{yx} = M_y - (M_x)(b_{yx})$

$= 47.5 - 39.5 \times 0.7$

$= 47.5 - 27.65$

$= 19.85$

(iii) $Y' = b_{yx} X + a_{yx}$

$= 0.7 X + 19.85$

Now $X = 50$

$Y' = 0.7 \times 50 + 19.85$

$= 35 + 19.85$

$= 54.85$

$\doteqdot 55$

The expected marks in Paper II is 55.

Example :

Find the two regression equations using the following data :

$\overline{x} = 90, \overline{y} = 80 \quad \sigma_x = 3 \quad \sigma_y = 4 \quad r = 0.6$

Find the expected value of

(i) y when x = 95

(ii) x when y = 78

Solution :

Predicting Y from X

(i) $b_{yx} = r_{yx}\left(\frac{\sigma_y}{\sigma_x}\right)$

$= 0.6 \times \frac{4}{3}$

$= 0.2 \times 4$

$= 0.8$

(ii) $a_{yx} = M_y - (M_x)(b_{yx})$

$= 80 - 90 \times 0.8$

$= 80 - 72$

$= 8$

(iii) $Y' = b_{yx} X + a_{yx}$

$= 0.8 X + 8$

Predicting X from Y :

(i) $b_{xy} = r_{xy}\left(\frac{\sigma_x}{\sigma_y}\right)$

$= 0.6 \times \frac{3}{4}$

$= 0.6 \times 0.75$

$= 0.45$

(ii) $a_{xy} = M_x - (M_y)(b_{xy})$

$= 90 - 80 \times 0.45$

$= 90 - 36$

$= 54$

(iii) $X' = b_{xy} Y + a_{xy}$

$= 0.45 Y + 54$

Now

$\because \quad Y' = 0.8X + 8$

$\therefore \quad$ For $X = 95$

$Y' = 0.8 \times 95 + 8$

$= 76 + 8$

$= 84$

$\because \quad X' = 0.45\,Y + 54$

For $Y = 78$

$\therefore \quad X' = 0.45 \times 78 + 54$

$= 35.1 + 54 = 89.1$

Example :

Find the two regression equations if $\overline{x} = 15$, $\overline{y} = 20$, $b_{yx} = 0.3$, $b_{xy} = 0.7$

Solution :

(i) $a_{yx} = M_y - (M_x)(b_{yx})$

$= 20 - 15 \times 0.3$

$= 20 - 4.5$

$= 15.5$

(ii) $Y' = b_{yx}\,X + a_{yx}$

$= 0.3\,X + 15.5$

Similarly.

(i) $a_{xy} = M_x - (M_y)(b_{xy})$

$= 15 - 20 \times 0.7$

$= 15 - 14$

$= 1$

(ii) $X' = b_{xy}\,Y + a_{xy}$

$= 0.7\,Y + 1$

The regression line can also be found by the following equations :

(i) Regression of Y on X is

$$(Y - \overline{Y}) = r\frac{\sigma_y}{\sigma_x}(X - \overline{X})$$

(ii) Regression of X on Y is

$$(y-\bar{y}) = r\frac{\sigma_x}{\sigma_y}(x-\bar{x})$$

These equations also represent straight line equation (i) is in slope point form and equation (ii) can also be expressed is slope intercept form.

CERTAIN PROPERTIES OF THESE REGRESSION EQUATIONS

(1) These two linear equations represent two straight lines. These two lines coincide when there is perfect correlation (positive or negative) between the two variables. In this case $r = \pm 1$

This can be verified as follows

$$(Y-\bar{Y}) = r\frac{\sigma_y}{\sigma_x}(X-\bar{X}) \quad ---- \quad (I)$$

$$(X-\bar{X}) = r\frac{\sigma_x}{\sigma_y}(Y-\bar{Y}) \quad ---- \quad (II)$$

substituting $r = \pm 1$ in (I) and (II) we get

$$(Y-\bar{Y}) = \pm\frac{\sigma_y}{\sigma_x}(X-\bar{X}) \text{ and}$$

$$(X-\bar{X}) = \pm\frac{\sigma_x}{\sigma_y}(Y-\bar{Y})$$

$$\therefore \sigma_y(X-\bar{X}) = \pm\sigma_x(Y-\bar{Y}) \text{ and } \sigma_y(X-\bar{X}) = \pm\sigma_x(Y-\bar{Y})$$

Hence, the two lines coincide.

(2) The two lines move away from each their as the value of coefficient of correlation decreases and they will be perpendicular to each other when there is no correlation.

(3) Two straight lines can be intersected only at one point. Therefore, there can be only one pair satisfying the two equations simultaneously i.e., $(\bar{X},\bar{Y})$ is the only pair which satisfies both equations simultaneously.

(4) There exists relation between the two regression coefficients and the coefficient of correlation.

$$b_{yx} = r\frac{\sigma_y}{\sigma_x} \quad \text{and} \quad b_{xy} = r\frac{\sigma_x}{\sigma_y}$$

Multiplying the two equations

$$(b_{yx}) \cdot (b_{xy}) = r\frac{\sigma_y}{\sigma_x} \times r\frac{\sigma_x}{\sigma_y} = r^2$$

$$r = \pm\sqrt{(b_{yx})\,(b_{xy})}$$

If r is positive, both the regression coefficients are positive and if r is negative both the regression coefficients are negative.

STANDARD ERROR OF ESTIMATES

The deviation between the predicted scores and the actual scores introduces an error. The deviations (Y–Y') and (X–X') can be squared, summed, arranged and then the square root extracted. This index of the discrepancies between the observed and the predicted values is called the standard error of the estimates. We predict on the basis of the regression equations, we need not calculate (Y–Y') or (X–X'). The standard error (SE) of the estimate can be calculated from the correlation coefficient and the standard deviations. The following formulae are used :

(i) S.E. of Estimate of predicting Y from X

$$\sigma_{yx} = \sigma_y\sqrt{1 - r^2_{xy}}$$

(ii) S.E. of Estimate of predicting X from Y

$$\sigma_{xy} = \sigma_x\sqrt{1 - r^2_{xy}}$$

The interpretation of S.E. of the estimate is like the S.E. of measurement.

Example :

Given the following data for two tests

History (X)	**English (Y)**	r_{xy}
Mx = 75.00 σ_x = 6.00	My = 70.00 σ_y = 8.00	0.72

(a) Work out the regression equation in score form.

(b) Predict the probable grade in English of a student whose History mark in 65. Find the $\sigma_{est.}$ of this prediction.

(c) If r_{xy} had been 0.84 (standard deviations and means remaining the same) how much would $\sigma_{(est).Y}$ be reduced?

Solution :

(a) Predicting Y from X :

(i) $b_{xy} = r_{yx}\left(\frac{\sigma_y}{\sigma_x}\right)$

$= 0.72 \times \frac{8}{6}$

$= 0.96$

(ii) $a_{yx} = M_y - (M_x)\ (b_{yx})$

$= 70 - 75 \times 0.96$

$= 70 - 72$

$= -2$

(iii) $Y' = b_{yx} + a_{yx}$

$Y' = 0.96\ X - 2$

(b) Predicting X from Y :

(i) $b_{xy} = r_{xy}\left(\frac{\sigma_x}{\sigma_y}\right)$

$= 0.72 \times \frac{6}{8}$

$= 0.54$

(ii) $a_{xy} = M_x - (M_y)\ (b_{xy})$

$= 75 - 70 \times 0.54$

$= 75 - 37.8$

$= 37.2$

(iii) $X' = b_{xy} + a_{xy}$

$X' = 0.54\ Y + 37.2$

(c) Marks in English (Y) = ? When Marks in History (X) = 65

$Y' = 0.96\ X - 2$

$= 0.96 \times 65 - 2$

$= 60.4$

The probable grade or marks in English would be 60.4

Now

$$\sigma_{yx} = \sigma_y \sqrt{1-r_{xy}^2}$$

$$= 8\sqrt{1-0.72 \times 0.72}$$

$$= 8\sqrt{1-0.5184}$$

$$= 8\sqrt{0.4816}$$

$$= 5.55$$

$$\doteqdot 5.6$$

σ_{est} of this prediction is 5.6

(d) Now value of r_{xy} = 0.84 all other values remain same.

$$\sigma_{yx} = \sigma_y \sqrt{1-r_{xy}^2}$$

$$= 8\sqrt{1-0.84 \times 0.84}$$

$$= 8\sqrt{1-0.7056}$$

$$= 8\sqrt{0.2944}$$

$$= 8 \times 0.5425$$

$$= 4.34$$

$$\text{Reduction in } \sigma_{yx} = 5.5 - 4.3$$

$$= 1.2$$

$$\text{\% reduction in } \sigma_{yx} = \frac{1.2}{5.5} \times 100$$

$$= 21.81$$

$$\doteqdot 22$$

If r_{xy} had been 0.84 (other values remaining the same) 22% would $\sigma_{est\ Y}$ be reduced.

ASSUMPTIONS

The setting up of regression equation, making predictions, and calculation of the SE of the estimate involves certain assumptions which are made clear.

(1) We assume that the relationship between the two variable is linear. It means that a straight line is the best way to describe the relationship. Linearity can be judged by making a look at the scatter diagram. Statistical tests of linearity also exist.

(2) We assume homoscedasticity which means that Y scores in any single column have essentially the same standard deviation.

(3) We assume that Y scores within any one column are normally distributed. This assumption is essential when we interpret the predicted scores by using normal distribution.

MULTIPLE PREDICTION

Simple regression is based on two variables – one independent and other dependent or criterion. Actual relationship in social sciences are not always simple. There could be two or more variables affecting or jointly related to a dependent variable. School marks may be a joint function of intelligence and the number of hours at study or a rural and urban setting. Hence, in such situations one has to keep in view multiple dependence instead of the idea of dependence of one variable on another single variable. Multiple dependence means the dependence of one variable on two or more variables. Success in sports may be related both to aptitude and training. Multiple dependence can be indicated by the coefficient of multiple correlation R.

THE COEFFICIENT OF MULTIPLE CORRELATION (R)

Multiple correlation indicates the strength of relationship between dependent variable and two or more dependent variables taken together. It is related to the inter-correlations with the dependent variables as well as to their correlations with the dependent variable.

The method of working out coefficient of multiple correlation (R) is illustrated in the following example.

Example :

Intercorrelation among four variables

Variable	X_2	X_3	X_4	X_1
X_2	-	0.50	0.60	0.70
X_3	0.50	-	0.20	0.80
X_4	0.60	0.20	-	0.90
X_1	0.70	0.80	0.90	-
M_x	73	55	60	78
σ_x	12	10	15	16

X_1 = Criterion or dependent variable

X_2, X_3, X_4, = Independent variables

Mx and σ_x = Means and Standard deviations of the four variables resp.

THREE VARIABLE SOLUTION

The coefficient of multiple correlation is calculated and then the regression equation is set up.

The formula for calculating R is

$$R^2_{1.23} = \frac{r_{12}^2 + r_{13}^2 - 2r_{12}\, r_{13}\, r_{23}}{1 - r_{23}^2} \quad \text{---- (I)}$$

where $R_{1.23}$ is the square root of $r^2_{1.23}$

$R_{1.23}$ = coefficient of multiple correlation between X_1 and a combination of X_2 and X_3

r_2, r_{34}, r_{13}, are correlation between pairs of variables as indicated by their subscripts.

Substituting the values we get

$$R^2_{1.23} = \frac{(0.70)^2 + (0.80)^2 - 2 \times (0.70) \times (0.80) \times (0.50)}{1-(0.50)^2}$$

$$= \frac{0.49 + 0.64 - 0.56}{1 - 0.25}$$

$$= \frac{0.57}{0.75}$$

$$= 0.76$$

$$R^2_{1.23} = \sqrt{0.76} = 0.87$$

Formula (I) can be modified to obtain multiple correlation among other combinations of variables. For example

$$R^2_{1.34} = \frac{r_{13}^2 + r_{14}^2 - 2r_{13}\, r_{14}\, r_{34}}{1 - r_{34}^2}$$

THE MULTIPLE - REGRESSION EQUATION

Here a multiple correlation has been calculated by taking a three variable problem. The same will be extended for the purpose of setting up the multiple regression equation for prediction of values of X, from the knowledge of the values of X_2 and X_3.

The equation for multiple prediction for our problem will be

$$X'_1 = a + b_{12.3}\, X_2 + b_{13.2}\, X_3$$

in which

X'_1 = the predicted or dependent variable

b coefficients = the multiplying constants or weights.

a coefficients = a constant to be added

To get the equation we must get the value of b coefficients. The various formulae are

$$b_{12.3} = \frac{\sigma_1}{\sigma_2} \beta_{12.3}$$

(Partial regression coefficient, keeping X_3 variable constant)

$$b_{13.2} = \frac{\sigma_1}{\sigma_2} \beta_{13.2}$$

(Partial regression coefficient, keeping X_2 variable constant)

in which σ_1, σ_2 and σ_3 are standard deviations of variables X_1, X_2, and X_3. $\beta_{12.3}$ and $\beta_{13.2}$ are standard partial regression coefficients. The first partials out or keep constant the effect of X_3, while the second that of X_2 as is done in partial correlation. The betas, $\beta_{12.3}$ and $\beta_{13.2}$ are found as below :

$$\beta_{12.3} = \frac{r_{12} - r_{13}\, r_{23}}{1 - r_{23}^2}$$

$$= \frac{r_{13} - r_{12}\, r_{23}}{1 - r_{23}^2}$$

(Standard partial regression coefficients or β weights)

in which correlation coefficients, for various combinations of variables have been indicated by the subscripts.

Values from the table are substituted. Thus,

$$\beta_{12.3} = \frac{r_{12} - r_{13}\, r_{23}}{1 - r_{23}^2}$$

$$= \frac{0.70 - 0.80 \times 0.50}{1 - (0.50)^2}$$

$$= \frac{0.70 - 0.40}{1 - 0.25}$$

$$= \frac{0.30}{0.75}$$

$$= 0.4$$

$$\beta_{13.2} = \frac{r_{13} - r_{12}\, r_{23}}{1 - r_{23}^2}$$

$$= \frac{0.80 - 0.70 \times 0.50}{1 - (50)^2}$$

$$= \frac{0.80 - 0.35}{1 - 0.25}$$

$$= \frac{0.45}{0.75}$$

$$= 0.6$$

b coefficients are calculated as follows

$$b_{12.3} = \frac{\sigma_1}{\sigma_2} \beta_{12.3}$$

$$= \frac{16}{12} \times 0.4$$

$$= 1.333 \times 0.4$$

$$= 0.533$$

$$b_{13.2} = \frac{\sigma_1}{\sigma_2} \beta_{13.2}$$

$$= \frac{16}{10} \times 0.6$$

$$= 1.6 \times 6$$

$$= 0.96$$

Now the **a** constant is calculated as follows :

$$a_{1.23} = M_1 - b_{12.3} M_2 - b_{13.2} M_3$$

in which and M_1, M_2, and M_3, are the means of the variables X_1, X_2, and X_3, respectively.

Substituting the values we get

$$a_{1.23} = 78 - (0.4)(72) - (0.6)(55)$$

$$= 78 - 28.8 - 33 = 16.2$$

Now substuting the values in the following equation

$$X'_1 = a + b_{12.3} X_2 + b_{13.2} X_3$$

$$= 16.2 + 0.533 X_2 + 0.96 X_3$$

It is now possible to predict the value of X_1 from the knowledge of the values of X_2 and X_3.

For example of $X_2 = 60$ and $X_3 = 40$

the predicted value of X'_1 score is

$$X'_1 = 16.2 + 0.533 \times 60 + 0.96 \times 40$$
$$= 16.2 + 31.98 + 38.4$$
$$= 85.58$$

Calculation of R from betas (β's) :

β-coefficients can also be used to calculate coefficient of multiple correlation (R) as follows :

$$R^2_{1.23} = \beta_{12.3}\ r_{12} + \beta_{13.2}\ r_{13}$$

substituting the values

$$R^2_{1.23} = (0.4)\ (0.7) + (0.6)\ (0.8)$$
$$= 0.28 + 0.48$$
$$= 0.76$$
$$R_{1.23} = \sqrt{0.76} = 0.87$$

Note the value of R agrees with R obtained earlier.

STANDARD ERROR OF ESTIMATE FROM MULTIPLE PREDICTION

Standard error of estimate from multiple prediction can be calculated to know as to how far the predicted values would deviate from the obtained ones. The formula for the purpose is.

$$\sigma_{1.23} = \sigma_1\sqrt{1 - R^2_{1.23}}$$

in which

σ_1 = SD of X_1

R = coefficient of multiple correlation.

in the given example

$$\sigma_{1.23} = 16\sqrt{1-(0.87)^2}$$
$$= 16\sqrt{1-0.7569}$$
$$= 16\sqrt{0.2431}$$
$$= 16 \times 0.4930$$
$$= 7.88$$

The interpretation of S.E. of estimate is similar to that in the case of simple regression.

□□□

CHAPTER X

FACTOR ANALYSIS

THE THEORY OF TWO FACTORS

I. FACTOR TESTS

In actual practice at the present day, this science of "Factor Analysis" is endeavouring to arrive at an analysis of mind based on the mathematical treatment of experimental data obtained from tests of intelligence and of other qualities, and to improve vocational and scholastic advice and prediction by making use of this analysis in individual cases. This science of "Factor Analysis" is thus a development of "testing" movement – the movement in which experimenters endeavour to devise tests of intelligence and other qualities in the hope of sorting mankind, and especially children, into different categories for various practical purposes – educational, administrative, vocational, etc. etc ...

Now, everyone, who has had anything to do with tests will readily agree that there are many psychologists who would deny that from the scores in such tests (or indeed from any analysis), we can even return to the full picture of an individual. However, the tester may be allowed to try to make his modest diagram of the individual better, more useful and if possible, simpler.

The broadest fact about the "results of test" of all sorts, when a large number of them is given to a large number of people, is that, every individual and every test is different from every other; and yet that there are certain rather vague similarities which run through groups of people or groups of tests, not very well marked off from one another but merging imperceptibly into neighboring groups at their margins. To describe an individual accurately and completely one would have to administer to him all the thousand and one tests which have been or may be devised, and record his score in each, an impossible plan to carry out, and an unwieldy record to use even if obtained. Both – practical necessity and the desire for theoretical simplification – lead one to seek for a few tests which will describe the individual. With sufficient accuracy, and possibly with complete accuracy if the right tests can be found. If there is some tendency for the tests to fall into groups, perhaps one test from each group may suffice. Such a set of tests might then be said to measure the "factors" of the mind.

II. FICTITIOUS FACTORS

Actually the progress of 'factorial' movement has been rather different, and the factors are not real but as it were fictitious tests which represent certain aspects of the whole mind. But conceivably it might have taken the more concrete form. In that case, the "factor tests" finally decided upon would be a set of standards which, like any other standards, would have to be kept inviolate, and unchanged except at rare intervals and for good reasons. There has been some tendency towards this. The Binet scale of tests is almost an international standard, and there is a general agreement that it must not be changed except by certain people upon whose shoulders Binets' mantle has fallen. But the Binet's scale is a very complex entity, and rather represents many groups of tests than any one test. By 'Factor tests' one would more naturally mean tests of a 'pure' nature, differing widely from one another so as to cover the whole personality adequately. And since actual tests always are more or less mixed, it is understandable why "factors" have come to be fictitious, not real, tests, to be each approximated to by various combinations of real tests so weighted that their unwanted aspects tend to cancel out, and their desired aspects to reinforce one another, the term approximating to a measure of the pure "factor".

But, the question is, how do we know a "pure" factor, how are we to tell when the actual tests approximate to it? And to give a preliminary answer to that question we must go back to the pioneer work of Prof. Charles Spearman in the early years of this century (1904). The main idea which still, rightly or wrongly dominates the factorial analysis was enunciated then by him, and practically all that has been done since, has been either inspired or provoked by his writings. Spearman's discovery was that the "coefficients of correlation" between tests tend to fall into "hierarchical order" and he saw that this could be explained by his famous "theory of two factors".

III. HIERARCHICAL ORDER

A coefficient of correlation is a number which indicates the degree of resemblance between two sets of marks of scores. If a school master, for example, gives two examination papers to his class, say (i) in arithmetic and (ii) in grammar, The will have two sets of marks are identical then the correlation is perfect, and the correlation coefficient, denoted by the symbol r_{12} is said to be + 1. If by some curious chance the one list of marks is exactly like the other one upside down (e.g., the best boy at arithmetic being worst at grammer), the correlation is still perfect, but negative, and $r_{12} = -1$. If there is absolutely no resemblance between the two lists, $r_{12} = 0$. If there is a strong resemblance, but falling short of identity, r_{12} may equal .9; and so on. There is a method of calculating such coefficients, given the list of marks.

The product – moment "formula is :

$$r_{12} = \frac{\text{Sum}(x_1\, x_2)}{\sqrt{(\text{Sum } x_1^2) \times (\text{Sum } x_2^2)}}$$

Where x_1 and x_2 are scores in two tests, measured from the average and the sums over the persons to whom the scores apply. The quantity –

$$\sigma^2_1 = \frac{\text{Sum of } x_1^2}{\text{Number of persons}} \text{ is called as the variance}$$

of test L, and σ_1 its standard deviation.

"Tests" can obviously be correlated just like examinations, and a convenient form in which to write down the intercorrelations of a number of tests is in a square chequer board with the names of the tests (say, a, b, c, ...) written along the two margin, thus :

	a	b	c	d	e	f
a	.	.48	.24	.54	.42	.30
b	.48	. .	.32	.72	.56	.40
c	.24	.32	.	.36	.28	.20
d	.54	.72	.36	.	.63	.45
e	.42	.56	.28	.63	.	.35
f	.30	.40	.20	.45	.35	.
Totals :	1.98	2.48	1.40	2.70	2.24	1.70

It was early found that such correlations tend to be positive. The tests can then be rearranged and numbered in the order of these totals; thus :

	1	2	3	4	5	6
	d	b	e	a	f	c
1 d	.	.72	.63	.54	.45	.36
2 b	.72	.	.56	.48	.40	.32
3 e	.63	.56	.	.42	.35	.28
4 a	.54	.48	.42	.	.36	.24
5 f	.45	.40	.35	.30	.	.20
6 c	.36	.32	.28	.24	.20	.

After the tests have been thus arranged, the tendency which Prof. Spearman was the first to see, and which he called "hierarchical order", is more seen. It is the tendency for the coefficients in any two columns to have a constant ratio throughout the column. Thus, in the above example, if we fix our attention on Columns a and f, say, they run (omitting the coefficients which have no partners) thus :

.54	.45
.48	.40
.42	.35
.	.
.	.
.24	.20

and every number on the right is five-sixths of its partner on the left.

Our example is a fictitious one, and the tendency to hierarchical order in it has been made perfect in order to emphasize the point. It should not be supposed that the tendency is as clear in actual experimental data.

IV. "g" SATURATIONS

This tendency to hierarchical order was explained by Prof. Spearman by the hypothesis that all the correlations were due to the "factor" only, present in every test, but present in largest amount in the test at the end of hierarchy. This factor is his famous "g" to which he gave only this algebraic name to avoid making any sort of suggestions as to its nature.

Suppose if Test d is saturated with so - and - so - much g; and Test b has less g in it than d has, it seems likely enough that b's column of correlations will all be smaller in that proportion.

We can, moreover, find what these saturations with g are. For, on the theory, each of our 6 tests contains the factor g, and another part which has nothing to do with causing correlation. Moreover, the higher the test is in the hierarchical ranking, the more it is saturated with g. Imagine now a fictitious test which had no specific, a test for g and for nothing else, whose saturation with g is 100% or 1 – 0. This fictitious test would, of course, stand at the heart of hierarchy, above our 6 real tests, and its row of correlations with each of those tests (their saturations) would each be larger than by any other in the same column. What values would these saturation take?

Before we answer this, let us see the diagonal cells of the "matrix" of correlations, – (a matrix is just a square or oblong set of numbers) – cells which we have upto the present left blank. Since each number in our matrix represents the correlation of the two tests in whose column and row it stands, there should be inserted in each diagonal cell the number "Unity", representing the correlation of a test with its own identical self. In these self – correlations, however, the specific factor of each test of course, plays its part. These self-correlations of unity are the only correlations in the whole table in which specifics do play any part in these unities, therefore, do not conform to the hierarchical rule of proportionality between the columns.

But the case is different with the fictitious test of pure g. It has no specific and its self-correlation of unity should conform to the hierarchy. If therefore we call the "Saturations" of the other tests r_{1g}, r_{2g}, r_{3g}, r_{4g}, r_{5g}, and r_{6g}, we see that we must have as we come down to the first two columns within the water –

$$\frac{r_{1g}}{1} = \frac{.72}{r_{2g}} = \frac{.63}{r_{3g}} = \frac{.54}{r_{4g}} = \frac{.45}{r_{5g}} = \frac{.36}{r_{6g}}$$

and similar equations for each other column with the g column, which together indicate that the 6 "saturations", are –

.9 .8 .7 .6 .5 .4

Further, each correlation in the table is the product of two of these saturations – Thus :

$$.72 = .9 \times .8$$

$$.42 = .7 \times .6$$

$$r_{34} = r_{5g} \times r_{4g}$$

	g	1	2	3	4	5	6
g	1	r_{1g}	r_{2g}	r_{3g}	r_{4g}	r_{5g}	r_{6g}
1	r_{1g}	.	.72	.63	.54	.45	.36
2	r_{2g}	.72	.	.56	.48	.40	.32
3	r_{3g}	.63	.56	.	.42	.35	.28
4	r_{4g}	.54	.48	.42	.	.30	.24
5	r_{5g}	.45	.40	.35	.30	.	.20
6	r_{6g}	.36	.32	.28	.24	.20	.

V. A WEIGHTED BATTERY

In the two factor theory, the important pure factor was g itself, and a test approximated to it the more, the higher it stood in the hierarcy. It's accuracy of measurement of g was indicated by its 'saturation'. And a battery of hierarchical tests could be weighted so as to have a combined saturation higher than that of any one member, each test for this purpose being weighted by a number proportional to $\frac{r_{ig}}{1-r^2_{ig}}$

where r_{ig} is the g saturation of Test i

VI. TETRAD DIFFERENCES

The discovery made by Prof. Spearman was that the correlation coefficients in two columns tend to be in the same ratio as we go up and down the pair of columns. That is to say if we take the columns belonging to Tests b and f, and fix our attention on the correlations which b and f make with d and e, we have :

	b	f
d	.72	.45
e	.56	.35

where $$\frac{.72}{.45} = \frac{.56}{.35}$$

This may be written :

$.72 \times .35 - .45 \times .56 = 0$, and in this form it is called a "tetrad difference". In symbols this one is—

$$r_{db} \times r_{ef} - r_{df} \times r_{eb} = 0$$

Spearman's discovery may therefore, be put thus :

"The tetrad differences are, or tend to be, zero"

The present day test for hierarchical order in a correlation matrix is to calculate all tetrad differences and see if they are sufficiently small.

It is, of course, not to be expected in actual experimenting that the tetrad differences will be exactly zero; no experiment on human material can be as accurate as that. What is required is that they shall be clustered round zero in a narrow curve, falling off steadily in frequency as zero is departed from. The number of tetrad differences increases very rapidly as the number of tests grow, and in an actual experimental battery, the tetrads are very numerous indeed.

VII. GROUP FACTORS

As time went on it became clear that the tendency to zero tetrad differences, though strong was not universal enough to permit an explanation of all correlations between tests in terms of g and specifics, with a few slight "disturbers" in the form of slightly overlapping specifics. It therefore became necessary to call in *group factors,* which run through many, though not through all tests, to explain the deviations from strict hierarchical order.

THE CENTROID METHOD

I. NEED OF GROUP FACTORS

The two factor method of analysis began with the idea that a matrix of correlations would ordinarily show perfect hierarchical order if care was taken to avoid tests which were unduly similar", i.e., very similar indeed to one another. If such were found coexisting in the team of tests, the team had to be "purified" by the rejection of one or other of the two. Later, it became clear that this process involves the experimenter in great difficulty, for it subjects him to the temptation to discover "undue similarity" between tests after he has found that their correlation breaks the hierarchy. Moreover, whole groups of tests were found to fail to conform; and so group factors were admitted, though always, by the experimenter trained in that school, with reluctance and in as small a number as possible. It had, however, become quite clear that the theory of two Factors in its original form had been superseded by a theory of many factors, although the method of two factors remained as an analytical device for indicating their presence and for isolating them in comparative purity.

Under these circumstances it is not surprising that some workers turned their attention to the possibility of method of multifactor analysis, by which any matrix of test correlations could be analysed direct into its factors. It was Thurston who saw that one solution to this problem could be reached by a **generalization of Spearman's idea of zero tetrad differences.**

II. RANK OF MATRIX AND NUMBER OF FACTORS

We know that when all the tetrad differences are zero, the correlations can all be explained by one general factor, a tetrad being formed of the interrelations of two tests with two other tests :

thus;

	3	4
1	r_{13}	r_{14}
2	r_{23}	r_{24}

and tetrad differences being

$$r_{13} \times r_{24} - r_{23} \times r_{14} = 0$$

Thurston's idea, though rather differently expressed by him, can be based on a second, third, fourth ....calculation of certain retrad differences.

To explain this let us take the correlation coefficients which three tests make with three others.

	4	5	6
1	r_{14}	r_{15}	r_{16}
2	r_{24}	r_{25}	r_{26}
3	r_{34}	r_{35}	r_{36}

This arrangement of nine correlation coefficients might have been called a 'N O N A D' by analogy with the tetrad. Actually by mathematicians it is called a "minor determinant of order three".

We can now, on the above three-rowed determinant, perform the following calculations : choose the top left coefficient as "*pivot*" & calculate the 4 tetrad differences of which it forms part, namely :

$$(r_{14} \times r_{25} - r_{24} \times r_{15}) \quad (r_{14} \times r_{26} - r_{24} \times r_{16})$$

$$(r_{14} \times r_{35} - r_{34} \times r_{15}) \quad (r_{14} \times r_{36} - r_{34} \times r_{16})$$

These 4 tetrad differences now, themselves form a tetrad which can be evaluated. If it is zero, we say that the three-rowed determinant with which we started "vanishes".

We can in this way examine the minors of orders two, three, four (and so on) of a correlation matrix, always avoiding those diagonal cells which correspond to the correlation of a test with itself. We may come to a point at which all the minors of that order vanish. Suppose these minors which all vanish are the minors of order five. We then say that the "rank" of correlation matrix is four (with the exception of diagonal cells). The *'rank'* of matrix is the order of its largest non-vanishing minor.

III. THURSTON'S METHOD USED ON HIERARCHY

Thurston's rule about the rank includes Spearman's hierarchy as a special case, for in a hierarchy the tetrads ____ that is, the minors of order two vanish. The rank is therefore one, and a hierarchical set of tests can be analysed into one common factor plus a specific in each. A simple way of introducing Thurston's hypothesis and his *"Centroid"* method of finding a set of factor saturations will be, to use it first of all on the perfect Spearman hierarchy – thus :

Tests	1	2	3	4	5	6
1	.	.72	.63	.54	.45	.36
2	.72	.	.56	.48	.40	.32
3	.63	.56	.	.42	.35	.28
4	.54	.48	.42	.	.30	.24
5	.45	.40	.35	.30	.	.20
6	.36	.32	.28	.24	.20	.

The first step in Thurston's method, after the rank has been found, is to place in the blank diagonal cells numbers which will cause these cells also to partake of the same rank as the rest of the matrix, numbers which are called *"Communalities"* In Spearman's example, that rank is one; that is the tetrads vanish. The Communalities, therefore, must be such numbers as will also make those tetrads vanish which include a diagonal cell : this enables them to be calculated. Let us, for example, fix our attention on the communality of the first test, which we will designate as h_1^2. Then the tetrad formed by Tests 1 and 2 with Tests 1 and 3 is –

	1	3
1	h_1^2	.63
2	.72	.56

and the tetrad difference has to vanish – therefore,

$$.56\, h_1^2 - .72 \times .63 = 0$$

$$\therefore h_1^2 = .81$$

Similarly, all the communalities may be calculated and found to be –

.81 .64 .49 .36 .25 .16

The method of finding the saturations of each test with the first common factor is then to insert the communalities in the diagonal cells and then add up the columns of the matrix thus :

Original Correlation Matrix

(.81)		.72		.63		.54		.45		.36
.72		(.64)		.56		.48		.40		.32
.63		.56		(.49)		.42		.35		.28
.54		.48		.42		(.36)		.30		.24
.45		.40		.35		.30		(.25)		.20
.36		.32		.28		.24		.20		(.16)
3.51	+	3.12	+	2.73	+	2.34	+	1.95	+	1.56 = 15.21

The column totals are then themselves added together (15.21) and the square root taken is 3.90. The "Saturations" of the first (and here the only) common factor are then the columnar totals divided by this square root, namely :

$$\frac{3.51}{3.90} \quad \frac{3.12}{3.90} \quad \frac{2.73}{3.90} \quad \frac{2.34}{3.90} \quad \frac{1.95}{3.90} \quad \frac{1.56}{3.90}$$

or .9 .8 .7 .6 .5 .4

As applied to the hierarchical case, this method of finding the saturations or loadings had been devised and employed many years previously by **Cyril Burt.**

In actual practice, Thurston and his followers do not calculate the minor determinants to find the rank and the communality. Instead, they adopt various approximations of which the simplest is to insert in each diagonal cell the largest correlation coefficient of the column.

IV. THE SECOND STAGE OF "CENTROID" METHOD

If there is more than one common factor, the process goes on to another stage. Even with our example we can show the beginning of this second stage, which consists in forming that matrix of correlations which the first factor alone would produce. This is done by writing the loadings along the sides of a chequer board and filling every cell of the chequer board with the product of the loading of that row with the loading of that column. Thus,

First Factor Matrix

	.9	.8	.7	.6	.5	.4
.9	.81	.72	.63	.54	.45	.36
.8	.72	.64	.56	.48	.40	.32
.7	.63	.56	.49	.42	.35	.28
.6	.54	.48	.42	.36	.30	.24
.5	.45	.40	.35	.30	.25	.20
.4	.36	.32	.28	.24	.20	.16

This is the "first factor matrix" which gives the parts of the correlations due to the first factor. This matrix has now to be subtracted from the original matrix to find the residues which must be explained by further common factors.

***Loading :** Very often in multiple factor-analysis, the "saturation" of a test with a factor is called the "loading".

❑❑❑

CHAPTER XI
CHI-SQUARE TESTS

The Chi-square test represents a useful method of comparing experimentally obtained results with those to be expected theoretically on some hypothesis. Some social research involves the counting of a number of persons, objects or responses as they occur under various categories of classifications. For example, students may be classified into groups like very good, satisfactory and poor. Adult subjects may be classified according to whether they are "in favour of", "indifferent to" or "opposed to" making Mathematics compulsory at S.S.C. level. In all such cases when the data are in the form of discrete categories and frequencies, Chi-square test is the most suitable test to compare the obtained set of observed frequencies in given categories with a set of theoretical or expected frequencies, occuring within them. It includes proportions, probabilities and percentages. The number of categories may be two or more and the observed frequencies are obtained empirically and the theoretical frequencies may be determined in a number of different ways depending upon the nature of the problem under consideration.

The equation for Chi-square (χ^2) is as follows :

$$\chi^2 = \Sigma \left\{ \frac{(f_o - f_e)^2}{f_e} \right\}$$

f_o = Observed frequency in a single category

f_e = Expected frequency, or theortical frequency or hypothetical frequency.

Thus, it is clear from the above equation that Chi-square (χ^2) is an index of the divergence of fact from hypothesis. If each of the observed frequency agreed exactly with the corresponding frequency the value of $\Sigma\,(f_o - f_e)^2$ would be zero and χ^2 would also be reduced to zero. The larger the divergence between the observed and theoretical frequency, the larger is the value of Chi-square.

It is to be noted Chi-square is based on the squares of the deviations i.e., $(f_o - f_e)^2$, hence it is always positive. It does not therefore take the direction of the deviations into account. This is a limitation of the Chi-square. To interpret the value of Chi-square we consider degree of freedom (df).

DEGREES OF FREEDOM (d*f*)

The number of degrees of freedom in a table of frequencies is the number of those frequencies to which we may assign arbitrary values and still satisfy the external requirements in terms of row and column totals. Consider the following 2 × 2 contingency table. The restriction imposed in this case is that the cell frequencies in each row and column must add upto a fixed total for that row or column.

(a) 10	(b) 30	40
(c) 27	(d) 18	45
37	48	

There are 4 cells here *viz.* a, b, c and d. The frequency of any one cell can be varied at will. The frequencies of the remaining three cells get fixed immediately to make up the row and column totals. Suppose we change the frequency of cell (a) from 10 to 15, the frequencies of cell (b), cell (c) and cell (d) will be fixed to 25, 22 and 23 respectively. Thus, in this table we have only one degree of freedom.

In 2 × 2 or larger contingency tables the df may be calculated as follows :

$$df = (r - 1)(c - 1)$$

where r = number of rows

c = number of columns.

Thus in 2 × 2 contingency tables

$$df = (2 - 1)(2 - 1) = 1 \times 1 = 1$$

In a 3 × 3 contingency tables

$$df = (3 - 1)(3 - 1) = 2 \times 2 = 4$$

It is thus clear from the above discussion that χ^2 test is a test of significance. It is a very useful device of checking observed frequencies against expected frequencies. It is a measure between a sample and an accepted theory or standard. The calculated value of χ^2 is compared with the table value for given degree of freedom and at a certain level of significance (e.g., 0.05 or 0.01 level). If the calculated value of χ^2 is greater than the table value at 0.05 or 0.01 level the hypothesis giving rise to theoretical frequencies is rejected.

Steps :

(1) State the null hypothesis (hypothesis of equal probability) H_0 and the alternative hypothesis H_1.

(2) State the level of significance (a) and the size of the sample (n).

(3) Determine the critical region based on degree of freedom and state the decision rule. Critical value of χ^2 will be found from the Chi-square table (Table F).

(4) Compute the value of χ^2 by using the formula

$$\chi^2 = \Sigma \left\{ \frac{(f_o - f_e)^2}{f_e} \right\}$$

(5) Take a decision to reject or not to reject the null hypothesis.

Testing the divergence of observed results from those expected on the hypothesis of equal probability (null-hypothesis).

Example 1 :

48 post-graduate students were asked to express an opinion on the issue. "Should India use an Atom Bomb?" by marking on a three point scale

(i) Yes (ii) Undecided (iii) No

24 of them marked 'yes', 12 were undecided and 12 marked No! Do these results indicate a significant trend against the hypothesis of equal probability?

Solution :

(1) Hypotheses :

H_0 = f (yes) = f (undecided) = f (No)

H_1 = f (yes) $\neq$ f (undecided) $\neq$ f (No)

(2) Decision Rule :

Given a = 0.5 and a 3 × 2 contigency table with

df = (r – 1) (c – 1) = (2 – 1) (3 – 1) = 2

Entering χ^2 table we find that χ^2 of 5.991 for df = 2 is significant at 0.05 level. Thus,

if χ^2 (observed) < 5.99 accept H_0. and

if χ^2 (observed) $\geq$ 5.99 reject H_0.

(3) Calculation :

The data is arranged in a contingency table.

	Responses			
	Yes	Undecided	No	
Observed frequency (f_o) →	24	12	12	48
Expected frequency (f_e) →	16	16	16	48
$(f_o - f_e)$	8	– 4	– 4	
$(f_o - f_e)^2$	64	16	16	
$\frac{(f_o - f_e)^2}{f_e}$	4	1	1	

$$\chi^2 = \Sigma\left\{\frac{(f_o - f_e)^2}{f_e}\right\} = 4 + 1 + 1 = 6.$$

(4) Interpretation :

Entering χ^2 table we find that χ^2 of 5.991 for df = 2 is significant at 0.05 level. Since the obtained value of 6 is greater than the table value we reject the equal probability hypothesis and conclude that the group favours the proposition at 0.05 level of significance.

Example 2 :

In 120 throws of a single die, the following distribution of faces was obtained.

	Faces						
	1	2	3	4	5	6	Total
Observed frequencies	30	25	18	10	22	15	120

Do these results constitute a refutation of the 'equal probability' (null) hypothesis?

Solution :

(1) Hypotheses :

$$H_0 = f_{(1)} = f_{(2)} = f_{(3)} = f_{(4)} = f_{(5)} = f_{(6)}$$

$$H_1 = f_{(1)} \neq f_{(2)} \neq f_{(3)} \neq f_{(4)} \neq f_{(5)} \neq f_{(6)}$$

(2) Decision Rule :

Given : a = 0.05 and a 6 × 2 contigency table with

df = (r – 1) (c – 1) = (2 – 1) (6 – 1) = 5

If χ^2 (observed) < 11.070 accept H_0 and

If χ^2 (observed) ≥ 11.070 reject H_0.

(3) Calculation :

The data are arranged in a contigency table

Faces

	1	2	3	4	5	6	Total
Observed (f_o)	30	25	18	10	22	15	120
Expected (f_e)	20	20	20	20	20	20	120
$(f_o - f_e)$	10	5	–2	–10	2	–5	
$(f_o - f_e)^2$	100	25	4	100	4	25	
$\frac{(f_o - f_e)^2}{f_e}$	5	1.25	0.20	5	0.20	1.25	

$$\therefore \chi^2 = \Sigma \left\{ \frac{(f_o - f_e)^2}{f_e} \right\} = 5 + 1.25 + 0.20 + 5 + 0.20 + 1.25 = 12.90.$$

(4) Interpretation :

Entering Table E we find in row df = 5, a $\chi^2 = 11.070$ while the χ^2 observed = 12.90.

As χ^2 observed > 11.070.

Reject H_0. The results indicate a trend significantly different from equal probability. Thus, the results in the given example constitute a refutation of the "equal probability" (null) hypothesis.

Example 3

Two hundred students were asked whether open book examination be instituted at the Post-graduate stage.

Their responses are given below –

Strongly approve	Approve	Indifferent	Disapprove	Strongly disapprove
46	36	48	34	36

Do these results differ significantly from equal preferences in the group?

Solution :

(1) Hypotheses :

$H_0 = f_{\text{Strongly approve}} = f_{\text{Approve}} = f_{\text{Indifferent}} = f_{\text{Disapprove}} = f_{\text{Strongly disapprove.}}$

$H_1 = f_{\text{Strongly approve}} \neq f_{\text{Approve}} \neq f_{\text{Indifferent}} \neq f_{\text{Disapprove}} \neq f_{\text{Strongly disapprove.}}$

(2) Decision Rule :

Given a = 0.05 and a 5 × 2 contigency table with

df = (r – 1) (c – 1) = (2 – 1) (5 – 1) = 4

If χ^2 (observed) < 9.488 accept H_0. and

If χ^2 (observed) $\geq$ 9.488 reject H_0.

(3) Calculation :

The data are arranged in a contigency table.

	Strongly approve	Approve	Indifferent	Disapprove	Strongly disapprove	Total
Observed (f_o)	46	36	48	34	36	200
Expected (f_e)	40	40	40	40	40	200
$(f_o - f_e)$	6	– 4	8	– 6	–4	
$(f_o - f_e)^2$	36	16	64	36	16	
$\frac{(f_o - f_e)^2}{f_e}$	0.9	0.4	1.6	0.9	0.4	

$$\chi^2 = \Sigma \left\{ \frac{(f_o - f_e)^2}{f_e} \right\} = 0.9 + 0.4 + 1.6 + 0.9 + 0.4 = 4.2$$

Entering Table E we find in row df = 4

χ^2 = 9.488 while the observed χ^2 = 4.20

As χ^2 (observed) < 9.488 the hypothesis H_0 is accepted, thus it is not significant.

Example 4

200 digits were chosen at random from a set of tables. The frequencies of the digits were :

Digit	0	1	2	3	4	5	6	7	8	9
Frequency	18	19	23	21	16	25	22	20	21	15

Use the χ^2 test to assess the correctness of the hypothesis that the digits were distributed in equal numbers in the tables from which these were choosen.

Solution :

If we take the hypothesis that the digits were distributed in equal numbers in the tables as correct, the expected frequencies of the digits would be as follows :

Digit	0	1	2	3	4	5	6	7	8	9	Total
Observed (f_o)	18	19	23	21	16	25	22	20	21	15	200
Expected (f_e)	20	20	20	20	20	20	20	20	20	20	200
$(f_o - f_e)$	–2	–1	3	1	–4	5	2	0	1	–5	
$(f_o - f_e)^2$	4	1	9	1	16	25	4	0	1	25	
$\frac{(f_o - f_e)^2}{f_e}$	0.2	0.05	0.45	0.05	0.8	1.25	0.2	0	0.05	1.25	

$$\chi^2 = \Sigma \left\{\frac{(f_o - f_e)^2}{f_e}\right\} = 0.2 + 0.05 + 0.45 + 0.05 + 0.80 + 1.25 + 0.20 + 0 + 1.25 = 4.30$$

The number of degrees of freedom df $= (c - 1)(r - 1)$

$= (10 - 1)(2 - 1)$

$= 9$

Entering Table E we find the 5% value of χ^2 for 9 degrees of freedom is 16.919. The calculated value of χ^2 is 4.30 which is much less than 16.919. Hence, the hypothesis is seen reasonable and correct and hence accepted.

CHI-SQUARE TEST AND NORMAL DISTRIBUTION HYPOTHESIS

Chi-square can be used to test significane of divergence of the observed results from those expected on the hypothesis of a normal distribution. The hypothesis may be set up in such a way that it asserts that the observed frequencies of an event follow a normal distribution instead of being equally probable.

Example 1 :

42 students, on the basis of the consensus of teachers were classified into three groups: very good, satisfactory and poor at Mathematics. Does this distribution of rating differ significantly from that to be expected of Mathematical ability if normally distributed?

Solution :

Steps of the Procedure

(1) Hypotheses :

H_0 = The observed frequencies are normally distributed.

H_1 = The observed frequencies are not normally distributed.

(2) Decision Rule :

Given a = 0.05 and 2 × 3 contigency table with

df $= (c - 1)(r - 1)$

$= (2 - 1)(3 - 1) = 2$

If χ^2 observed < 5.99 accept H_o and

If χ^2 observed $\geqslant 5.99$, reject H_o.

	Good	Satisfactory	Poor	Total
Observed (f_o)	16	20	6	42
Expected (f_e)	6.7	28.6	6.7	42
$(f_o - f_e)$	9.3	– 8.6	– 0.7	
$(f_o - f_e)^2$	86.49	73.96	0.49	
$\frac{(f_o - f_e)^2}{f_e}$	12.90	2.59	0.07	

$$\chi^2 = \Sigma \left\{\frac{(f_0 - f_e)^2}{f_e}\right\} = 12.90 + 2.59 + 0.07 = 15.56$$

HOW TO FIND EXPECTED FREQUENCIES?

(i) First divide the base line of a normal curve (taken to extend over 6σ) into 3 equal segments of 2σ each.

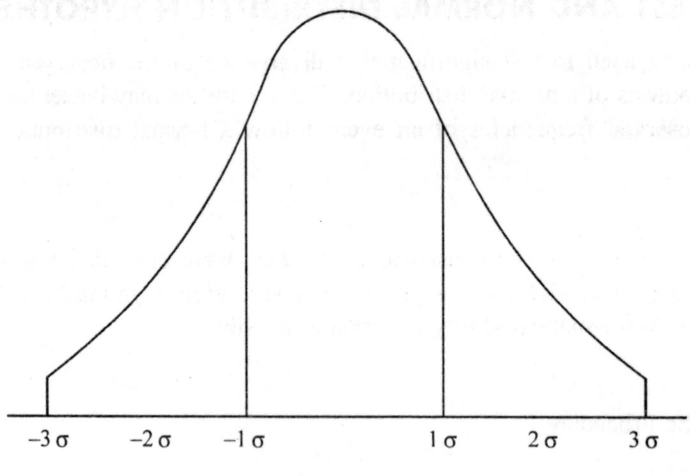

(ii) Segment	Proportion	Frequencies out of 42
Between + 3σ and + 1σ	0.16	$0.16 \times 42 = 6.7$
Between + 1σ and – 1σ	0.68	$0.68 \times 42 = 28.6$
Between - 1σ and – 3σ	0.16	$0.16 \times 42 = 6.7$

Note : Entries under proportion have been calculated with the help of area under the normal curve.

INTERPRETATION

Entering χ^2 table, it is seen that the obtained value of χ^2 is greater than the table value for the significance at 0.05 level (or even at 0.01 level) Hence, the hypothesis of normal probability distribution is rejected.

Example 2:

Sixty students were rated on "Co-operativeness" by a group of their teachers. The ratings were done by consensus on a three fold classification.

(i) generally co-operative (20 students)

(ii) some time co-operative (32 students)

(iii) seldom co-operative (8 students)

If co-operativeness is persumed to be normally distributed in this population of students, does this distribution of ratings differ significantly from normality?

Solution :

(1) Hypotheses :

H_o = The observed frequencies are normally distributed.

H_1 = The observed frequencies are not normally distributed.

(2) Decision Rule :

Given a = 0.05 and a 2 × 3 contigency table with

$$df = (r-1)(c-1) = (2-1)(3-1) = 2$$

If χ^2 observed < 5.99 accept H_o and

If χ^2 observed ⩾ 5.99, reject H_o

(3) Calculation :

	Generally co-operative	Sometime co-operative	Seldom co-operative	Total
Observed (f_o)	14	38	8	60
Expected (f_e)	9.6	40.8	9.6	60
$(f_o - f_e)$	4.40	-2.8	-1.6	
$(f_o - f_e)^2$	19.36	7.84	2.56	
$\frac{(f_o - f_e)^2}{f_e}$	0.02	0.19	0.27	

$$\chi^2 = \Sigma\left\{\frac{(f_o - f_e)^2}{f_e}\right\}$$

$$= 2.02 + 0.19 + 0.27 \quad = 2.48$$

COMPUTATION OF EXPECTED FREQUENCIES

(i) Divide the base line of a normal curve (taken to extend over 6σ) into three equal segments of 2σ each.

(ii)

Segment	Proportion	Frequencies out of 60
Between $+3\sigma$ to $+1\sigma$	0.16	$0.16 \times 60 = 9.6$
Between $+1\sigma$ to $+-1\sigma$	0.68	$0.68 \times 60 = 40.8$
Between -1σ to -3σ	0.16	$0.16 \times 60 = 9.6$

Note : Entries under Proportion have been calculated with the help of area under the normal curve.

INTERPRETATION

The value of observed Chi-square is 2.48 which is less than the critical value of Chi-square required for significance at 0.05 level and with df = 2. Hence H_0 is accepted. It may be concluded that the distribution of observed frequencies is not significantly different from normality.

Example : 3

Eighty four teachers were classified into three categories - very good, average, and poor - by a consensus of team of inspectors. If the teaching proficiency is distributed normally, does this distribution differ significantly from the normal distribution? The observed frequencies are :

Good = 32, Average = 40, Poor = 12.

Solution :

(1) Hypotheses:

H_0 = The observed frequencies are normally distributed.

H_1 = The observed frequencies are not normally distributed.

(2) Decision Rule:

Given a = 0.05 and a 2 × 3 contigency table with

$$\begin{aligned} df &= (r-1)\,(c-1) \\ &= (2-1)\,(3-1) \\ &= 2 \end{aligned}$$

If χ^2 (observed) < 5.99 accept H_0 and

If χ^2 (observed) $\geq$ 5.99 reject H_0.

(3) Calculation :

	Good	Average	Poor	Total
Observed (f_o)	32	40	12	84
Expected (f_e)	13.44	57.12	13.44	84

$(f_o - f_e)$	18.56	− 17.12	− 1.44
$(f_o - f_e)^2$	344.5	293.1	2.1
$\frac{(f_o - f_e)^2}{f_e}$	25.6	5.1	0.15

$$\chi^2 = \Sigma\left\{\frac{(f_o - f_e)^2}{f_e}\right\} = 25.6 + 5.1 + 0.15 = 30.85$$

COMPUTATION OF EXPECTED FREQUENCIES

Segment	Proportion	frequencies out of 84
Between + 3 σ to + 1 σ	0.16	0.16 × 84 = 13.44
Between + 1 σ to − 1 σ	0.68	0.68 × 84 = 57.12
Between − 1 σ to − 3 σ	0.16	0.16 × 84 = 13.44

INTERPRETATION

The value of observed Chi-square is 30.85 which is greater than the critical value of Chi-square required for significance at 0.01 level with df = 2. Hence H_0 is rejected. It may be concluded that the distribution is significantly different from normality.

Example 3 :

The following judgments were classified into six categories taken to represent a continuum of opinion.

	Categories						
	I	**II**	**III**	**IV**	**V**	**VI**	**Total**
Judgments	48	61	82	91	57	45	384

(a) Test given distribution versus "equal probability" hypothesis.

(b) Test given distribution versus normal distribution hypothesis.

Solution :

(a) Given distribution versus equal probability hypothesis (null).

(1) Hypotheses :

$H_0 = f_I = f_{II} = f_{III} = f_{IV} = f_V = f_{VI}$

$H_1 = f_I \neq f_{II} \neq f_{III} \neq f_{IV} \neq f_V \neq f_{VI}$

(2) Decision Rule :

Given a = 0.05 and 6 × 2 contigency table with

$$df = (r-1)(c-1) = (2-1)(6-1) = 5$$

If χ^2 observed < 11.070 accept H_0 and

If χ^2 observed $\geq$11.070 reject H_0.

Given a = 0.01 and 6 × 2 contigency table with
df = 5

If χ^2 observed <15.086 accept H_0 and

If χ^2 observed $\geq$15.086 reject H_0

(3) Calculation :

The data are arranged in a contigency table.

	Categories						
	I	**II**	**III**	**IV**	**V**	**VI**	**Total**
Observed (f_o)	48	61	82	91	57	45	384
Expected (f_e)	64	64	64	64	64	64	384
$(f_o - f_e)$	-16	-3	18	27	- 7	- 19	
$(f_o - f_e)^2$	256	9	324	729	49	361	
$\frac{(f_o - f_e)^2}{f_e}$	4	0.14	5.06	11.39	0.76	5.64	

$$\chi^2 = \Sigma \left\{ \frac{(f_0 - f_e)^2}{f_e} \right\}$$

$$= 4 + 0.14 + 5.06 + 11.39 + 0.76 + 5.64$$

$$= 26.99$$

INTERPRETATION

Entering table E we find in row df = 5 under 0.01 level of significance χ^2 = 15.086 while the observed χ^2 = 26.99.

As χ^2 observed > 15.086. The hypothesis H_0 is rejected.

Thus P is less than 0.01 and hence the hypothesis of 'equal probability' must be discarded.

(b) Given distribution versus normal distribution hypothesis :

Solution :

(1) Hypotheses :

H_0 = The observed frequencies are normally distributed.

H_1 = The observed frequencies are not normally distributed.

(2) Decision Rule :

Given a = 0.05 and a 6 × 2 contigency table with

$$df = (r-1)(c-1) = (2-1)(6-1) = 5$$

If χ^2 observed < 11.070 accept H_0 and

If χ^2 observed ≥ 11.070 reject H_0.

Given a = 0.01 and a 6 × 2 contigency table with

$$df = (r-1)(c-1) = (2-1)(6-1) = 5$$

If χ^2 observed <15.086 accept H_0 and

If χ^2 observed ≥ 15.086 reject H_0.

(3) Calculation:

	Categories						
	I	**II**	**III**	**IV**	**V**	**VI**	**Total**
Observed (f_o)	48	61	82	91	57	45	384
Expected (f_e)	7.7	53.8	130.6	130.6	53.8	7.7	384
($f_o - f_e$)	40.3	7.2	– 48.6	– 39.6	3.2	37.3	
$(f_o - f_e)^2$	1624	51.8	2361.9	1568.2	10.2	1391.3	
$\frac{(f_o - f_e)^2}{f_e}$	210	0.97	18.1	12	0.19	180.7	

$$\chi^2 = \Sigma\left\{\frac{(f_0 - f_e)^2}{f_e}\right\}$$

$$= 210 + 0.97 + 18.1 + 12 + 0.19 + 35.37$$

$$= 276.63$$

COMPUTATION OF EXPECTED FREQUENCIES

(i) Divide the base line of a normal curve (taken to extend over 6σ) into six equal segments of 1σ each.

(ii) Segment	Proportion	frequencies out of 384
Between $+3\sigma$ to $+2\sigma$	0.02	$0.02 \times 384 = 7.7$
Between $+2\sigma$ to $+1\sigma$	0.14	$0.14 \times 384 = 53.8$
Between $+1\sigma$ to 0σ	0.34	$0.34 \times 384 = 130.6$
Between 0σ to -1σ	0.34	$0.34 \times 384 = 130.6$
Between -1σ to -2σ	0.14	$0.14 \times 384 = 53.8$
Between -2σ to -3σ	0.02	$0.02 \times 384 = 7.7$

INTERPRETATION

Entering Table E we find in row df = 5 under 0.01 level of significance $\chi^2 = 15.086$ while the observed $\chi^2 = 276.63$

As χ^2 observed > 15.086 H_o is rejected.

CALCULATION OF CHI-SQUARE FOR 2 X 2 CONTINGENCY TABLES

A frequently occurring type of contigency table is the 2×2 or four fold contingency table. The value of Chi-square can be calculated without calculating expected values.

The following example illustrates the method.

Example :

In the following table 60 students have been placed in four cells according to their teacher's ratings as 'good performers' and 'poor performers' and success/failure on an intelligence test item. Is the performance independent of the intelligence?

Test item

	Fail	**Pass**	
Good Performers	(A) 13	(B) 14	27 = (A+B)
Poor performers.	(C) 18	(D) 15	33 = (C+D)
	31 (A+C)	29 (B+D)	65 N

Chi-square can be calculated by using the formula.

$$\chi^2 = \frac{N\,(AD - BC)^2}{(A+B)\,(C+D)\,(A+C)\,(B+D)}$$

in which

N = Total Number in the table

A, B, C, D = Frequencies in each of the four cells.

AD, BC = Cross products of the cell frequencies A × D and B × C resp.

(A+B), (C+D), (A+C), and (B+D) = Marginal total of frequencies.

$$\therefore \chi^2 = \frac{65\,\{(13 \times 15) - (14 \times 18)\}^2}{(13+14)\,(18+15)\,(13+18)\,(14+15)}$$

$$= \frac{65\,(195 - 252)^2}{27 \times 33 \times 31 \times 29}$$

$$= \frac{65\,(-57)^2}{27 \times 33 \times 31 \times 29}$$

$$= \frac{65 \times 3249}{801009}$$

$$= \frac{211185}{801009}$$

$$= 0.26$$

In this example

df = (r – 1) (c – 1)

= (2 – 1) (2 – 1)

= 1

The critical value of Chi-square with df = 1, on a = 0.05, is 3.84. The observed value of Chi-square is not significant. Hence the data do not provide enough evidence that the test item differentiates between individuals on the basis of their performance (as rated by their teachers).

When entries in 2 × 2 fold contingency table are very small (e. g., 5 or less), χ^2 is subject to considerable error unless a correction for continuity (called Yate's correction) is made. The following corrected formula is then used

$$\chi^2_c = \frac{N\,(|AD - BC| - N/2)^2}{(A+B)\,(C+D)\,(A+C)\,(B+D)}$$

Where |AD - BC| means the absolute difference of the two cross products i.e., the difference is to be taken positive, Thus, from the data

| AB-BC | = | 195-252 | = | -57 | = 57

Applying the formula to the data given above we get

$$\chi^2_c = \frac{65\,(\,|\,195 - 252\,|\, - 65/2)^2}{27 \times 33 \times 31 \times 29}$$

$$= \frac{65\,(\,57\; - 65/2)^2}{801009}$$

$$= \frac{65\,(\,57\; - 32.\,5)^2}{801009}$$

$$= \frac{65\,(\,24.5)^2}{801009}$$

$$= \frac{65 \times 600.25}{801009}$$

$$= \frac{39016.25}{801009}$$

$$= 0.0487$$

This value is smaller than that of the uncorrected Chi-square. Yate's correction will always reduce the size of the Chi-square. Its effect is more crucial when entries are small. When χ^2 is marginally significant the χ^2_c may well fall below the level set for significance. However, if χ^2 is already not significant, χ^2_c will be even less.

YATE'S CORRECTION FOR CONTINUITY

Chi-square is subject to considerable error in the following two situations and requires the use of Yate's correction for continuity.

(1) When working with 2x2 tables : Chi-square is based on the assumption that adjacent frequencies are connected by a continuous and smooth curve (like the normal curve) and are not discrete numbers. In 2x2 tables this continuity of the curve is broken and hence needs a correction.

(2) When the table entries are very small : Chi-square is not stable, When computed from a table in which any experimental frequency (f_o) is less than 5. Hence, a correction of continuity is required.

Yate's correction for continuity requires subtracting of 0.5 from each (f_o-f_e) difference as shown in the following example.

	Right	Wrong	
Observed (f_o)	8	2	10
Expected (f_e)	5	5	10
($f_o - f_e$)	3	3	
correction (–.5)	2.5	2.5	
$(f_o - f_e)^2$	6.25	6.25	
$\frac{(f_o - f_e)^2}{f_e}$	1.25	1.25	

$$\chi^2 = \Sigma\left\{\frac{(f_0 - f_e)^2}{f_e}\right\} = 1.25 + 1.25 = 2.50$$

The value of χ^2 falls far below the 0.05 significance level which requires a critical value of 3.841. However, the uncorrected value of χ^2, of calculated comes to 3.6 which approaches nearer to the critical value.

CHI-SQUARE FROM PERCENTAGES

Chi-square test can be used when table entries are in terms of percentages or proportions. However, the chi-square test should not be used with percentage entries or proportions unless a correction for size of sample is made. It is because of the fact that percentage does not indicate whether the actual frequency from which percentage has been calculated was large enough. A coin to fall head 8 times in 10 tosses and a coin to fall head 80 times in 100 tosses give the same percentage but the latter is more significant.

The calculation of Chi-square from percentages is shown with the help of an example below. N in this case is 10.

	Right	Wrong	
f_o	80%	20%	100%
f_e	50%	50%	100%
($f_o - f_e$)	30%	30%	
correction (–5%)	25%	25%	
$(f_o - f_e)^2$	625	625	
$\frac{(f_o - f_e)^2}{f_e}$	12.5	12.5	

$$\chi^2 \% = \Sigma\left\{\frac{(f_o - f_e)^2}{f_e}\right\}$$

= 12.5 + 12.5

= 25

$$\chi^2 = \chi^2\% \times N/100$$

$$= 25 \times 10/100 = 2.5$$

The $\chi^2\%$ based on percentages must be brought back to its proper value in terms of original number by multiplying it by N/100 as shown above.

Example : N = 12

	Right	Wrong	
f_o	75%	25%	100%
f_e	50%	50%	100%
$(f_o - f_e)$	25%	25%	
correction (–5%)	20%	20%	
$(f_o - f_e)^2$	400	400	
$\frac{(f_o - f_e)^2}{f_e}$	8	8	

$$\chi^2\% = \Sigma \left\{ \frac{(f_o - f_e)^2}{f_e} \right\}$$

$$= 8 + 8$$

$$= 16.$$

$$\chi^2 = \chi^2\% \times N/100$$

$$= 16 \times 12/100$$

$$= 1.92$$

ASSUMPTIONS OF THE CHI-SQUARE TEST

Chi-square test is based on the following assumptions :

(i) The two samples are independent from one another. This implies that different and unrelated sets of subjects are selected.

(ii) The subjects within each group must be randomly and independently sampled.

(iii) Each observation must qualify for one and only one category. It implies the f's in each cell must be distributed in mutually exclusive categories.

(iv) The samples size must be relatively large.

The two important assumptions of normality of distributions and homogeneity of variance which underlie all important parametric tests do not apply to chi-square.

THE ADDITIVE PROPERTY OF χ^2 :

When several Chi-squares have been computed from independent experiments (i.e., from tables based on different samples; these χ^2 may be added to provide an overall test of hypothesis. In such cases df for the new Chi-square = the sum of the separate df's.

Suppose sex difference with respect to an attitude to a certain question is expected (e.g., comparison of performance of boys and girls in Arithmetic test) then

(1) The repetition of the experiments is carried out for certain time (say three times)

(2) Each repetition of the experiment should be on samples of almost equal size and drawn independently; and at random.

(3) Let the separate Chi-squares found not be significant.

(4) These chi-squares are added to get new Chi-square.

(5) df for the new chi-square = the sum of the separate dfs.

(6) Table E is referred to know the significance of the new chi-square.

Thus, combining the data from several experiments will often yield a conclusive result, when separate experiments, taken alone, provide only indications.

Example :

Five chi-squares computed from four-fold tables in independent replications of an experiment are 0.50, 4.10, 1.20, 2.79 and 5.41. Does the aggregate of these tests yield a significant Chi-square?

Solution :

df for each chi-square = 1

df for the new chi-square = the sum of the separate df's

= 1+1+1+1+1

= 5

These separate χ^2 s are added to get new χ^2

New Chi-square = 0.50 + 4.10 + 1.20 + 2.79 + 5.41

= 14

Table E is referred to know the significance of the new chi-square. It is seen that the aggregate of these test yield a significant chi-square and P lies between 0.02 and 0.01.

NON-PARAMETRIC STATISTICAL TESTS

Many tests of significance are called parametric tests because these involve the estimation of at least one population value or parameter. For example in F test a population variance estimate is needed as the error term. Some tests are called non-parametric tests because they do not involve the estimation of any parameter or population value. The assumption of normality of distribution is the pre requisite in parametric tests such as F, t and Z. In non-parametric test, the assumption of normality is also not made. Such methods are called non-parametric or distribution free. The χ^2 test for example is a non-parametric technique.

WHEN TO USE NON-PARAMETRIC TESTS

Non-parametric tests are generally preferred to parametric tests in the following situations :

(1) When making tests of the significance of the difference between two means, we assume that scores upon which our statistics are based are normally distributed in the population. What we actually do-under the null hypothesis - is to estimate from our sample statistics the probability of a true difference between the two parameters. When N is very small or the data are badly skewed, so that the assumption of the normality is doubtful, "parametric methods" are of dubious value or are not applicable at all. In such cases "non-parametric methods" are used. In short, when samples are not from a normal distribution, non-parametric tests are preferred to parametric tests.

(2) When measurements are in terms of nominal and ordinal scales, the use of non-parametric tests are more appropriate, In other words, when data can be expressed only in grades or ranks, non-parametric tests are used. (the rank-difference correlation coefficient 'rho' is for example a non-parametric technique used when data is expressed in ranks).

(3) Non-parametric tests are prefered to parametric tests when N is small.

THE SIGN TESTS

This is the simplest and most generally applicable of the non-parametric tests.

Example : S and C represent two tasks, S the spelling of 25 words presented separately, and C the spelling of 25 words of equal difficulty presented as an integral part of a sentence (i.e., in context) Which condition is favourable to higher scores?

Solution : The data have been arranged in the following table. The null hypothesis to be tested is that any difference will be positive is equal to the probability that it will be negative. Under null hypothesis $^1/_2$ of the differences should be positive (+) and half should be negative (–).

Hypotheses $H_o : P_{negative} = P_{positive} = \frac{1}{2}$

$H_1 : P_{negative} \neq P_{positive} \neq \frac{1}{2}$

Decision Rule :

If $P_{obs} > .05$ Accept H_o

If $P_{obs} \leq .05$ Reject H_o

Ratings of the two Groups

Matched Pair	C	S	Sign difference (C-S)
1	15	12	+
2	18	15	+
3	9	10	–
4	15	16	–
5	18	18	0
6	12	10	+
7	15	12	+
8	16	13	+
9	14	12	+
10	22	19	+

Number of Zero differences = 1

Number of negative differences = 2

Number of positive differences = 7

Of the 10 differences 7 are plus, 2 are minus and one is zero. Since zero differences are neither plus nor minus they are excluded from N. In the given example there are thus 9 pairs out of which 7 are positive and 2 are negative.

To test the hypothesis is whether condition C is significantly superior to condition S? We shall first expand the binomical $(p + q)^9$ in which

p = the probability of a +

q = the probability of a – .

$$(p+q)^9 = p^9 + 9p^8q + 36p^7q^2 + 84p^6q^3 + 126p^5q^4 + 126p^4q^5 + 84p^3q^6 + 36p^2q^7 + 9pq^8 + q^9$$

The total number of combinations = sum of all the coefficents of the terms of the expression

$$= 2^N$$

$$= 2^9$$

$$= 512$$

In the given expression p^9, $9p^8q$ and $36p^7q^2$ contain 7 or more plus signs. By adding the numerical coefficients of the first three terms (i.e., $p^9 + 9p^8q + 36p^7q^2$) the number of combinations which contain 7 or more plus signs out of 9 is obtained which is 46.

The probability of the occurrence of 7 or more plus signs out of $9 = \frac{46}{512}$

$$= 0.089$$

$$\doteqdot 0.09$$

It is clearly not significant.

This is one tailed test since our hypothesis states that C is better than S. If the hypothesis at the outset had been that C and S differ without specifying which is superior, we would have had a two tailed test.

The two tailed probability is then 2 x 0.09 = 0.18. Using a = 0.05 for two tailed test we accept H_o because P > .05 For one tailed test also, the H_o cannot be rejected because P >.10.

ASSUMPTIONS OF SIGN TEST

The assumptions underlying the sign test are :

(i) The differences are continuously distributed and

(ii) The differences are independent of each other.

As stated earlier, no assumption regarding the form of the distribution or homegeneity of variance is required.

Example : In a group of 15 identical twin pairs one member of each pair is given special training, the other member of the pair acting as a control. In a final test, 10 of the trained twins were superior to their twin controls, 4 were interior, and in one pair the scores were the same. Were the trained twins superior to the untrained? Apply the sign test.

Solution :

Hypotheses $H_o : P_{negative} = P_{positive} = \frac{1}{2}$

$H_1 : P_{negative} \neq P_{positive} \neq \frac{1}{2}$

Decision Rule :

If $P_{obs} > .05$ Accept H_o

If $P_{obs} \leq .05$ Reject H_o

Ratings of Two Groups

Matched pair	Experimental	Control	Sign of difference
1	Superior	Inferior	+
2	"	"	+
3	"	"	+
4	"	"	+
5	"	"	+
6	"	"	+
7	"	"	+
8	"	"	+
9	"	"	+
10	"	"	+
11	Inferior	Superior	–
12	"	"	–
13	"	"	–
14	"	"	–
15	same	same	0

Number of zero differences = 1

Number of negative differences = 4

Number of positive differences = 10

There are 14 pairs out of which 10 are positive and 4 are negative (zero differences are excluded from N).

To test the hypothesis whether experimental group is significantly superior to control group. We shall first expand the binomial $(p + q)^{14}$ in which

p = the probability of a +

q = the probability of a –

$$(p+q)^{14} = {}^{14}C_{14}p^{14}q^{14-14} + {}^{14}C_{13}p^{13}q^{14-13} + {}^{14}C_{12}p^{12}q^{14-12} + {}^{14}C_{11}p^{11}q^{14-11} + {}^{14}C_{10}p^{10}q^{14-10}$$

$$+ {}^{14}C_{9}p^{9}q^{14-9} + {}^{14}C_{8}p^{8}q^{14-8} + {}^{14}C_{7}p^{7}q^{14-7} + {}^{14}C_{6}p^{6}q^{14-6} + {}^{14}C_{5}p^{5}q^{14-5}$$

$$+ {}^{14}C_{4}p^{4}q^{14-4} + {}^{14}C_{3}p^{3}q^{14-3} + {}^{14}C_{2}p^{2}q^{14-2} + {}^{14}C_{1}p^{1}q^{14-1} + {}^{14}C_{0}p^{0}q^{14-0}$$

$$= {}^{14}C_{14}p^{14} + {}^{14}C_{13}p^{13}q + {}^{14}C_{12}p^{12}q^{2} + {}^{14}C_{11}p^{11}q^{3} + {}^{14}C_{10}p^{10}q^{4}$$

$$+ {}^{14}C_{9}p^{9}q^{5} + {}^{14}C_{8}p^{8}q^{6} + {}^{14}C_{7}p^{7}q^{7} + {}^{14}C_{6}p^{6}q^{8} + {}^{14}C_{5}p^{5}q^{9}$$

$$+ {}^{14}C_{4}p^{4}q^{10} + {}^{14}C_{3}p^{3}q^{11} + {}^{14}C_{2}p^{2}q^{12} + {}^{14}C_{1}p^{1}q^{13} + {}^{14}C_{0}p^{0}q^{14}$$

$$= p^{14} + 14p^{13}q + 91p^{12}q^{2} + 364p^{11}q^{3} + 1001p^{10}q^{4}$$

$$+ 2002p^{9}q^{5} + 3003p^{8}q^{6} + 3432p^{7}q^{7} + 3003p^{6}q^{8} + 2002p^{5}q^{9}$$

$$+ 1001p^{4}q^{10} + 364p^{3}q^{11} + 91p^{2}q^{12} + 14pq^{13} + q^{14}$$

---

* The numerical coefficients of the terms can be obtained by using the general formula $^{n}C_{r} = \dfrac{n!}{(n-r)! \times r!}$

e.g.,

$$^{14}C_{14} = \frac{14!}{(14-14)! \times 14!} = \frac{14!}{0! \times 14!} = 1 \quad (\because 0! = 1)$$

$$^{14}C_{13} = \frac{14!}{(14-13)! \times 13!} = \frac{14!}{1! \times 13!} = \frac{14 \times 13!}{1 \times 13!} = 14$$

Note 5 ! = 5 x 4 x 3 x 2 x 1

The total number of combinations $= 2^N$

$= 2^{14}$

$= 16384$

In the given expression $p^{14}, 14p^{13}q, 91p^{12}q^2, 364p^{11}q^3$ and $1001p^{10}q^4$ and contain 10 or more plus signs. By adding the numerical coefficients of the first 5 terms (*viz.* $p^{14} + 14p^{13}q + 91p^{12}q^2 + 364p^{11}q^3 + 1001p^{10}q^4$) the number of the combination which contain 10 or more plus signs out of 14 is obtained which is :

1 + 14 + 91 + 364 + 1001 = 1471.

The probability of occurrence of 10 or more plus signs

out of 14 $= \frac{1471}{16384}$

$= 0.089$

$\doteqdot 0.09$

It is clearly not significant

We accept H_o because. $P > 0.05$.

THE MEDIAN TEST

It compares the medians of two independent samples. This test allows to test whether two independent groups have been drawn from populations with same median. The test can be used for unequal groups also.

The hypothesis to be tested can be stated either in non-directional (two tailed test) or directional terms (one tailed test).

The computation requires the following steps :

(1) The two groups are thrown together and a common median is found.

(2) Both sets of scores are dichotomized separately at the common median and the data is put in a 2 x 2 contingency table as given below :

	Group I	Group II	Total
Number of scores above combined Median.	A	B	A+B
Number of scores below combined Median.	C	D	C+D
	A+C	B+D	$N = n_1 + n_2$

If the two groups have been drawn at random from the same population, $\frac{1}{2}$ of the scores in each group should lie above and $\frac{1}{2}$ below the common median.

(3) The chi-square test is used.

(4) If the P yielded by the test is equal or less than a, H_o is rejected.

(5) If some scores fall at the combined median then –

(i) They are dropped from analysis if they are only a few and $n_1 + n_2$ is large, or

(ii) The groups are dichotomized as

(a) those scores which exceed the median and

(b) those scores which do not exceed the median.

The troublesome scores (which fall at the combined median) are included in category b.

Example :

The attitude towards the Church scale is administered to a group of 78 sophomores. Of the 78, 57 had a course in religious education and 21 had not. Suppose that 37 of the 57 are above common median of the whole group of 78 and that only 15 of the 21 are above the common median. Are the groups significantly different ? Apply median test.

Solution :

Hypotheses : H_o : No. of scores below combined Median for experimental group = No. of scores below combined Median for control group

H_1 : No. of scores below combined Median for experimental group No. of scores below combined Median for control group

Decision Rule : Given a = 0.05 $n_1 + n_2 > 20$ df = 1

If $\chi^2_{obs} < 3.84$ Accept H_o

If $\chi^2_{obs} \geq 3.84$ Reject H_o.

	Below Median	Above Median	Total
Experimental group.	(A) 20	(B) 37	57 (A+B)
Control group.	(C) 6	(D) 15	21 (C+D)
	26 (A+C)	52 (B+D)	N = 78

$$\chi^{-} = \frac{N\,(|AD - BC| - N/2)^2}{(A+B)\,(C+D)\,(A+C)\,(B+D)}$$

$$= \frac{78\,(|300 - 222| - 78/2)^2}{57 \times 21 \times 26 \times 52}$$

$$= \frac{78\,(|78| - 39)^2}{57 \times 21 \times 26 \times 52}$$

$$= \frac{78\,(78-39)^2}{57\times 21\times 26\times 52}$$

$$= \frac{78\,(39)^2}{57\times 21\times 26\times 52}$$

$$= \frac{78\times 39\times 39}{57\times 21\times 26\times 52}$$

$$= \frac{118638}{1618344}$$

$$= 0.073$$

INTERPRETATION

Since the observed Chi-square of 0.073 is less than 3.84 accept H_0. The two samples do not differ significantly with respect to their medians.

Note : χ^2 is generally applicable in the median test. However, when n_1 and n_2 are small (e.g., less than about 10) the χ^2 test is not accurate and exact method of computing probabilities should be used.

THE SUM OF RANKS TEST

The sum of ranks test is used to test the hypothesis of two independent groups of observations (e.g., scores or other data) have been drawn at random from the same population and hence that there is no real difference between them. This general hypothesis requires a two tailed test. One tailed test is suitable when the hypothesis of one group is higher or lower than the other group.

Example :

Two groups of graduate students 8 in each group earn the following scores.

A : 19, 28, 14, 23, 14, 17, 12, 15

B : 25, 23, 29, 15, 27, 21, 24, 20

Do the groups differ significantly? Apply the sum of ranks test.

Solution :

First the entire sets of 16 (i.e., $N_1 + N_2$) scores is ranked in 1-2-3 order from smallest to largest.

Group A Scores	(N_1 = 8) Ranks	Group B Scores	(N_2 = 8) Ranks
19	7	25	13
28	15	23	10.5
14	2.5	29	16
23	10.5	15	4.5
14	2.5	27	14
17	6	21	9
12	1	24	12
15	4.5	20	8
	R_1 = 49		R_2 = 87

The sum of ranks is obtained separately for each group. As a check, note that $R_1 + R_2 = \frac{N(N+1)}{2}$

In the given example

$R_1 + R_2 = 49 + 87 = 136$ and

$$\frac{N(N+1)}{2} = \frac{16(16+1)}{2} = \frac{16 \times 17}{2} = 136.$$

When N_1 and N_2 are each equal or larger than 8, we can calculate σ-score for each rank total by the following formula.

Sample A :

$$Z_1 = \frac{2R_1 - N_1(N+1)}{\sqrt{\frac{N_1 N_2 (N+1)}{3}}}$$

Sample B :

$$Z_2 = \frac{2R_2 - N_2(N+1)}{\sqrt{\frac{N_1 N_2 (N+1)}{3}}}$$

These Z's may be referred to the normal distribution and their probability of occurrence is determined. The two Z's should equal each other with opposite signs.

In the given problem

$$Z_1 = \frac{2 \times 49 - 8\,(16+1)}{\sqrt{\dfrac{8 \times 8\,(16+1)}{3}}} \qquad Z_2 = \frac{2 \times 87 - 8\,(16+1)}{\sqrt{\dfrac{8 \times 8 \times 17}{3}}}$$

$$= \frac{2 \times 49 - 8 \times 17}{\sqrt{\dfrac{64 \times 17}{3}}} \qquad = \frac{2 \times 87 - 8 \times 17}{\sqrt{\dfrac{64 \times 17}{3}}}$$

$$= \frac{98 - 136}{\sqrt{\dfrac{1088}{3}}} \qquad = \frac{174 - 136}{\sqrt{\dfrac{1088}{3}}}$$

$$= \frac{-38}{\sqrt{362.6}} \qquad = \frac{38}{\sqrt{362.6}}$$

$$= \frac{-38}{19.04} \qquad = \frac{38}{19.04}$$

$$= -1.995 \qquad = 1.995$$

From Table A it is seen that 2.33% (.5000 - .4767 = 0.0233 = 2.33%) of the normal curve lies to the right of 1.995 σ and 2.33% lies to the left of -1.995 σ.

INTERPRETATION

The two groups differ significantly at the 0.05 level.

Some precautions in the use of non-parametric test :

(1) When measurements are in terms of interval and ratio scales, the transformation of the measurements, on nominal or ordinal scales will lead to the loss of much of information.

(2) In situations where the assumptions underlying a parametric test are satisfied and both parametric and non-parametric tests can be applied, then the parametric tests should be preferred.

(3) Non-parametric tests, provide a means for avoiding the assumption of normality of distribution. But these methods do nothing to avoid the assumptions of independence on homoscedasticity wherever applicable.

(4) We do not have the problem of choosing stastical tests for categorical variables. Non-parametric tests alone are suitable for enumerative data.

(5) Non-parametric methods are especially useful when few assumptions can be made or are tenable under the conditions of the problem.

APPENDICES

TABLE A Fractional parts of the total area (taken as 10,000) under the normal probability curve, corresponding to distances on the baseline between the mean and successive points laid off from the mean in units of standard deviation.

Example : between the mean and a point $1.38\sigma \left(\frac{x}{\sigma} = 1.38\right)$ are found 41.62% of the entire area under the curve.

$\frac{x}{\sigma}$	.00	.01	.02	.03	.04	.05	.06	.07	.08	.09
0.0	0000	0040	0080	0120	0160	0199	0239	0279	0319	0359
0.1	0398	0438	0478	0517	0557	0596	0636	0675	0714	0753
0.2	0793	0832	0871	0910	0948	0987	1020	1064	1103	1141
0.3	1179	1217	1255	1293	1331	1368	1406	1443	1480	1517
0.4	1554	1591	1628	1664	1700	1736	1772	1808	1844	1879
0.5	1915	1950	1985	2019	2054	2068	2123	2157	2190	2224
0.6	2257	2291	2324	2357	2389	3422	3454	2486	2517	2549
0.7	2580	2611	2642	2673	2704	2734	2764	2794	2823	2852
0.8	2851	2910	2939	2967	2995	3023	3051	3078	3106	3133
0.9	3159	3186	3212	3238	3264	3290	3315	3340	3365	3389
1.0	3413	3438	3461	3485	3508	3531	3554	3577	3599	3621
1.1	3643	3665	3686	3708	3729	3749	3770	3790	3810	3830
1.2	3849	3869	3888	3907	3925	3944	3962	3980	3997	4015
1.3	4032	4049	4066	4082	4099	4115	4131	4147	4162	4177
1.4	4192	4207	4222	4236	4251	4265	4379	4292	4306	4319
1.5	4332	4345	4357	4370	4383	4394	4406	4418	4429	4441
1.6	4452	4463	4473	4484	4495	4505	4515	4525	4535	4545
1.7	4554	4564	4573	4582	4591	4599	4608	4616	4625	4633
1.8	4641	4649	4658	4664	4671	4678	4686	4693	4699	4700
1.9	4713	4719	4726	4788	4793	4798	4803	4808	4812	4817
2.0	4772	4778	4830	4834	4838	4842	4846	4850	4854	4857
2.1	4821	4826	4830	4834	4838	4842	4846	4850	4854	4857
2.2	4861	4864	4868	4871	4875	4878	4881	4884	4887	4890
2.3	4893	4896	4998	4901	4904	4906	4900	4911	4913	4916
2.4	4918	4920	4922	4925	4927	4929	4931	4932	4934	4936
2.5	4938	4940	4941	4943	4945	4946	4948	4949	4951	4952
2.6	4953	4955	4956	4957	4959	4960	4961	4962	4963	4964
2.7	4965	4966	4967	4968	4969	4970	4971	4972	4973	4974
2.8	4974	4975	4976	4977	4977	4978	4979	4979	4980	4981
2.9	4981	4982	4982	4983	4984	4984	4985	4985	4986	4986
3.0	4986.5	4986.9	4987.4	4987.8	4988.2	4988.6	4989.9	4989.3	4989.7	4990.0
3.1	4990.3	4990.6	4991.0	4991.3	4991.6	4991.8	4992.1	4992.4	4992.6	4992.9
3.2	4993.129									
3.3	4995.166									
3.4	4996.631									
3.5	4997.674									
3.6	4998.409									
3.7	4998.922									
3.8	49999.277									
3.9	4999.519									
4.0	4999.683									
4.5	4999.966									
5.0	4999.997133									

TABLE C Conversion of a pearson *r* into a correspoinding Fisher's z coefficient*

r	z	r	z	r	z	r	z	r	z	r	z
.25	.26	.40	.42	.55	.62	.70	.87	.85	1.26	.950	1.83
.26	.27	.41	.44	.56	.63	.71	.89	.86	1.29	.955	1.89
.27	.28	.42	.45	.57	.65	.72	.91	.87	1.33	.960	1.95
.28	.29	.43	.46	.58	.66	.73	.93	.88	1.38	.965	2.01
.29	.30	.44	.47	.59	.68	.74	.95	.89	1.42	.970	2.09
.30	.31	.45	.48	.60	.69	.75	.97	.90	1.47	.975	2.18
.31	.32	.46	.50	.61	.71	.76	1.00	.905	1.50	.980	2.30
.32	.33	.47	.51	.62	.73	.77	1.02	.910	1.53	.985	2.44
.33	.34	.48	.52	.63	.74	.78	1.05	.915	1.56	.990	2.65
.34	.35	.49	.54	.64	.76	.79	1.07	.920	1.59	.995	2.99
.35	.37	.50	.55	.65	.78	.80	1.10	.925	1.62		
.36	.38	.51	.56	.66	.79	.81	1.13	.930	1.66		
.37	.39	.52	.58	.67	.81	.82	1.16	.935	1.70		
.38	.40	.53	.59	.68	.83	.83	1.19	.940	1.74		
.39	.41	.54	.60	.69	.85	.84	1.22	.945	1.78		

*r's under .25 may be taken as equivalentto z's.

TABLE D Table of *t*, for use in determining the significance of statistics

Example : When the *df* are 35 and $t = 2.03$, the .05 in column 3 means that 5 times in100 trials in divergence as large as that obtained may be expected in the positive *and* negative directions under the null hypothesis.

Degrees of Freedom	Probability (P) 0.10	0.05	0.02	0.01
1	$t = 6.34$	$t = 12.71$	$t = 31.82$	$t = 63.66$
2	2.92	4.30	6.96	9.92
3	2.35	3.18	4.54	5.84
4	2.13	2.78	3.75	4.60
5	2.02	2.57	3.36	4.03
6	1.94	2.45	3.14	3.71
7	1.90	2.36	3.00	3.50
8	1.86	2.31	2.90	3.36
9	1.83	2.26	2.82	3.25
10	1.81	2.23	2.76	3.17
11	1.80	2.20	2.72	3.11
12	1.78	2.18	2.68	3.08
13	1.77	2.16	2.65	3.01
14	1.76	2.14	2.62	2.98
15	1.75	2.13	2.60	2.95
16	1.75	2.12	2.58	2.92
17	1.74	2.11	2.57	2.90
18	1.73	2,10	2.55	2.88
19	1.73	2.09	2.54	2.86
20	1.72	2.09	2.53	2.84
21	1.72	2.08	2.52	2.83
22	1.72	2.07	2.51	2.82
23	1.71	2.07	2.50	2.81
24	1.71	2.06	2.49	2.80
25	1.71	2.06	2.48	2.79
26	1.71	2.06	2.48	2.78
27	1.70	2.05	2.47	2.77
28	1.70	2.05	2.47	2.76
29	1.70	2.04	2.46	2.76
30	1.70	2.04	2.46	2.75
35	1.69	2.03	2.44	2.72
40	1.68	2.02	2.42	2.71
45	1.68	2.02	2.41	2.69
50	1.68	2.01	2.40	2.68
60	1.67	2.00	2.39	2.66
70	1.67	2.00	2.38	2.65
80	1.66	1.99	2.38	2.64
90	1.66	1.99	2.37	2.63
100	1.66	1.98	2.36	2.63
125	1.66	1.98	2.36	2.62
150	1.66	1.98	2.35	2.61
200	1.65	1.97	2.35	2.60
300	1.65	1.97	2.34	2.59
400	1.65	1.97	2.34	2.59
500	1.65	1.96	2.33	2.59
1000	1.65	1.96	2.33	2.58
∞	1.65	1.96	2.33	2.58

TABLE E **X^2 Table. *P* gives the probability of exceeding the tabulated value of X^2 for the specified number of degrees of freedom (df). The values of X^2 are printed in the body of the table.***

df	0.95	0.90	0.50	0.70	0.50	0.30	0.20	0.10	0.05	0.02	0.01
1	0.00393	0.0158	0.0642	0.148	0.455	1.074	1.642	2.706	3.841	5.412	6.635
2	0.103	0.211	0.446	0.713	1.386	2.408	3.219	4.605	5.991	7.824	9.210
3	0.352	0.584	1.005	1.424	2.366	3.665	4.642	6.251	7,815	9.837	11.345
4	0.711	1.064	1.649	2.195	3.357	4.878	5.989	7.779	9.488	11.668	13.277
5	1.145	1.610	2.343	3.000	4.351	6.064	7.289	9.236	11.070	13.388	15.086
6	1.635	2.204	3.070	3.828	5.348	7.231	8.558	10.645	12.592	15.033	16.812
7	2.167	2.833	3.822	4.671	6.348	8.383	9.803	12.017	14.067	16.622	18.475
8	2.733	3.490	4.594	5.527	7.344	9.524	11.030	13.362	15.507	18.168	20.090
9	3.325	4.168	5.380	6.393	8.343	10.656	12.242	14.684	16.919	19.679	21.666
10	3.940	4.865	6.179	7.267	9.342	11.781	13.442	15.987	18.307	21.161	23.209
11	4.575	5.578	6.989	8.148	10.341	12.899	14.631	17.275	19.675	22.618	24.725
12	5.226	6.304	7.807	9.034	11.340	14.011	15.812	18.549	21.026	24.054	26.217
13	5.892	7.042	8.634	9.926	12.340	15.119	16.985	19.812	22.362	25.472	27.688
14	6.571	8.547	9.467	10.821	13.339	16.222	18.151	21.064	23.635	26.873	29.141
15	7.262	9.312	10.307	11.721	14.339	17.322	19.311	22.307	24.996	28.259	30.578
16	7.962	10.085	11.152	12.624	15.338	18.418	20.465	23.542	26.296	29.633	32.000
17	8.672	10.865	12.002	13.531	16.338	19.511	21.615	24.769	27.587	30.995	33.409
18	9.390	10.651	12.857	14.440	17.388	20.601	22.760	25.989	28.869	32.346	34.805
19	10.117	11.651	13.716	15.352	18.338	21.689	23.900	27.204	30.144	33.687	36.191
20	10.851	12.443	14.578	16.266	19.337	22.775	25.038	28.412	31.410	35.020	37.566
21	11.591	13.240	15.445	17.182	20.337	23.858	26.171	29.615	32.671	36.343	38.932
22	12.338	14.041	16.314	18.101	21.337	24.939	27.301	30.813	33.924	37.659	40.289
23	13.091	14.848	17.187	19.021	22.337	26.018	28.429	32.007	35.172	38.968	41.638
24	13.848	15.659	18.062	19.943	23.337	27.096	29.429	33.196	36.415	40.270	42.980
25	14.611	16.473	18.940	20.867	24.337	28.172	30.675	34.382	37.652	41.566	44.314
26	15.379	17.292	19.820	21.792	25.336	29.246	1.795	35.563	38.885	42.856	45.642
27	16.151	18.114	20.703	22.719	26.336	30.319	32.912	36.741	40.113	44.140	46.963
28	16.928	18.939	21.588	23.647	27.336	31.391	34.027	37.916	41.337	45.419	48.278
29	17.708	19.768	22.475	24.577	28.336	32.461	35.139	39.087	42.577	46.693	49.583
30	18.403	20.599	23.364	25.508	29.336	33.530	36.250	40.256	43.773	47.962	50.892

* Adapted from R. A. Fisher's *Statistical Method for Research Workers,* Oliver & Boyd, by permission publishers.

BIBLIOGRAPHY

(1) Allen, W.G. : **Cumulative Pupil Records,** Bureau of Publications, Teachers Columbia University, New York, 1943.

(2) Anderson R. L. and T.A. Banerot (1952), **"Statistical Theory of Research"**. New York : Mc Graw Hill Book Company.

(3) Blommers, Paul and E.F.Lindquist (1960), **"Elementary Statistical Methods in Psychology and Education."** New Delhi: Oxford Book Company, 528 pp.

(4) Blum, J.R. and Fattu, N.A. (1954), **"Nonparametric Methods"**. Review of educational Research 467-487.

(5) Bradfield & Mordock; **Measurement & Evaluation in Education,** MacMillan, New York, 1957.

(6) Cocharn, W.G. (1963) **"Sampling Technique"**. Indian Edition, Bombay. Asian Publishing House, 413 pp.

(7) Cocharan, W.G. (1954), **"Some Methods for Strengthening the common χ^2 tests"**. Biometrics

(8) Coombs, C.H. (1962), **"A theory of Psychological Scaling"**. Bull University Michigan Engng Research.

(9) Cronbach, Lee J. : **Essential of Psychological Testing**. Harper & Brothers, New York, 1960.

(10) David, F.N. (1969), **"Probability theory for Statistical Methods"**. New Yrok : Cambridge University Press.

(11) Edward, A.L. (1964), **"Statistical Methods for the Behavioural Sciences"** New York : Rinehart. Elhance D.N. (1964), **"Parctical Problems in Statistics"** Kitab Mahal Private Ltd., Allahabad.

(12) Ferguson, G.A. (1966), **"Statistical Analysis in Psychology and Education"**. New York : Mc Graw Hill Book Company, 446 pp.

(13) Fisher, R.A. (1936), **"Statistical Methods for Research"**. Workers : Edinburg Oliver and Boyd.

(14) Fisher, R.A. (1955), **"The Design of Experiments"**. Edinburg : Oliver and Boyd.

(15) Freund, J.E. (1952), **"Modern Elementary Statistics"**. New York : Prentice Hall.

(16) Garrett, H.E. (1969), **"Statistics in Psychology and Education"**. Bombay. Vokels Feffers and Simons Ltd., 491 pp.

(17) Green, E. B. : **Measurement of Human Behaviour,** Obyssey Press, New York, 1941.

(18) Green, Jorgenson & Gerberich : **Measurement & Evaluation in the Secondary School,** Longmans Green & Co., New York, 1957.

(19) Guilford, J. P. : **Fundamental Stasistics in Psychology & Education,** McGraw-Hill Book Co., New York, 1950.

(20) Guilford, J.P. (1954), **"Psychometric Methods"**. Bombay : Tata Mc Graw Hill Publishing Co., Ltd., 597 pp.

(21) Jordan, A.M. : **Measurement of Education,** McGraw-Hill Book Co., New York, 1953.

(22) Jorgerson, T.L. & Adams, G. S. : **Measurement & Evaluation for the Elementary School,** Dreyden Press, New York, 1954.

(23) Kelly, T. L. : **Interpretation of Educational Measurement,** World Book Co., Yonkers, 1939.

(24) Kendall, M. G. (1948), **"Rank Correlation Methods",** London : Griffen.

(25) Kerlinger, Fredan N. (1964), **"Foundations of Behavioural Research"**. New York : Holt Rinhert and Winston, 741 pp.

(26) Lindquist, E.F. (1968), **"Design and Analysis of Experiments in Psychology and Education".** Boston : Houghton Mifflin Company, 393 pp.

(27) Lindquist, E.F. (1956), **"Design and Analysis of Experiments in Psychology and Education".** Boston : Houghton Mifflin Company, 393 pp.

(28) McCall, W.A. : **Measurement,** The MacMillan Co. New York, 1939.

(29) McNemar, Q. : **The Revision of the Stanford-Binet Scale,** Houghton Mifflin, Boston, 1942.

(30) McNemar, Q. : **Psychological Statisitcs,** John Wiley & Sons, New York, Chapman & Hall Ltd., London.

(31) Micheels, W. J. and Karnes, M. R. : **Measuring Educational Achievement,** McGraw-Hill Book Co., New York, 1950.

(32) Mood, A. M. (1950), **"Introducation to Theory of Statistics".** New York : Mc Graw Hill.

(33) Moses, L. E. (1952), **"Nonparametric Statistics Psychological Research"**. Psychological Bull. 49, 122-143.

(34) Rawat, D. S. : **Statistics & Measurement in Education,** Bharat Publication, Agra, 1956.

(35) Remembers, H. H., and Cage, N. L. : **Education Measurement and the Evaluation,** Harper and Brothers, New York, 1943.

(36) Ross, G. C. and Stanley, J. C. : **Measurement in Today's Schools,** Prentice - Hall, New York, 1954.

(37) Savage, L.J. (1954), **"The Foundation of Statistics"**. New York : Wiley.

(38) Siegel, Sidney (1956), **"Nonparemetric Statistics for the Behavioural Sciences"**. New Delhi Mc Graw Hill Book Company, 312 pp.

(39) Sharma, R.A. (1993), **"Fundamental of Educational Research"**. Meerut : International Publishing House, 453 pp.

(40) Sharma, R.A.(1996), **"Parametric and Non parametric Statistics"**. Meerut : Surya Publication.

(41) Simpson, G. and F. Kaffka (1971), **"Basic Statistics"**. New York : Mc Graw Hill Book Company.

(42) Smith, B. O. : **Logical Aspects of Educational Measuement,** Columbia Universtiy Press, New York, 1938.

(43) Snedecor, G.W. (1958), **"Statistical Methods"** Iowa State college Press.

(44) Tata, M.W. (1955), **"Statistics in Education"**. New York Mac Millan Company.

(45) Thomas, R. M. : **Judging Student Progress,** Longmans, London, 1955.

(46) Thomson, G. H. : **The Factorial Analysis of Human Ability,** Houghton Mifflin, Boston, 1939.

(47) Tiffin, J. : **Industrial Psychology,** Prentice-Hall, New York, 1942.

(48) Thorndike, E. L. : **An Introducation to the Theory of Mental & Social Measurement,** Colubia University, New York, 1904.

(49) Thorndike, R. L. : **Personal Selection, Test and Measurement Techniques,** John Wiley & Sons, New York, 1949.

(50) Thorndike, R. L. and Hagen, E : **Measurement & Evaluation in Psychology & Education,** John Wiley & Sons, New York, 1955.

(51) Travers, R.M.W. : **Education Measurement,** MacMillan & Co. New York, 1955.

(52) Vernon, P. E. : **The Measurement of Abilites,** University of London Press, London, 1956.

(53) Walker, H. W. **Elementary Statistical Methods,** Henry Holt & Co., New York, 1943.

(54) Walker, Helen M. and Joseph Lev, **"Statistical Inference"**. Calcutta : Oxford & IBH Publishing Company, 510 pp.

(55) Winer, B. J. (1971), **"Statistical Principles in Experimental Design"** London : Mc Graw Hill KogaKusha Ltd., 907 pp.